An Endless Road Of Words

Sir M.J. Wasik

ThePoorKnight.com

For The Muse

Caged in the fears and sorrows of our own making
But the night can never last forever
For her eyes are the light of the coming dawn

Clouds thick in our mind, winter's bight all around
But the flowers of spring still bloom in our heart
For her smile is the warmth of our life

Dreams of yesterdays and tomorrows, of hopes and desires
But the waking world is where we want to be
For paradise is found when her laughter is in the air

An artist insanity brought on by perfection unexpressed
But she is in every song, painting and sculpture
For hers is the beauty at the heart of every masterpiece

To love, to want, and then she is gone
But the happiness she inspired remains
For that is the gift the Muse leaves behind

Contents

Foreword..1

Reformation Remix 6

Show Me..9

The White Rose of Faith...10

The Red Rose of Charity 12

What Shall I Do? 14

The Sorrow of Our Time 15

Teachers of the Word 20

A Little Fire 27

A little Salt..29

Leadership 31

The Ten Companions of Lumpy..............................34

Desperate Prophesies...36

Fighting Fire with Fire...38

Godly Training 40

Holy Innocence...42

Not By Works..44

No worth except its name 47

For The Love of Death 51

Thought Crimes..52

Faith Alone 53

Justified by Grace 57

Saved by His Will...59

The Changing of the Guard 62

Not in my lifetime 65

Preach the Gospel 69

The Truth in Love...72

Feel the Yaboo..79

I'll Help You If I Can..81

The Rise and Fall of a Xristzen 82

A Chaotic Twist..85

Lent, Mortification and Hubris 87

Our Glory in Christ 90
The Faith Divide... 93
Moral Philosophy 97
A request for aid 101
Moral Exhibitionists Need Not Apply 105
Shadows of a Midlife Hangover.................................... 114
Beauty in the Eye of the Mystic 119
A Suicide Note (Version 1)... 129
Outcasts of the Tyrannies of our Churches. 130
Ethics and social collapse... 142
Age of Accountability 149
The Object of Faith 153
Faith as a Mystery 156
I Like to Sin.. 159
Moral Sanctification... 162
The Ruby in The Dark... 166
Hold onto Faith... 166
The Now of God's Will... 170
Maturity of the Faith 173
Saved for a Purpose.. 178
Surrendering Love... 182
Judgment 188
The Circle of Harmony 190
Sanctification.. 193
Balanced Grace 196
Resist Temptation... 199
Beyond Religion... 201
Tradition of Scripture 205
Frustration of the Flesh 210
Idols of Prayer 213
In His Name 216
Truth and Spirit 219
Illumination 222
Inspiration.. 225
Spirit and Truth 227
Mortification... 231
Trust in Christ... 235
More words than Sense 238
Repentance 242

Love and the Cross 246
Hypocrisy, Partiality and Self-Seeking 249
Journal of the Poor Knight 255
    Great Folly.. 256
    Freedom... 259
    Returning To the Road 260
Epilogue...263

Foreword

When we were young artists, it was easy to dream of fame, of fortune, of respect. Easy to dream of creating a legacy, a masterpiece which outlives our mortal coil. At some point, however, an artist must face that the dreams themselves are an illusion. Illusions which once fueled creation, eventually turn to hinder it. There is no fame, no fortune, no respect and the fate of our works will ultimately be judged by that youth sitting in the library of the future imagined. Judged to be genius or insane by those not even born yet. We spend our lives in a futile attempt to truly capture the rhythm of the rain, to draw out that poem found in the heart of the cloud. There is no goal, no dream of expressing of higher truths, no meaning to our art, only the next idea in which to give shape, only an endless road of words in the unpacking of our hearts.

I have tried to give up writing several times. To be normal, to be responsible. To take to heart the words of Voltaire's father 'one who chooses literature as a profession is one who wants to be useless to society, a burden to their family and to die of hunger'. Or in more common vulgate, there is nothing worse than an aging hippie. But I cannot help but to string an endless road of words together. I am possessed by my art, addicted, driven to write. Metaphysics, as philosopher use the word, is my playground. But what is the point of spending countless hours exploring ideas and concepts if it is not to express them. And of course, to be a writer and a philosopher is simply to be doubly useless. I have of late felt most inadequate in my writing, an uncommon feeling for me to be sure, but still one which is not without logic. It is most difficult, and seemly useless for me to address the heresies, superstations and downright silliness found in the Church today when our society has lost all sense of reason.

The problem, in my opinion, is that about fifty years ago (give or take) our society as a whole started a slow decline into an intellectual collapse. Blame the television if you would. Blame the decadence in which our success as a nation has created. Blame whatever you like. But all in all, just as the Church was slow to adjust to the Industrial Revolution and the masses of poor it created, we have not adjusted to the post-literate culture we are now in. Indeed, I think for the most part we do not even recognize the shift that has happened. The purpose-driven, or rather market-driven churches who sell cheap enlightenment have. Create shallow sermons calculated to titillate the crowds who really just wants to be entertained. And it has been solved on the flip-side of the same record, by those dry-leaved churches who cater to those who only want to be told a set of rules to live by. Those who pat each other on the back on how much better they do church then others, or what version of the Bible they read. Such things may solve the problems a church may face with membership, but it does not address the problem of which the Church faces.

The question of our time is not in how to pull in the masses, or how to keep them lined up like good little ducks. The question is one of Christian philosophy, of apologetics, of explaining the Faith in a post-literate age. The Medieval Church fed the ignorance and superstation of the peasants by an endless road of Latin words, that the village priest very often could not understand himself. And much of our theological debates sound very much like Latin to the average Christian. Do not mistake me, those who fight for theological purity have an important role. One in which helpful to people like me. For the average Christian, for one without my scholarly inclination, it does little good to prove with endless road of Scripture verses that what they are being taught is heresy, superstation or downright silliness. Bad theology is not the problem but one of the symptoms. The problem and the battle are over the purpose of our salvation.

The truth is, we have it easy. That is, we but have to appeal to an understanding that every Christian has. A knowledge that all who is saved knows. The argument starts with the indwelling of the Spirit of God, and ends with the Perfection of God. I am not referring to Theology, to intellectual pursuits, though for me that has always been a large part of it. I am writing about that place we have all been. At that moment when we look around church and ask if this is all there is to it. Is there not more to the Faith than this? When all the church stuff seems shallow and, if we are honest, a tad delusional. This happened to me in my physical youth and it happened in the youth of my Faith, though with a radically different view. Maybe I was saved in my youth and fell away, that time which I call my conversion was simply a time for me to stop my running. Maybe I was not saved, and only had been given a pre-regenerative Grace as some call it. It all depends on where you draw the line. I do not feel like I was ever saved until my conversion. Regardless though, I did not know God in a personal and real way until I bent my knee and submitted to Christ as Lord of my life.

I could blame the church I grew up in for not telling me that was the more I was looking for. But they most likely did and I was simply unwilling to listen. I have long known that God did not reveal Himself to me then, allowed me to run like Jonah in the manner I did according to His will, so I would have the understanding I needed for my part in His will. But, in the ignorance and arrogance of youth I set the goal for myself to become perfect in myself instead of seeking His perfection. There was some logic involved. It is, after all, a common enough knowledge that all our problems and the problems of the world will go away if we can just obtain perfection, gain some form of enlightenment. My conversion really did not change that view, only redefined what is perfect. In a way I can excuse myself. After all, God did promise that peace of perfection if I followed Him. I just did not realize at the time that the perfection is that which is to come. Yet, in truth, much if not most of the turmoil I experienced in the first ten years of my Faith came not from the lack of perfection but from not accepting my imperfections. Or if you would, the hardest struggle I have in finding peace in God's will is accepting that I will struggle to do God's will. But then, whether or not I find peace is not as important as doing God's will, now is it?

As a death-to-self-will mystic that is an important part of my Tradition. Which has been the reluctance to write this. As the mystic tradition is rather individualistic in nature. We do not have a denomination nor a church structure which gives us a seal of authority which is why we have such a difficulty dealing with our heretics. We do have our heretics, and at times it seems to be all we have. Those who see the Nothing as the same as the Void, or those who see our tradition as a means of forcing God to titillate them with vision and raptures. But then that seems to be the norm for this time in Church history.

I know, I know, there are a good many Protestants which think all mystics are heretics, which I find rather humorous considering how much of the Reformation is based on the old mystical tradition. But their anti-mystic bigotry does not concern me, and considering what has been passing for Christian within mystic circles over the last hundred years I can agree with them. In fact, the ones most likely to dismiss me out of hand for being a mystic are, in fact, usually defining aspect of our tradition, death-to-self-will. They are just calling it Lordship theology, instead.

I feel for them, of course. Us old-school mystics have had a hard go, well, even before the Reformation because of the teaching. But beyond an occasional poke and jab, I normally do not involve myself in the squabbles of other people's Traditions. This would be a shrug and a sigh, and next please. Except the heresy which it introduces into the Church is one which is especially prevalent among mystics. No, I am not calling the free-grace crowd heretics. From what I read so far, the serious theologians among them make some valid points in regard to salvation. But then again, in regard to salvation the whole debate centers around the question on whether or not one can be saved and not made their knightly vow of obedience to God. In that I do not know, but I do know that whether or not one makes the vow, one who is saved is simply going to obey.

I had an idea in this I want to flush out, but my rambling thoughts and endless roads of words here, is really about making the point that the theological argument in this is more or less lost on the masses. We can appeal to reason easy enough. That God is perfect, and His will is perfect. A straightforward computation that submission to His will is the most logical thing. God is perfect, and the His Spirit which dwells in us works on us to do and desire that perfect will. There is simply no way, theologically or logically, that if one is saved that they can avoid the understanding that obedience is expected of them. But, humans by nature are not reasonable animals. Indeed, if we were as logical as we believed ourselves to be most of the messes in the world would not exist.

But the appeal of our arguments is not on our theology, but in how we live our lives. Not just in avoiding vice, but striving for virtue. The proof of our Faith is not in our ability to transform the world, but in the ability of God to transform our hearts into the image of Christ. When you examine the years of your Faith, has there not been convictions, times when you were being rebellious, simply not doing or doing what you ought not to do? Maybe big horrible things we do not bring up, maybe just those stubborn I do not want to kind of things. Were these not the most horrible times of your early Life? That as we matured, we have learned to take these convictions in stride, whether they come from our study, from someone else, or directly from the Spirit. Indeed, have we not learned to be grateful for the conviction and that the Spirit dwells in us, transforming us? This has been a large part of maturing in the Faith, has it not? That there is a peace, in knowing that God's will is perfect, far better than your own?

The theologians can argue about salvation, but all things considered, for most of us it is good enough just to know that we are saved. That we are free from having to prove our worthiness, and so are free to seek to be pleasing to God from a love for Him, rather than a fear of Him. I think it is far better to start a person of in the Faith with the understanding that they will need to submit to the work of the Spirit. That the struggle is submission to Christ as our King. Because it is in those struggles, we learn, come to truly understand that His Will is the expression of His Love for us.

As always, you have to make up your own mind. Maybe me and the older mystics are wrong when we said that Grace is not to be found in works of our body, or our minds but is given according to God's will. That our struggle, our only real struggle is to submit our will to His. The death to our self-will so that we may find pleasure in His. And so on. I can say, without a doubt, that if you want to know God as I do, or rather be known by God as I am then it requires a submission, a subjugation of your own will to the will of God. It requires you to get on your knee and pledge your life, and your sword to God. and then to spend the rest of your life trying and struggling and failing, struggling some more and praying many times for the strength to keep that pledge. It requires that you submit to the work the Spirit is doing in you, indeed and facing all those ways which you are not in accord with Him. That is, I know no other way of reaching for God rather than submitting to His will, His perfection, and accepting whatever He gives.

And let me end this here before it does become an endless road of words.

Reformation Remix

Romans 8:

You will live…if by the Spirit you put to death the deeds of the body.

You are joint heirs with Christ…if you suffer with Him.

You are not in the flesh…if the Spirit dwells in you.

You are children of God…if you are led by the Spirit of God

There is no condemnation…for those who are in Christ Jesus.

But if anyone does not have the Spirit of Christ then they are not His

There were many things, and questions that were rattling around inside me for the past month. My thoughts, my studies and my prayers returned to that same question I have been asking all along. Returning me to the proposition I made long ago. That what needs to be expressed today is what it means to us today that Christ is Life. Salvation is understood, for as we will have Life because we are in Christ. But the theology needed is not in the perfect which will come, but the Life we have in this age. And while we wait for some theologian to get on it, you will have to suffer through my ramblings on the topic. And it starts with an understanding that if one is saved, they have the Spirit of God dwelling in them.

Sometime over the last four-hundred years something has gone horribly wrong with the doctrine of saved by Grace through Faith alone. While there is much of the Reformation which I think was derived from the flesh, and my fondness for the Catholic Tradition, I am still a Protestant at heart because ultimately, I have to agree that we are saved apart from works of the law, that Grace does not come to us from the rituals of our tradition but through Faith. For all its faults, I am at agreement with the Reformation as a rebellion against a ritual and membership-based salvation. Were our doctrine has gone wrong, where we have fallen short is that we leave off the qualifier which is so central to what St. Paul was writing in Romans. As I have been writing for years, what has gone wrong is that our doctrine stops at justification and does not progress beyond salvation. We are saved by Grace through Faith to-be-sure, but being saved we are in Christ. We have the Spirit of God dwelling in us, and our life is found in putting to death our flesh by His Spirit.

I used to simply dismiss people as never being saved as I have no understanding how one can be in Christ and not understand the demands the Spirit places on us. Is it possible for one to be saved and not have the Spirit of God? Surely not! But is it possible for us to have the Spirit dwelling inside us and not have Him place any demands on us? Is it possible for the Spirit to be dwelling in us and for Him not to work on us the death of our self-will, the deeds of the body? We can see in Scripture that it is, or maybe that it is. More likely, the exhortations found in Scripture is in regard to those times when we are being rebellious about the work the Spirit is doing in us. I have been at this for a while now, have exhorted and been exhorted, and usually it amounts to reminding me when I am being stubborn or simply not paying attention.

Basically, we already know that if we belong to Christ then His Spirit dwells in us, and the Spirit works in us to put to death the deeds of the body, to put an end to sin in our lives. And I think now that the problem I have had with my writings, from the very beginning is my assumption that we all already know that, that we all agree with that. My first foray into church culture ended horribly because I had not yet understood that not everyone who believes is saved. My second would end just as horribly because I had not yet understood many, if not most Christians do not want to be led by the Spirit, they just want to get into heaven. This of course, has had me questioning the doctrine of Perseverance of the Saints, and wondering whether or not there are in fact those who are saved, truly saved, yet risk losing it because of their refusal to be led by the Spirit. Can there be those who are saved, who have the Spirit of God within and not want to put to death the deeds of the body?

I can certainly understand not liking it. I have had my share of tantrums, of pouting. Those of you who have been with me from the beginning have read your share of whining from me. Though I am not prone to outward decadence, I can even understand Jonah, that if I just run far enough away then God cannot find me. That is, I certainly understand that not everyone who is saved wants to submit to the work of the Spirit of God, and at times we do not want to. I even except the possibility that there are those who are so stubborn that they are still resisting God after three days in the belly of the whale, or in doing God's will never learn the lesson of the vine. What I have trouble understanding, what I have always have had trouble understanding is how one could be saved, have the Spirit of God and not know His movements. Not be driven to know and do what God would have of us.

Obviously as a mystic I have experienced God in a way which is not normative, but that is not what I am writing about. God trains us not only to do His will, but also to desire it. That the demands of the Spirit work by transforming us into desiring that which God would have of us. That is, the Spirit leads us, not by decree as the Law was given, but by changing of our heart and minds. Not imposed from the outside, as the Law was, but one written on our nature by virtue of being reborn into Christ. We do good, desire and live according to God's way not so we will be saved but because we are saved. Not so we will be resurrected into glory but because we will be. I mean, really. If the only purpose for salvation was so we will escape God's wrath then why the Spirit?

Show Me

Show me not a beauty perfected
By adding here, and taking there
With nip and cut and tuck
But show me a beauty real
With crooked noses
And lopsided smiles

Show me not a house perfected
By marble countertops
And golden floors
But show me a home made real
With the stress of hardships
And the unity of love

Show me not a vision perfected
If men had wings
And women could fly
But show me a vision made real
With the arm of the Warrior
And the heart of the Poet

Show me not a world
Where a few are perfected
By the sacrifice of the many
But show me a Faith real
Where hearts are justified
By the sacrifice of the Son

The White Rose of Faith

Romans 4: Abraham believed God, and it was accounted to him for righteousness…who, contrary to hope, in hope believed…he did not waver at the promise of God through unbelief, but was strengthened in Faith, giving glory to God.

White, in the imagery of the knight and traditionally, is the color of purity, righteousness and holiness. This most likely comes from the fact that prior to modern detergents it was very hard to keep white clothing white. Clays, wine, and general grime which came from living would permanently stain clothing, and no amount of washing could make them truly white again. As such the white robes have done well as a metaphor for our souls, for our longing to have a pure and innocent spirit, untouched by the evils and darkness in the world around us. Uncorrupted by darkness of the world, or the evil of which we are capable.

I have heard it said that we must first be saved before we have this longing. This indeed holds true to a good number of people who see themselves as good. Such people are not kept up at night from their sins, because they do not get in the way of their goals. To them the only sins are those which prevent them from being rich, or famous, or popular. The greatest sins for them are the ones in which others of their circle question their goodness. Indeed, many an activist considers their anger and hatred justified because it gives fuel to their activities.

There are others, however, many others who look at their hearts and see something wrong. That even when their anger is truly justified, such as in an abuse victim, they still do not want to give into the hatred, to use the anger as a way of avoiding the pain. They do not want being a victim to be an excuse to victimize others, not using their pain as an excuse to cause pain to others. Basically, they long not to use the fact that another has sinned against them as an excuse to sin against others. Many of these, after trying to do so, will then learn that they cannot do it on their own.

Hours spent in therapy. The large numbers flocking to some religious leader claiming they can give peace for a price. Or the self-help gurus who claim all you need is to retrain your thought process.

Indeed, the longing for the peace which comes from a pure heart, to put away the darkness is common enough that it is written into the cannons of every serious religion and is used as a means of control in every cult. They all center around the idea that one must purge the darkness of their heart, either through meditation or following some moral code. Christianity differs only in that the Grace of our purification comes not through our works, but through our Faith.

I chose white for the Rose of Faith for just that reason. There are those who care only for justification, to be saved from God's wraith against the wicked is there primary concern. For them Faith is a rose because justification is the sweetest smell, for me it is a rose because it is through Faith we are sanctified, being purified, made holy, able to better each day live according to the Life we have been given. Forgiveness of our sins is part of the fragrance to be sure, but it was the rebirth, the regeneration, being a new creature with the Grace to overcome, to put an end to our sin is a far sweeter smell to me. Faith is a rose because in so much as it is the fulfillment of the love for God it is not just believing and trusting that God will save us through His work on the Cross, but us wanting God to save us. It is not simply wanting to be saved, but to be saved by God. Not simply wanting Life, but our Life to be in Christ. Not simply the desire to have a pure and innocent heart, Faith is the desire for such a heart which is pleasing to God and trusting in Him to get us there.

The Red Rose of Charity

1 Corinthians 13: though I bestow all my goods to feed the poor, and though I give my body to be burned, and have not charity, it profits me nothing…now abide faith, hope, charity, these three; but the greatest of these is charity.

Because of the Cross, long before the red rose was a symbol of romance it was used to represent the highest form of love. The Love which comes from God. In the symbolic language of the knight, red is the color of Charity. Not in the mediocre understanding of the world today, but as the symbol of the blood, both literally and metaphorically, one sheds for the Faith and for their fellow knight. The red rose represented the greatest of loves, the laying down of one's life for each other, as Christ gave His life for us. Red is the traditional color of Love, and I saw no reason to change that. I retained the rose because thorns which come with Charity are often far sharper and seemingly more painful than the thorns of sins which concern us with our purity.

Which is probably why the red rose became associated with romance. Though it is rarely recognized now, romantic love, if it is love and not simply lust, is a sacrificing love. Once upon a time, the red rose was not simply saying that 'you make me feel good' but 'I will sacrifice myself for you'. The rose represents love as and action and not simply the feeling. We may do all those things which love requires from a desire to gain some feeling, or some reaction from another, but when we love we do it because we are motivated by what is best for our beloved. This is true in romance, it is true in friendship and family. And it is true with Charity.

The Red Rose of Charity is a mystical love, for we may do acts of Charity without having Love. We may have the warm feelings of affection, and even go to great lengths in our works and not have Charity. It is a mystical love because unlike romantic or familial love, it is one in which only God can give us. It is loving, not with human love but with God's Love. It is the Love derived not by human affection or shared interest but from the fellowship of the Spirit. It is the Love which, or at least should be the basis for the unity of the Body of Christ for it is the Love we have for each other as members of that Body. (Philippians 2)

Though it is lost in our modern culture, Charity comes from the Grace we have through our Faith, it comes from being in Christ. We are saved by Grace through Faith, and we fulfill the ministry of the Church by Grace through Charity. Faith is the individualism of the Church, Charity communal. Faith is the means through which we seek sanctification by Grace, Charity is the means in which we seek to help others in their sanctification. And while the work may seem thorny, when you pursue Charity, after you have spent time truly seeking to Love, the thorn which stays with you are the one in which you could not help.

What Shall I Do?

What shall I do?
So many choices, so many paths
Its seems such a waste to pick just one
But to choose many paths and live all trials
Burns my life up way to fast

What shall I do?
Which way to live, which way is right
Shall I do what I should,
And fight the noble and righteous fight
Or should I give in and take all that I might

What shall I do?
How should I express myself to you
Write you, tell you, show you
Or just wait and do nothing but hope

What shall I do?
Try to fight, try to love
They make it so hard and say it's so easy
Dare to live, dare to give
Dare to find out just what's after death

The Sorrow of Our Time

For the past week, I have woken each morning with a reason to praise God fresh in my mind. A few weeks ago, it was by wondering if what I was feeling what emotional based thinkers means by 'being happy.' I think it was and praised God as I could sing a lumpy song and dance a lumpy dance simply because I was happy.

It did not last, as emotions never do for me. So, I praised God as I could sing a lumpy song and dance a lumpy dance simply because the quiet desperations of our lives are not so quiet. God is equally worthy of praise in our works, hardships and struggles as He is in our celebrations. For those of us who have been born of God's purifying fire, carved and formed by the pain of the sins of others and our own, there is a joy to be found in the sorrow that lasts forever. Indeed, there are no prayer more fruitful, for us at least, than the tears of Godly sorrow. (Mark 14)

Do not ask why the eye sheds prayerful tears. I might just be tempted to show you through the eye that burns. For I can find joy now in 'la tristesse durera toujours', the memory is still fresh in my mind when it was not pleasing to me. I remember clearly that day some years ago spent sitting on the stairs praying, begging God to take my life for the sorrow was too much for me. And even today that is true. the pain I find in Charity is past enduring without God, a burden too heavy to carry without the Cross. And that is the sorrow of our time, that we have forgotten that our Life is in Christ. (John 16)

A world in which liberty is the highest virtue and the pursuit of pleasure is the highest goal, is it no wonder that people speak of love only as a path to happiness. Is it only in a Church compromised by the spirit of such a world we would teach of God's Love void of His tears, void of His Righteousness? It is only in apostasy in which we can preach a Gospel void of the Cross, preach forgiveness without the horror of sin. The sorrow, the great sorrow of our time is that we do no longer understand that Godly Love requires Godly sorrow. (Luke 10)

It is proper and just to rejoice and find pleasure in our salvation. But the sweetness of our forgiveness is in direct proportions to the bitter taste of our sins. Forgiven much, love much.

Undoubtedly in the maturity which leads to ministry we come to enjoy the bitter-sweet flavor of the Cross. Without a doubt dealing with the knightly paradox of being both sinner and saint we learn that the Fire of God's condemnation of our sin is in perfect harmony with the Water of His forgiveness. God's condemnation, the conviction which His Spirit brings is as much a product of His Love as His forgiveness bought by the Cross, for to love perfectly as He is perfect is to find even the smallest of sins horrid. Even the smallest sin is a burden too heavy to carry, a pain past enduring. And having gained some taste of the perfection we will have in the next age, we gain some small understand what it means that Christ took our sins to the Cross with Him. (Romans 7)

It is a shame, a great shame that we are taught to avoid our Godly sorrow. For it is the maturing in our election by the sorrows of living at the threshold of eternity in which God trains us for our calling. It is not the sins we hate but the ones we grieve which shape us the most. For we hate the sins we do not do, but we grieve with a Godly sorrow those sins which we do not want to do, but do none-the-less. We have no need to repent for the sins we do not do, but for the sins we do we return to the Cross. In the maturing of our election, we learn to trust in Christ, and Christ alone in our justification and sanctification so that in our ministry we can confirm it boldly. So that we will know, and are able to tell others that in Faith God is both the source and the answer to the sorrow that never ends. (Luke 6)

It would have been so easy to slip into a contemplative life and put away the sorrows of the youth of my Faith. How tempting it was to allow apathy to take over and not go through the struggle to make sure my calling was secure. Indeed, I could beat my chest and say it is not fair that I should weep and struggle for your benefit when you do not care. If life was fair, none would escape hell. And there are those who weep and struggle and care. But make no mistake, it is for them and only them in which I continue on the path God has me on. And make no mistake it is for our sake, for the sake of his mystical body, the invisible Church in which God now brings His purifying Fire.

Do you not know that God is a jealous God? Do you not know that all with Faith belongs to Him, and we can have no other god? How long did you think that He would allow you to chase after your five-point plans for overcoming? How long did you think He would put up with a Gospel without a Cross, a Cross without repentance, repentance without Him? How long did you think that God would let His people chase idols, be corrupted by teachers teaching falsely and prophets prophesying falsely. Do you not yet see why I weep, do you not understand the sorrow of our time. As you would not be purified by the tears of His Love, how long did you think it would be before His Love would purify by Fire?

God gave you teachers equipped by the Spirit and Scriptures but we would not learn. We wanted something new so refused to be encouraged and taught endurance by what was written. We thought it was a new age so we needed new words, and sought teachers which would discard both the Spirit and Scriptures. (Romans 5). So God sent the judges equipped by the Spirit and Scripture but we would not discern. We wanted the glory for ourselves so refused to forsake those who feed our pride. We thought only how they made us feel so followed preachers who would distract us from our sorrows. (Galatians 3) So now God sends prophets equipped by the Spirit and Scripture to declare to you only one thing… You will be Justified by the Cross or not at all. You will have Faith in Christ, or you will have none at all. You will weep from Godly sorrow now or you will weep and gnash your teeth latter…you will repent or you will perish.

The first question is whether or not you are really saved. Much of my life, much of what I ever have to say or write makes little sense, and is considered unimportant to those who do not have a union with God through Christ. Not that everyone who has been regenerated is going to find me helpful, it is only as a knight I lean heavily towards obedience to God, but it is all for not if one does not already have that indwelling of the Spirit of God. One cannot be a knight to a lord they do not know. How can one expect to be trained by God if they do not already known by Him? One must first 'Examine yourself as to whether you are in the faith. Test yourselves. Do you not know yourselves, that Jesus Christ is in you? – unless indeed you are disqualified.' (2 Corinthians 13)

It would be over the issue of obedience in which I would turn my back on God in my youth. I could blame problems in the church, hypocritical Christians, that vague but dreadful sense of what obedience would cost me, but it was pride, pure and simple. The only cost I feared was the death of self-will, the subjection of my own will to the will of God was not a sacrifice I was willing to make. Much of my youth was focused on gaining the power control of my own fate. It would be that desire which motivated me to go into occult practices which would bind me into a fate crafted by unclean spirits. Though part of that delusion that I was free, unable to see the chains which trapped me until they were broken by Christ as my conversion.

Because I was raised in a church, believed in the right things, even baptized, some people would prefer to see my conversion as a rededication. I cannot because for the first time in my life I knew, really knew what it meant to be condemned, the first time I got a glimpse of what it meant to be saved. What I believed about the Gospel of Christ did not change, but it was the first time I saw, knew the Gospel as 'the power of God to salvation for everyone who believes.' It was the first time I understood that 'it is the righteousness of God is revealed from faith to faith'. (Romans 1) I do not consider myself saved at any time prior to that hot summer night in ninety-seven because before then I had never been united with God in Christ. Faith suddenly became a real thing to me.

I am no stranger to epiphanies. I had a Gnostic view of spirituality. Truth built upon truth until understanding came. Enlightenment was one awaking after the next which requiring an adjustment to my view of reality. And there is a kind of bonding and sharing which occurs with the occult practice of binding spirits. My conversion was not much different in a way, except in its totality. God was not simply added to my old views, He replaced them. What was planted in me that day shattered the philosophy of life I had so carefully crafted. Destroyed everything I rested my views on and replaced it with Christ. God became my only truth, my union with Him became my only reality, my Honor found only in service to the Jesus Christ, our King. I do not consider myself saved or regenerated prior to my conversion for the same reason I rarely refer to Christ as light. Without a doubt the Spirit of Christ is the Light in which shines from us and guides our way. No one who knows Jesus stays in darkness (John 8, 12).

But there are many who are like I once was and consider the darkness as light. They will talk about their darkness as the light, because without the Light of Christ the light we may have seems bright compared to the darkness of the world. How could they see it differently for 'If the light which is in you is darkness how great is the darkness' (Mathew 6). They will talk about embracing the god or even the God within because without knowing God the Father, Creator of heaven and earth, we can seem like gods. Indeed, God Himself told us to 'See to it that the light within you is not darkness' (Luke 11)

Of course, I would not have you be overly concerned about your salvation either. Though I have never struggled with that doubt, with having Hope, I know some do. I have never struggled with the doubt that Christ's work upon the Cross justified me, I have struggled with the doubt that through the Spirit He would sanctify me. And what I have learned has been that Hope is found not in placing trust in our own natures but in the nature of God. His righteousness and His Love, His power to redeem us. By Grace through Faith I know 'that He is a rewarder of those who diligently seek Him.' (Hebrew 11)

Teachers of the Word

As I pointed out sometime last year, the last time we have seen this level of conflict, mystics rising to such a level of predominance, was just prior to the Reformation. The Catholic Church took a long time responding to Luther because he was literally just one of thousands of 'heretics' running around. The rebellion against Rome started long before Luther. We think of it today in terms of the Reformation because, well as the saying goes, truth will win out. With all the good, the bad and the ugly we have today. The only difference now is our communication system, and that we have no Rome to rebel against. Well, that and they were on the verge of becoming a literate culture while we are on the verge of becoming a post-literate culture, if we are not already there.

Now I want you to mark the times in Church history when there seemly no mystics, and the word itself was regulated to fringe groups and spiritualists. The party line is that we did not exist then because there was no need. You know, God has raised us up for this time because He has some new revelation, a new reformation or to rethink the Faith etc. In the youth of my Faith, I agreed with that. After all, God dealt with me in extraordinary way, so He must have extraordinary plans for me. Right? Pride, of course, and a teaching which I think is formulated as an appeal to hubris. I have a different theory now. We do not see mystics during the times when the Church is doing well because, then nor now, there is no such thing as a mystic. As in something distinct from any other Christian, you know different from any other person who is actually regenerated.

Basically, when church culture is actually taking us in the direction God wants us to go, then there are no mystics. But when church is pushing us one way, and God another we have to make a choice. We have to choose between social pressure and the guiding of the Spirit. That is, of course, something that we all have to deal with, throughout our Life. But it is different, and what I mean by the Church doing well, is when the Teachers are actually teaching. You know, educating us in Scripture. You ever wonder why the insides of churches look like classrooms? Or maybe I should put it when Teachers, real teachers are behind the pulpits and not someone like me.

The problem which I am pointing out is what happens when someone has to make that choice before they have matured. That is, when one knows something is wrong but cannot put their finger on it. Is there really something wrong, or am I just being rebellious? Well, for me it was sometimes both. Let me use myself as an example, as of course everything is about me, at least in my own mind. I left the first church I attended after my conversion under some controversy, or I should write because of the collateral damage it was causing. I was accused of saying that doctrine was unimportant, which now I find humorous considering the whole thing started from my opposition to Benny Hinn. But the question was about that rebellion, that is what do you do when you disagree with the leadership at your church. Ego's clashed and I got into an argument with a jr. pastor.

I might have avoided the argument now, maybe it would be worse. I still think Benny Hinn is either delusional or a charlatan, but back then all I had was a reaction to him, and to the church moving into direction towards the prosperity superstation. My mistake was going to my sister's church, her being far more social than me. But I had actually gone for one reason. I wanted to know what happened to me, or more to the point what was still happening to me. My conversion I understood, the whole born again thing, was covered in what I learned from growing up in a church. But I could not rap my head around the fact that God continued to be active in me, work on me. I wanted to understand that and what I got instead was a worksheet to discover your gifts, or small group discussions on whether or not a Christian can be possessed.

Now it seems so simple, so obvious. Sanctification, maturing in the Faith, that work the Spirit of God does on us, throughout the rest of our lives. The convictions, the entirely different way of seeing Scripture, and especially the desire to know and conform to God's will. These are things I knew from the beginning in the abstract, but did not understand how the Bible related to them, so did not know why all the babbling and obsession with the Gifts seemed so wrong. If I was wiser, humbler, that is, if I was already mature enough, I would have looked for a church that actually had a teacher teaching from Scripture, truly teaching the Word rather than twisting it.

I left that church very much asking what was wrong. Even

more so during our failed rebellion at the ministry some of us worked for. I, of course, had a lot of time to think about it living with the hillbillies during my exile. I think asking what is wrong is a normal, a good reaction. In both cases I concluded was bad theology. I did not know it then, because I had not yet matured enough to discern those subtle heresies. The problem is that we often latch onto a specific issue and then judge everything by it. Obsession on signs and wonders, a lack of a focus on God, the lack of Love, using prayer as a form of spellcraft, and so on. For me it was the Lordship issue, people simply do not take their Faith seriously. All these issues are true, but they are all covered by Scripture.

As it is late, and I am starting to ramble and repeat, let me sum up my point, and maybe return on it tomorrow. The Church always has people like us. We simply are not noticed when the church is staying true to Scripture, helping us grow, in our sanctification by teaching Scripture. All of Scripture, the whole council of God. Not only what Christ did for us (though even that seems to lacking today), but also the work the Spirit does in us. Not only justification, but sanctification. But when it does not, we go looking for what it means to be saved, what is 'beyond salvation'. That is, when we have not matured enough to see it in Scripture ourselves, and those who are supposed to be showing it to us are not, we go off looking for that 'thing', that whatever we are supposed to be doing.

Do not mistake me, I am not blaming the teachers. (Romans 14). What I am pointing out is that in a world where real Teachers of the Word are few and far apart, the immature has to be careful who they pay attention to. That in that searching, we are too apt to listen to someone teaching heresy because they preach that 'thing' which was lacking in those who taught us before, or for that matter we may fall into error our self by thinking that that 'thing' which is needed for our sanctification is found in Scripture, instead of it being Scripture. I am tired, and will have to finish tomorrow, but I do not like that last line. Basically what I mean, is that tendency to get hung up on some detail of the Faith and warping our theology around it, instead of basing our theology on all of Scripture.

Sometimes we have felt, shall I say irritated by being lumped together with the other 'heretics', as Luther was. Not to be listened to and swiped aside as just another malcontent. And now that we are older, so we are past, or at least should be past our bitterness at a system which chewed us up and spit us out. By now we have come to terms, come to understand that most of the time we were expecting too much of the old guard when we expected them to know that our questions were not challenges but honest. That we had the hubris of youth so common with the moderns. Like our parents, and our younger siblings we are rebels of rebellious generations in a time of malcontent. We have spent our lives looking for that 'thing' which will set it right, which is the heart of activism, and it is the 'thing' which is at the heart of what is going on now.

What the 'thing' is differs, and we are broken into camps depending on what we think the problem is. Obviously, in so much as it is unavoidable to be in a camp, I have thrown my lot with the bible-thumpers. Not that I think that the Bible is the 'thing', but that all the 'things' are addressed in Scripture. This view came about when I started looking at the Church and not just individual Christians. That is, my personal 'thing' is sanctification, the work the Spirit of God does on us after the Grace of Regeneration, beyond salvation. It was, and is my opinion that the Church does not do a good enough job helping us mature, to grow in the Faith. We spend a lifetime sitting in a church but never growing.

Sanctification is a 'thing', important to be sure, but just one strip out of the whole cloth we call Faith. As I have mentioned before, I started studying salvation theology only because I noticed that how we view justification, affects our sanctification. That when we make it only about what Christ did for us for escaping God's wraith (hell), and forget that His work also allows the Spirit to work in us, on us, sanctification becomes unknown. Or the reverse, as I was more prone, when we ignore that His work saves us from the affects, the rightful judgment we deserve, sanctification becomes more about being perfect for perfect's sake rather than a means to give God glory for our salvation. Love is a 'thing', a thing often neglected but when we make it 'the thing', it distorts the theological map. Unitary, righteousness etc. and so on.

Obviously the 'thing' issue is not new. It is something that often happens, many denominations and cults (new religion rather than common use of the word) were and are based on a 'thing.' The difference is that today people looking around, claiming they have found the 'thing' is the rule now. And if you look back at what made us outcasts and rebels, was not so much that we were malcontents but that we dared to question 'the thing'. Not to brush aside my own pride, but I had no idea about the vineyard movement or its influence on the ministry I worked for, and so did not understand that my talk about transformation in terms of, well being transformed in the Image of Christ was an attack on their 'thing'. The point I made, or tried to make before was if I had been more educated in a theological sense, I still would have rebelled. It would not have sent me looking for what was wrong. I would have made the choice with eyes wide open.

From my view I have no one to blame but myself, my hubris and such, and lesson learned. And it is a lesson which I am expressing now. God is our Ground, Christ is our foundation, and there is a peace we have for that reason alone. We too often think of theology only in terms of building on that foundation. Something extra, if you would. I started my study in theology proper in order to make sure that what I was saying was orthodox, to make sure that I was not leading you cockeyed. What I discovered though was that theology, proper study of Scripture has given me a better image of Christ. That it has increased my peace and strength in God through Christ, by showing me more of the foundation we have in Him then I knew before.

I will, and have argued against those who basically make the sanctification that Scripture brings a Grace by Works. The study of Scripture is a Vehicle of Grace, but it is still the Spirit which works that Grace in us. Which brings me to the point of all this, Teachers, trust and 'the thing'. Those of how who have experienced that growth that the Spirit brings through the study of Scripture will, at this moment, have given me give me a certain amount of trust, is less likely to be critical to what else I have to write now. So, as you now trust me a bit more, let me say that trust is wrong.

Obviously, I am not meaning that I am untrustworthy. I work very hard to make sure what I say is as true as I can. Only that it is a technique of rhetoric, a way of manipulation. (Of course, I am not very good at it because I have yet to master the one-page memo. But anyway…). Because I speak the truth about Scripture, you are inclined to trust, to be less critical of what else I have to say. Or, on the other hand you will be more critical if you have a low view of

Scripture. So, let me turn my attention to Love as it seems the most popular, or at least my own readership peaked when it was my primary thing. Obviously Love, Charity, the love we have for one another as siblings in Christ, is lacking in a good number of churches. So, preach on love, God is Love, love is great. I am down with that being a long-hair peacenik and all. It is important, very, after all if we say we love God yet do not love our fellow Christian we are a liar.

But you will notice that those who restrict themselves only to Love, that say God is Love, but mean God is Only Love thing has to ignore a large portion of Scripture which clearly shows that His love is neither unconditional nor equal. He is Righteous as well as Loving, His will is wrath as well as mercy. Also, note their arrogance in that they think that their thing is the most important thing. Or for those who have been with me from the start, see the pride in what I wrote which made each 'thing' the most important thing needed when I was writing it. No balance, no completeness. More germane, focusing on single points, on single or limited 'thing' greatly limit the growth in the Faith we desire.

Notice how many of the superstars contending to be the new guard, the names representing the Church, are basically saying trust them because they understand the 'thing' you were looking for. Again the 'things' are important. There is a need to preach on things. People like me have our uses. I can be a bit motivating at times, at least I have been told such. I can explain things well, even if I do ramble way too much for the post-literate. The problem is it should never be 'trust me'. It is never about how well I string an endless road of words, or how much I can relate to you, but what I am pointing to.

Let me restate something. I am not trustworthy. I try very hard to have everything I write and say to be true, but am I God that I should be perfect always? I have had raptures and visions, been shown many 'things' but how do you know that? Is preaching from the authority of such things, from a 'thing' not the same as saying 'trust me'? Have Faith in me? Can you see the problem with that? Is that not just a betrayal of the very calling of those who preach, teach and minister, really every function and calling within the Church? That is a choice every preacher has to make, whether they are behind a pulpit or simply a writer such as myself. We either can grow your faith in us, or help your Faith in God grow. And not only in that 'thing' but growth in the entirety of Faith, in all the 'things' which make up that thing we call Faith.

And that really is 'the thing' is it not? The fullness of the Faith, the entire Image of Christ. That is all I am saying really. Teachers who do not teach the Word of God, teach all of the Word are not doing us any favors. They may help us, and may gain a following by teaching the 'thing' we need to hear at the moment. But are only hindrances when we need to hear the other 'things' we need to here. And the only way to make sure that we have all the 'things', the whole counsel of God by learning Scripture. Otherwise, we just end up focusing on those 'things' we want to hear.

A Little Fire

'Wolves...Further battles at this time hold no hope for victory, only the needless spilling of Blood. Blood which is still needed....I order an end to this fighting which spills the Warrior's Blood in vain...I do not doubt that you will once again stand when your are needed...'
- Loosely based on General Kleeberge's order of October 5th, 1939.

It seems to be that time, for my heart is pierced with sorrow. As it is apparent now that the old guard is passing away, one can expect there to be much ado as many try to be the new guard. One can already see the increase in people pressing their ideology, trying to gain followers and power so that they may claim to be the new guard. And all the preaching, finger pointing, stone throwing, in all the attempts to claim the moral high ground, I just have to ask; where is Christ is all this?

Betrayed with a kiss, indeed. Much of the Church today has traded God for Ideologies. And to be blunt, that is not my concern. I have made my choice, and as such I must say that Faith is not about ideology, but about God. If salvation is found, it is to be found in Christ, not in belief. And if you take a moment and think on who just wrote that. I, who has dedicated my life to philosophy, to find understanding and wisdom in all which can be understood under God, and in God. I, whose only benefit to the world around me is my understanding, say that what I believe and all my understanding is unimportant, of no use, pointless without God. I am nothing, and my words are nothing. It is that worship and fighting over ideology which is leaving the Church without the strength to resist the darkness. It is that war, that darkness which bloodies the 'land beyond the hill'.

Because of such statements when I look to the future, my future, and I could see a day when I am going to end up nailed to a social cross, crucified. Persecuted? Nay, I deserve far worse than anything mere humans can do to me. There simply comes that day when you have crossed the line, when one is no longer simply preaching, teaching, speaking the Word but living it. When one is no longer pointing to Virtue, The Beatitudes, as an ideal, but are living some measure of them. When one gains, in some small way that perfected Life in Christ. And when that day happens, when the Light in your heart can no longer be hidden, the World and the Church of Ideologies will join forces, however reluctantly, to nail you to a cross.

I spent years thinking that the problem was a lack of Love. While it is true that there is a considerable lack of Charity in the Church today, but that is a symptom not the disease. It is obvious to me now, in that I have been stupid not to notice it before, but the true illness which inflicts His Body, is the lack of a head. That after all these years, I have finally come to see that what we Christians are missing is Christ. The crucified Christ, the Living Christ, the Way, the Truth, the Life. Do not mistake what I am saying, one does not have to have those mystical experiences which have marked my life, but one must, I say again, one must have a communion with the Spirit of God.

I should, of course, make it clear that it is not I saying that, it is God. It is echoed in the heart of every Christian I know, all who hear what the Spirit is saying. I though, have no problem putting it in the harsh way. The time in which one could be lukewarm, could try to serve two masters is coming to an end. It now time to choose. Seek God and be blessed, or hold onto your ideologies and be handed over to the darkness.

A little Salt

My thoughts are seemingly scattered all over the place, but I think what fish see as only random threads here and there are in fact the net which catches them. Yes, I am calling you fish. The only real question is what kind of fish are you? Are you a small fish dreaming of being a big fish? Are you a big fish, dreaming that your pond was bigger? Or are you that fish tired of ponds all together. One dreaming and struggling to make it to the Ocean so you can find out just what kind of fish you are?

But you may not be in a pond at all but swimming around in an aquarium? So, you may not have noticed the drought. One by one all of the ponds are drying up, so all that is left are those fish that live in the Ocean and those here and there that have found a home in an aquarium. You may not see it. Your church may have plenty of water. Temperature controlled, live plants, even one of those scuba dudes floating up and down. Little flakes coming down out of nowhere that you can gobble up. Life is grand and the only fear you might have been that green net of death will come and scoop you out of the tank. But if you want to know what I am talking about take a look on the other side of the glass. See how dry it is out here, see how God is withholding the Rain.

But then again you may not want to see God withholding the Rain, because then you would have to ask where the water for your tank is coming from. It is refusal to answer that question, to keep asking it, is a reason, if not the main reason the Church culture is dead today. Because we have not the taste for salt.

We seek only sweet water for our aquariums. We know what the salt means, that once tasted enough, once it transforms us, we have little choice but to head to the Ocean, to seek the Source. Once we come to need the salt in our water, we can find no rest outside of the Ocean, outside of God.

So, I ask again, from where is the water in your tank coming? As there is no more Rain, and the water evaporates must be replaced, it must come from somewhere. But I am not really asking that, for we all know it is through individuals, the bond-servants out of who the water flows.

There is only one Way, one Path we can travel on, which

means only two directions we may head. Towards the Ocean, towards Christ, or we may move into the mud. So, the only new Water which can be coming, is either salty or muddy.

Which means I am really asking what is the quality of the Water flowing out of us. It is a question that every Bond-Servant should be asking every day. As in this time, like all dry seasons, that we are the jugs which overflow with water, the instrument of the refreshing of the water supplies, what is the nature of the Water coming from us? Is it salty, getting them accustom to the taste, helping them find the Source of the water, the Ocean, teaching them to have Faith, to rely on God? Or is it muddy, with only the appearance of substance and wisdom, teaching them only to put their faith in us, to look to us as the Source of the Water? Look to it, for the Word from God has never been clearer; death is what awaits all tyrants

Leadership

Do you ever get the desire to strip off all vestiges of civilization and run with the wolves, to hunt, to howl? To race the wind, pushing with everything you have until you collapse? Do you ever have the urge bubble up from deep inside to throw yourself into a tornado just for the pleasure of the ride? Do you ever dream of being a great samurai facing an opponent, not even questioning whether you will win or lose, not caring about victory or defeat but finding pleasure in the fight itself? The question is, no matter how it manifests, do you feel that pull, that longing deep inside to live, to truly live?

Maybe not. Maybe you are too old, maybe you say that is for the young, any passion you had for life dried up a long time ago. But I do not see age as a factor. I know people much older than me who live a life of gusto, and I know people half my age who find no passion in life, who have given up. The majority that I meet have a look in their eyes that tells that they long to live. They long for passion. They long, for most of them, something they cannot put into words. Their spirits scream out 'this cannot be all there is, there has to be more.'

Passion! Forget oil, forget electricity and defiantly forget money. Passion is the energy which truly runs a nation. Forget technology, forget information, what are these compared to the will to use them? It is passion that people seek. Not wealth, not glory, not power but passion, to feel alive, to be filled with life so abundantly that there are no more questions about the meaning of life, for you can feel what it means to be alive. If I could point to the sky, and crack open the heavens you would see passion perfected, the Resurrection. In that fleeting moment you would weep, for you would know what it means to be alive. And in that moment, you would weep because you would understand the cost for life. There is always a cost, the Cross.

Life is not possible without suffering, and suffering is pointless unless it is redemptive, unless it brings life. The life you have today was bought for you by the sufferings of others and yourself. Your mother's suffering to carry and birth you, your parent's suffering to care and provide, your friends' wiliness to care and your own suffering to endure and suffer for others. Suffering is the cost of life, the cost of passion. Without the Cross there could be no Resurrection, but without the Resurrection, the Cross would be pointless.

God allows, even wills us to suffer because it is by that suffering that we learn how to be alive, how to find joy in living, how we learn to use the life we have. Suffering, the wiliness to allow ourselves to suffer, does not only make those moments when we are not suffering a pleasure, it is also the cost of wisdom.

If I had to give a definition to wisdom, it would be the perfect balance between passion and intellect. It would be not only knowing how to act, but having the will to act. But the question is not how I define wisdom, but how a society defines it. All other social assumptions fall secondary to the nation's ideal of the concept we call wisdom. Morality or social norms, economics, culture, and public policy all derive from the wisdom that society has, how they define what is wise. And as the wisdom of a community flows not from its leader but from its elders, then that community's ideal of an elder is of vital importance.

Even with this understanding, I am ill equipped to describe what an elder should be, or even could be. I am like a man who has been trained in a profession to the point in which they can name and use each of the tools of their trade, and then goes to try to explain what it like to be a member of that profession. Or I am like one who, at seeing a figure far off in the distance, proceeds to gives a detailed description of that person. Life is like that. The future is like that. We look to the future and see what might happen, and even when we what will happen, we never fully understand it until it does happen.

I could point to that elder I will be some day. I could try to describe the wisdom that he will have. But the truth is, I would not be describing the future, I would be describing and image of the future created by the understanding of the now. Nor can I really speak of wisdom. It is funny that almost a life time as a philosopher, one who seeks to acquire wisdom, just to learn that, for the most part, wisdom is an illusion. Just as suffering is pointless unless it is redemptive, so is wisdom useless unless it is used to benefit the community. Which, in all honesty is where I am starting with my ideal of an elder, the first of the steps towards my future self.

The wisdom of an elder does not differ from others in either quality or quantity but in focus. A leader needs wisdom, they must be able to determine how to secure the welfare of the People, in the now, and they must wise enough to listen to the wisdom of the elders. The elder's wisdom is focused less on the now, and more on the future. I do not mean that they must be prophets, what I mean is that they must be able to weigh, to balance the welfare of the People in the now with the welfare of the People in the future.

I could go on, and on, and on, but like I said I have only really begun to understand what this means, at what level this really needs to be at. We do not need friends, or stars, or even for you to 'understand' us. What we need from you is your wisdom. If we have any hope of a better tomorrow, our work will have to be guided by you, your experience, and the wisdom that the sufferings of life have taught you. And as wrote in my journal this is a simple statement of fact, a cry of desperation, and a plea for mercy: We need elders!

The Ten Companions of Lumpy

The Bear, the Wolf and the Bat,
    The three which I know
    The three which know me
    Faithful companions
    Form birth, to death
    Everything in-between
The Horse, the Buffalo and the Raven,
    The three which I call
    The three which call me
    Loving companions
    Arriving and departing
    Always according to need
The Crow, the Spider, and the Mouse,
    The three which harmed me
    The three which I have harmed
    Helpful companions
    Into woe, or into healing
    The course set by my desires
Ten companions do I have
Nine I have given names
The Tenth I dare not
For what name can I contrive:
    To encompass all eternity?
    To describe all mysteries?
    To bind the boundless?
    To give form to the formless?
    To limit the limitless?
Call the Tenth what you will
Knowing a name is not enough
To make one a companion
For that, one must travel alongside:

The Truth Eternal
The Way Mysterious
The Life Boundless
The Hope Formless
The Love Limitless

Desperate Prophesies

I am downloading a very large file at the moment, so as often happens when I must be patient, I retreat into my own head. And I was thinking about all the financial crisis talk, and about how we are trying so desperately to get back to normal. And somewhere in the chaos I call my thoughts an idea kept surfacing from the murky depths... That maybe where we are at now is normal. Maybe decay and turmoil are the natural state of things. That hardships and struggle is the normal parts of life, and the good times are simply holidays, momentary glimpses of the sun in an otherwise bleak and stormy sky.

Obviously, there is more to it. That it goes with other things I have been thinking about. You know, as the storm has hit, and as the long night was brought by the Northern Wind, I move into the time in which the call for the Wolves will be put out. That, I was expecting, what has caught me a bit off guard is that I must now be looking to build some stability in my life, financial and what not. Odd timing don't ya think, but then again God has never really made since in that regard with me. It has taught me trust, though.

To speak plainly, I praying about this, you know, trying to make sure my course was correct. God told me, as He always does, not to worry, that it will happen soon. That is not all that odd, I almost always know what is going to happen in my life, even though I rarely know how it is going to happen. That odd thing is I need to talk about it before it before it does. Let other's know that I am about to be financially stable. It is not really like you care. I mean, I know people care about me, but I am sure that you have your own worries.

But here is the thing, it does let me make this point. I hear a lot of people say this or that is going to happen. Prophecy, if you can forgive a misunderstanding that the common use of the word implies. Being rather familiar with the Gift, in a personal way, the first question, the first thing I examine is where does it point. Just me and that judging my heart by where my focus is. That is, the purpose of prophecy is to edify the Church, to help in the Following of Christ. Or to be blunt, I have had it drilled into me, in that deep painful way God has of drilling us, that the primary purpose of prophecy it to reassure us that God is still with us. Us, not me, or I,

36

or that special person, but with us, the Church, the Body of Christ.

It is easy to feel, in times such as these, that God has abandoned us. Indeed, you do not have to search long to find someone preaching such. That God leaves us, or worse, punishes because of some sin. But has He? Has God abandoned, turned His back on those who follow Him? If feels like it sometimes, trust me I know that feeling, but it is never true. All these years of digging and searching, I have learned well that God always gives us what we need, even if we do not like it. That all this talk about God punishing us for our sin, I have to ask, what does that have to do with us, His Church? Does God punish the innocent for the crimes of the wicked, or does He simply cause the rain to fall on both?

The point being, that those who say that God is not with us, are not much different than those who say God is dead. He is still there, for those who seek Him. He is still God, and the only difference between now and ten years ago is whether or not we are letting our current struggles distract us from seeking Him.

Fighting Fire with Fire

From time to time, I make fun of my insanity. I know some do not like it. Maybe because you care about me and think I am being self-derogatory. For others, you may catch the touch of sarcasm, realizing that by pocking a finger at myself, I am also trolling your sanity. That what I am more often than not pointing out is that, by all worldly standards, Faith is insanity.

I believe in God. Insane. God speaks to me. Just crazy. I know, I have no doubt that nothing, nothing is impossible for me, with God, for the sake of the Gospel of Jesus the Christ. Which makes me completely out of my mind. Yet that is the measure of the Grace of Faith I have. I but have to ask and mountains will flatten for the sake of the Gospel. But a simple request and clouds will withhold their rain, for the sake of the Gospel. That a host of Messengers will fight for me on behalf of the Gospel. That there is absolutely nothing which will be withheld from me to do His will. Now, tell me I am not insane. Who in their right mind believes that they but only have to ask and God will move heaven and earth for the sake of the Gospel? I mean really, really believes.

Such is the measure of the Grace, the Faith I have. But as I said before the hard part is not getting the Grace, it is living up to it. Which there are two points here. The first is that belief is not the same thing as doing, trusting is not the same thing as asking. While I have no doubt, the struggle is stepping out in that Faith. For you that might be an issue of fear, and I cannot say that there is none, only my struggle has more been in that area of insanity. That feeling of it is just silly.

It has always been that feeling that it is just a silly, insane thought that God can do anything, that God would do anything, everything for the sake of Gospel. But that aspect, that struggle has been much easier for me since I took a hard look at my life and drew a conclusion. That if I am insane, if my life for the last eleven years has been some fantasy, then my life, and the life of those around me, are much better than when I was sane. Of course, my view is that I am the sane one and most of the world is the ones living in a fantasy. But that is hardly an argument which can show one's sanity.

As I have said before, being judgmental I will leave to others, because the real struggle, the one which will ruin more than any other has nothing to do with not claiming the Grace, but the temptation to abuse it. If one does not except the responsibility God is trying to give, then that one simply no longer grows. If one betrays that Sacred Trust, the harm those around them, hinders and maybe even destroys their growth.

I have spoken and written about with God all things are possible. You will notice this time, I have put in the words; for the sake of the Gospel. That which is given to us is not given to glorify us, but God. That everything which has happened to and for me in the last eleven years and even my conversion, my road to Damascus, kneeling at the foot of Christ, pledging sword and life in service to Elohim, has been for the sake of the Gospel. While it has been a great benefit to me, to be sure, it is so that I can declare with that power that only Truth can give you, as only an eye-witness can, that Christ rose from the dead. That Christ is alive…that Christ is Life. Woe to me if I think that it was for any other reason, that there is any other reason for my Life.

Godly Training

It does not bother me that I am one of those people who are so focused on the spiritual that I have no worldly use. It does not bother me because I know it is not true. That is, I have a worldly use to a person in direct proportion to how important the inner-life is to that person. But it does bother me sometimes that there are those within Christianity, of which being a Christian is of great importance to them, that they cannot see what use I can be. I do not mean that if one does not find me helpful that they lack Faith, not at all. I mean only that I do not understand, that I do doubt if one has Faith if they cannot see how some might find me helpful.

I might be bias. I mean, with rare exceptions I do not find sitting and listening to some pastor helpful, but I can understand listening to them why many would find them so. But thinking about it, I would have to say that it does not necessarily mean a lack of Faith, it could simply be a lack of humility. I mean, for me humility for a large part was having to accept that I am a genius.

That may not sound humble, but when I considered myself only average in intelligence, I considered my intelligence the standard in which to measure intelligence. Or if you would, I considered myself only average, then everyone who was really average I considered stupid. That the only reason that the average person was not understanding, did not already know what the preacher was saying for the hundredth time was because they were too lazy to think about it.

Of course, for many that is true, but I am pointing out something here. That my intellect and wisdom count for nothing, if it is not bent, subjugated to the Will of God. Oh, I am sure it would if I was focused on giving worldly advice, to helping people succeed in the outer-life. But my advice, and what I write is about the Inner-Life, about being that person God wants you to be, of becoming who it is in you to become. And being such, my focus, my advice must always be centered on what God is trying to teach the person who I am advising.

In truth, I do not feel like I even give advice. It is more like simply putting into words what the person already knows. Helping the person find the understanding of what God has placed in their hearts. And see now, I bring up humility because my role is always secondary, a very minor one compared to the person's willingness to seek that understanding. Their willingness to have God change their heart, to be and move according to God's will.

Holy Innocence

They are calling it the great recession. For me, it is simply that I am unemployed, broke, no prospects and all that jazz. I have nothing left to give but to words, and as I have made it clear, my words are nothing as I am nothing. So, as you might imagine, by prayers have been rather self-centered, even selfish of late. That when I sit down to pray, I can think of only one thing, can only seem to ask God for one thing. To increase my Love.

For many that may not seem selfish. Indeed, for many should be spending more time petitioning God for such, but I call it selfish for me because I have caught a glimpse of something. Something wonderful, something beautiful, something so great that I long to have it. Something which I can only describe as a holy innocence.

I have written about it before, even though I have never called it such. I do not know any other words to describe my new understanding, but I do know that if comes only from Love. That it is only Love, Agape, Charity, the Grace to Love which only God can give us, which allows one to be as innocent as a dove, while still being as shrewd as the serpent. I am sure I will write more about it when I have a better understanding, once I have grown towards it a bit. But the point of this is to state that sometimes it is alright, even needed for us to be self-centered, even selfish in our prayers.

Obviously, I do not mean that it is acceptable to treat prayers like rubbing a lamp. I mean it in that way as Christ said, that before you can take the speck out of your brother's eye, you need to get rid of your own plank. That is needed, especially when we are young in the Faith but also even with the mature, to spend time focused on the changes needing to be done in our own heart. Time set aside, or even better a lifestyle and attitude of allowing, accepting, seeking the changes that God is performing in us.

It might not be Love at this moment, it could be Faith, or Hope, joy or peace or so on. But the thing is, there is something which God is trying to show you. That at this moment, every moment of every day, God is trying to nurture your growth in the Inner-Life. Others can help us to understand, maybe give us that kick we need, remind us, exhort us, but in the end, the choice is always up to us. That the bottom line is that our growth, our progress towards being that person who it is in us to be, is entirely up to whether or not we are seeking to follow the Way, Christ, or whether we are being stubborn and trying to do it our way.

Not By Works

My hands are shaking as I write this. The fast for Holy Week tore me up in a way I have not been in a long time. A heart stripped naked, week, vulnerable, with more questions then answer. It threw me into turmoil, cause me to question, doubt the foundation of my life. A fire which burned away all my defenses and ripped away harshly all that which protects me from the cold and cruel reality of this world we live in. So tired, torn and raw that it is only by Grace that I have the strength to even breathe. Not feeling more worthy, more holy, but less, as chief among sinners. My sins grating on me like sandpaper underwear. In short, it was a good fast.

As I was looking around to see what people are saying about mortification I read many silly things. The most common view is that fasting is giving up a pleasure to get favor from God. and maybe that is your view, sacrifice a bit to earn a reward. Or that we fast because it supercharges our prayers. That our prayers are more powerful when we fast. It is not that these views are wrong, it is that it places power in the wrong place. To use the pointy end of the sword, this is simply a form of Christian spell craft. Doing something in order to get God to do what we want. That God rewards us for simply going through some ritual, or doing some work. It is a misconception, and a dangerous one, that Grace comes to us because of our sacrifice, rather than because we have a heart of mercy.

I can easily say that you will not become all you could be with God without fasting. But I could also easily say that you will not become all you could be with God with fasting. What one may become with God is without limit, so let me not speak on that at all for the moment. It is not easy to say, nor do I see any truth in saying that you must fast. Fasting, mortification, sacrifices of any kind are not required. But a heart, a humble heart that is willing to sacrifice is a requirement, something one must have. Works will not save but if one has Faith, that Faith will produce works, right? I am not saying that if you have Faith then you will fast. What I am saying is that if you have Faith, you will have Charity, and the works we perform from that Charity will require sacrifice. And fasting is one of those things which is useful for understanding and training in self-sacrifice.

No one enters the Kingdom of Heaven without doing the Will of the Father. As I have written before, the smallest of works in God's Will is greater than all of the combined works outside of His Will. Obedience is a requirement, but we are not commanded directly to any specific outer works. We are commanded to Love, and out of that Love works will come. Mercy is greater than sacrifice, for without mercy a sacrifice counts for nothing, and with mercy, it stops feeling like a sacrifice.

When we are immature our focus is on the Law. That in the beginning we see the sacrifice, the need to resist temptation, to beat down the flesh. But as we mature we see that it was no sacrifice at all, that those self-centered and selfish search for pleasures were doing us more harm than good. Of course, there are many, many time many who will not see this, that think they have done a great work because they can resist temptations. But look at how sour their face is. Where is the laughter, the peace and the Joy which is promised us?

One resists temptation, fights and bites against the flesh, is a way of showing mercy to one's self. As I love myself, then I will not harm myself, even if I long for those things which do me harm. And though I love myself, and desire what is best, I still do what is wrong, I must learn to forgive myself for those sins which I offend, harm myself with. To give myself time, to rely on the Mercy from above until that day in which I will not need it. Which I am not sure how it will happen, but I do know I will already be dead when it does.

Fast, do not fast, it makes little difference, but regardless we are all called to a life of mortification, to face and bare those pains which Loving requires. As I wrote in the Cost of Grace, that the real fast, the real mortification is found in subduing the self so that we may Love.

Every parent understands, or at least should understand, that struggle. The fight to put aside what they want for the sake of what is best for their children. Is that not what St. Paul was speaking about with spouses? That when one marries they no longer live for themselves but sacrifice their self for the sake of their spouse. Is it not the same with ministry, for those who are called to be bond-servants? That those who would be greatest in the Church, must be a servant, a slave to all. That we no longer sacrifice for ourselves but take into our flesh that which is lacking in the suffering of Christ?

In the Cross, in Christ and Him crucified we see the real lesson of mortification. It was not the pain, torture, and death which is the message, but that God so Love the world. It is that Love which brought Christ to Golgotha, not the sacrifice itself is something which I learn anew with each fast. That as works are dead when one does not have Faith, sacrifice is pointless if one does not have Love.

No worth except its name

The other day I woke up with the thought that I am enlightened…but that's ok, I'll get over it. And then I laughed, the kind of laugh which resonates through your entire being. If you understand why I laughed then you too are enlightened…but do not worry about it, you too will get over it…

I wrote to some of you personally a meeting and the request for my presence. Now the purpose for me to go was not, will be not be so I can impart any great wisdom. They have little need for me in that area, but so they can test me to see if I am the one they are waiting for. This may seem an odd thing to say considering I have no idea who these people are. In fact, I was a bit reluctant to share it (the reason I did not put it in my last email), for reasons I do not fully understand it is important that I share it now. See the point is not whether or not I am this person they are looking for, nor is it important if whether or not they are the elders I am looking for. What is important is what I am.

Few understand how close I came to becoming a priest, or more to the point, how difficult it was not to. The reason is simple, it is my vocation…it is who I am. The problem I have been having is asking the question of whom besides the Catholics comprehends who I am, or more importantly takes it into account enough to have a place in their tradition for me. I have been focusing on that question because when I find the answer then I will find the place I belong. What I should have been asking is who am I, which makes me laugh because I have spent most of my life searching for that answer. Yet, in many ways they are one in the same question.

Now I have said that the time of the wolf is over, and it is not time for the bears to rise. I in no way mean that it is time for bears to supplant wolves, what I mean by this is…the time to kill has passed, it is now time to heal. Any wolf worth the title must come to realize that the time for conquest is over, that the crusade to end all wrongs must itself come to an end. That all the fighting and struggles of the cultural war is counterproductive at best. It is time to gather the People together and heal our wounds, to heal our spirits, to heal the land.

When you look back over your life and examine why you

have suffered, not what caused the suffering but what the suffering as worked in you, you but cannot help but to view the pain as petty and minor things compared to what they have taught you. We often think that it is those pleasurable moments when Elohim takes us to the peaks of understanding are where we learn. This is true, if we speak of learning only in terms of knowledge. Yet, what we know is not who we are, it is the suffering and pain which we endure which is strong enough to etch our souls.

Pains we should call irritations, pains so intense that it burns all which it comes in contact and everything in between are the chisel which God used on us. To live is....to suffer, and the suffering does not cease, and even becomes worse until that moment we allow the suffering to do its work. The pain may continue for some time but the suffering ends when we allow ourselves to be the person God is trying to create. And the pain continues...and continues...and continues...waiting for the next time it is to be used...it becomes a constant companion, a friend. We grow so used to it that we could not imagine a life without it...we grow to want it, admire it, even love it...and I will ask the same question of you which God has recently asked of me... why are you still clutching the chisel and fire close to your heart now that their work is finished?

I will not, we must not, deny that we have been wronged. That society and individuals have wounded us and caused us to suffer. We cannot deny that society and individuals will wound us, and are wounded themselves. I cannot, we cannot forget that we too wound. It is a huge, bloody and vicious cycle, and it must be broken. It is time for us to admit honestly that we have felt the pain of life sting us most severe. It is also time for us to take a stand and say that it ends here and now, with me. It is time to say that I will take into my flesh all the suffering the world has to offer and...absorb it. To say with conviction and the resolve to accomplish it that I will not pass on the violence which has been to me. I will not slap another because I have been slapped...I will not even slap back.

I have a dear friend which a long time ago pointed out that when we go out and fight evil its blood which spills on our clothing will seep into our flesh and start to corrupt us. I have since found this to be true, not only personally but collectively. There is a time in which we must retreat and care for our wounded. It is time to mend some fences, to tend to the sheep, to prune the peach trees and maybe plant a few more.

This may seem like giving up, and this takes wisdom to understand, that sometimes you must give up land in order to win the war. There are times when you must let the enemy have the fight, so you can gather the strength to continue it. If you remember that I shared about the coming of three battles. And how the People, or at least those who I will call my people, must not involve themselves with the first two. They must do this because if to gather their strength so they will not have to fight the third one. We must spend the time to reach out to God, (and let me not forget - each other) to heal the wounds which cut so deeply across our individual and collective spirit.

So, you understand the importance of what I am saying I will say that it is not I but God who says thus. It is hardly necessary, is it though? You already know that we, as individuals, as families, as churches, as the Church, as communities and the nation as a whole, are in desperate need of healing. It is what we want, what we always wanted. Or at least it is what I always wanted. Writing this I have come to realize not only what I am about to write but also that this healing is what I meant by the word revival. In a way I already knew that. I knew what it would look like, feel like. My view was incorrect on the means of getting there. That I too looked upon it as a crusade, rid this or that evil and it will begin. But that is not the way.

Do not mistake what I am saying, healing is a fight in its own way. Just as anyone who has struggled (and those of you struggling) with their personal healing. It is a fight in which both combatants are yourself, and you do not heal until that moment you stop fighting with yourself. When you forgive yourself, when you are willing to admit God has forgiven you, why you let go of your pride and forgive, when you…well there as many ways of putting it as there are people, but is that not what we, the People, are doing? It is more than politics which are partisan it is our nation…it is our hearts.

Every once in a while, you will hear talk of a coming civil war. There are differing theories on what the sides will compose of, some make it about race, others religion. On that I have neither opinion, nor insight nor Word. If I could bring you to a higher, spiritual view of our nation you would see…we are already in a civil war. Not of blood and bullet but of ideology. But just because people are not being shot (even though some are in our very streets and homes) at does not mean they are not being wounded by it. (Every sensitive growing up during the evil empire eighties knows what I mean)

I am not saying that we should stop seeking righteousness or that we should stop teaching what that means, what I mean is: why are we taking it personally? Where is all the anger and frustration coming from if it is not coming from things not being the way we want it? Is it possible that we are motivated far less from the Charity to see their wounds healed then we think we are, and instead acting far more from the pain of our own wounds then we should be? We should give this much thought and prayers, not only from the social viewpoint but from a personal one as well. For the healing of a nation starts when individuals make a stand and say we will not pass the hurt on any more.

On that note I will leave you one more question to ponder. If I think of my brother as an enemy, can we still be called a family, if we name our neighbors the enemy can we still be called a community?

For The Love of Death

Death, oh sweet death
I welcome you with open arms
I do not fear you like others do
But enjoy your noble embrace

I fear not death
Only of living in vain
Have I not left my mark in the world?
But who will read and understand that mark when I'm gone

I fear not death
For there is an equality after death
Not like the equal now
But the sameness that someday will come

I fear not death
There is a beauty to be found in death
The leaves that fall in autumn die in such a way

I fear not death
Only not doing what is right
I try so hard and it seems so easy
Then why so many mistakes over a life

Death, oh sweet death
Come and take your prize of me
I will not fight you like so many others
The victory belongs to me
For being with my lord Jesus
Comes out of what others call death

Thought Crimes

Here is a simple fact for your consideration: the arguments which makes the most sense to you, the ones which will be the most convincing to you, relies not on reason but on your inability to reason, your desire to take the easy way out and not to opine for yourself. Indeed, you judge a statement as true only if it gives you pleasure, that sublime delight of confirming what you already hold to be true…I know, I know, I should have put that in the less offensive 'our, we, and they'. I know to put it down such only raises that spiked walls of the intellect defending itself. To cause that feeling, that desire to argue, to prove that your view is well reasoned. And knowing this, the question quickly becomes: did I not just control your attitude with nothing more than words?

You too may argue that this is not the case. There seems to be this base instinct not to admit that we are persuaded by others. And that unwillingness to admit that others have an influence on us is the same reason we are so easily controlled. The very idea that those in authority, that our leaders, our media, our teachers, preachers and parents may be the origin of our ideas and views creates the feeling that we have not control of our own lives. Others maybe, those masses of the unenlightened to be sure, but never us, never you, never me. Yet in avoiding to accept the discomfort that we may not be in control, by failing to recognize that it is others of whom we owe much of our ideas, ideals and opinions, creates a blind spot in which those who have the talent in the subtle means of persuasion to influence us.

It is one of those paradoxes of the human heart that the more we accept, the more we allow for the influence's others have on us, the less we are influenced by them. We are influenced, constantly and without cease, by those we meet and talk with, the books we read, the music we listen to, the shows we watch. Every smallest piece of data our sense reports influences us, mixes in that construct of the self-view and shapes who we are, who we become. But by admitting to ourselves that we are indeed influenced by our environment, that even an asocial Aspie such as myself is socialized, we can learn how to shape the influence. It is the first step in deciding what affect it has on us.

Faith Alone

I have met more than a few who believe if they can just experience what I have all their problems in their Faith will go away. Indeed, there are whole denominations and mega-churches built on little more than preaching such. For me, even though they have been grand and have had an effect, they also have also been cause of more than a few struggles. This centered mostly around my pride and turning my experiences into an idol, seeking them instead of Him. The mystical nature of my Faith would also be at the center of my crisis of Faith. It would make it hard to answer the question of how do I know my Faith is real.

Though I called myself Christian my entire life, and I delved into dark mysteries that we are not meant to know, my first religion was the High Art of Reason as it fits well with my natural analytical thought process. I am not without emotions, but my view of life tends towards the factual rather than emotional. The internal structure of my thought process is very much taking one fact and weighing it against others. The problem is that mystical experiences of every sort are, by their nature, subjective. It is a fact that I had them, but everything beyond that is conjecture. For the first ten years this was not much of an issue, as the fruits of my Faith confirmed my conversion. But a few years back, when my primary idol finally came crashing down, I found that the radical change in my life was not enough proof for me.

Though I prided myself on my self-awareness, but that I am fully aware of the great duplicity of the human heart. (Jeremiah 17) I had considerable turmoil over the question whether or not I have been hoodwinked for all these years. I struggled with pride. I still do just not in the same way. But pride is just another way of saying that we are making an idol out of ourselves. In pride I could feel assured that my experience was from God, because there was no doubt in my early years. But when I was less confident in my own ability to judge, when I was no longer seeing myself as the judge I had to doubt.

If my Faith had remained simply a personal thing then I most likely would not have had to face that long doubt. Then again, maybe it is a universal aspect of sanctification. I cannot say that strongly, but for me it was a time, the first time in which I doubted the reality of my Faith. I doubted my sanity. I doubted my experiences. But I never doubted God, or that He was the author of my Faith. I started to doubt, I had to make sure. Before I could minister I had to be sure that my election and calling was true, and not simply some megalomania on my part. I had to know that it was my Faith was really resting on, so I studied. I approached Scripture in way in which theologians do it, rather than simply for my own edification.

Faith alone? Grace alone? They are nice slogans but they do not capture the complexity of Scripture. Nor have they given me much comfort or guidance. I disliked Infralapsarianism for more than it being a long word never used in conversation by the average person. I do not think any of the positions truly take into account the fact the God as the Creator is beyond time as He transcends space. I found the arguments of Faith verse works, and by Grace verse by choice simply too shallow to answer the questions I had. Obviously there must be Faith (John 3), and we are saved by Grace (Ephesians 2). When I did my own study I counted at least seven other conditions which are mentioned in Scripture.

From the Scriptures of Acts (10) I removed baptism (1 peter 3) from the list as falling under obedience, done after the initial salvation. Unless, of course, you believe that one can have the Holy Spirit and not be saved. As act of baptism is useless unless one also has Faith, and it was showed to me that it clearly falls under obedience (Mark 16).

Confession of our belief (Romans 10) is an interesting one to me. I would be inclined to treat this as an obedience except our Lord saying that He will deny anyone who denies Him. But this returns to Faith because one must truly believe 'in their hearts' which makes it proclaiming the Faith they have. The same can be said about calling on the Lord (Acts 2, Romans 10), because of course not everyone who calls Him Lord will enter the Kingdom. Being saved in hope (Romans 8) might seem strange if it was not the hope found in our Faith. That by having the Spirit we know that we are saved, and we hope, long and desire the age to come. One cannot have hope without Faith, as it is the Gospel which gives us our hope.

Which, besides Grace through Faith, leaves repentance, love and obedience. Love is interesting in that it can be seen both as obedience and one of the changes of character (fruits) the Spirit works on us. I have written much on it over the years, and I am sure that I will write much of it in this work. I am going to skip over obedience (Philippians 2) for a moment to focus on repentance as it is the first recognizable component of salivation in which we partake.

Repentance which lead to salvation is a Godly sorrow (2 Corinthians 7).   Too often we think of repentance as our remorse or guilt for a sin. It is obviously more than simply hating our behavior, and it is even more than changing it. Even those without Faith can do that.   Repentance is not only turning away from sin but turning to God in that remorse (Acts 20). This is true at conversion, and it is true throughout our Life as repentance is returning to God. Sometimes it happens, we are tempted to lose our focus on God. To leave Him and His will. We are tempted away from God and towards sin, or we do not like where God is taking us. Or not happy about where God has us at the moment. Sometimes these are nothings, we fall, we get up and keep going, with little more than feeling stupid. Other times we lose hold of our Faith. We start being ashamed. We start having that doubt that maybe God is going to be so angry at us that He will not want us back. And this returns us again to Faith, for we must be trusting of God's loves, and His willingness to forgive us if we but turn to Him.

Which returns us to obedience. Only those who do the will of the Father will enter the kingdom of heaven (Mathew 7). Obedience is simply another word for work, not only of our hands but also of our minds and hearts. And it too returns to Faith, because it is not the works that saves but the obedience to God which flows from our Faith. Our sanctification, our calling all of it comes through the work of the Spirit on us. If we do not have this then we do not have Faith (James 2).

When I gathered and organized my all my notes, it was clear that my answers were not too be found in them. In the end I had to simply accept the subjective and abstract nature of Faith. I would have to spend some time laughing at my own stupidity. Because the answer was staring me in the face the whole time. While indeed we are saved by Grace through Faith in Christ, I know my Faith is real because I know that salvation is found only in Christ. (1 Corinthians 15).

Justified by Grace

Those who are evangelists have a saying that before one can accept Christ as their savior, they must first be convinced that they need to be saved. I am more on the Augustine side when it comes to the theology of how we are saved. Saying that first God must show a person that they are a condemned before we can convince them that it is their sins which condemns them. It is not something I talk about much, in part because Grace of Salvation is a Mystery in which God alone is the judge. There is obviously more involved than simply saying some words, simply believing the right things (Romans 10). That we must die and be reborn, that there must be a moving of His Spirit not only to receive that Grace but to understand that we need it. Does the Spirit work because we will it, or does God work in us because He wills it? And when God wills that we are to be saved, He puts us to death. His justice requires, because we have sinned, a punishment of death. Though I use the hyperbole of death, I also use it literally in a mystical way, for in order for us to be justified we must die.

The paradox of justification is that it is not enough to be considered a reformed sinner, we require to be righteous according to the Law. In order to be justified we must possess the righteousness which satisfies all the demands of the Law, and satisfies them perfectly. In our modern world, it is not enough that we have been declared guilty and then pardoned. Justification is a precise term, in which one is declared innocent. It is a judgment that we are right, that we did not committed the crime, as if we have never sinned.

Obviously then, our justification cannot be based on that we have lived, or live perfectly, but because Christ did. We have died as the Law has required, and we are no longer bound by that Law because of that death. The old wineskin is gone, our old self is dead in fulfillment of the Law by sharing in Christ's death. Because of His life, Christ was able to be the perfect sacrifice, and able to perform the perfect sacrifice. Because of His Sacrifice, His death, we are given Christ's righteousness. (2 Cor. 5:21, Rom. 4:6-8) to fulfill the Law. Faith is what justifies us, saves us from God's wraith on the wicked, for Faith is the condition of our heart when the Spirit gives us the righteousness of Christ (Rom 1, 3, 20, 22. Phil 3. Gal 2).

So too, our justification cannot be found in our own death. While that would indeed fulfill justice, we would be condemned for our sins. If all there was to Faith was simply a matter of killing the sin within ourselves, then enlightenment philosophy would be enough, almost. But we do not just die, but are given Life, born anew. Just as we have been justified, pardoned from our sins, we are sanctified, separated into Christ, reborn as a slave of righteousness and of God. (Romans 6). Not only separating us from the world, but bringing us the unity with God in Christ which we call collectively the Church, His Body. While justification is God forgiving our sins, sanctification is God making us sacred, holy. Justified so we are separated from the world of sin, and sanctified so we are separated into righteousness. Separated not only so we may be saved but that we may be of use to Him.

Faith, that Grace of Salvation, is not just justification but also sanctification. There simply cannot be one without the other. Justification is the putting away of the old wineskin, sanctification is the receiving the new wineskin. Justification kills our old self, sanctification is receiving Life, the righteousness of Christ. Justification fulfills the Law, sanctification allows us to live it. Being united with Christ, in His death and in His Life, we have it in us not only to put away what is wrong, but to do what is right. For a faith without works cannot save for it is a faith without sanctification, without a union with Christ, without Life.

Saved by His Will

Shortly after my conversion I struggled with trying to understand what happened and why it happened. One of my first questions to God was why it happened when it did instead of earlier in my life. As arrogant as I was, and still am I have never been under the impression that I found God, but rather He had revealed Himself to me. Trying to adjust and learning what happened, what the whole repentance thing was all about, I had to face why we repent. Before conversion, I did not know what sin was, saw it only as the Law or simply the rules of the game. Before being born again I did not know God's righteousness and so really had nothing which to compare my own. Part the regeneration which Grace brings through Faith is that 'the righteousness of God is revealed' to us. (Romans 1)

Knowing the horror of sin, and that God can reveal Himself at any time, why did He choose to reveal Himself when He did, after I embraced the Darkness instead of before? God responded by telling me it was so I would have the understanding, that it was part of my training to fulfill His purpose for me. So that I might do His will. In my pride, and the Gnostic views I was still holding onto I thought of this in terms of power and crusades, of empires and great tasks. I was still thinking that God revealed Himself to me because of my greatness, my importance. I was still thinking in terms of worldly greatness, in terms of my will instead of His. In time I would learn that for all of us, God 'has saved us and called us with a holy calling, not according to our works, but according to his own purpose and grace. (2 Timothy 1)

I have always had a sense of purpose to my life. Much of the rebellion of my youth was an attempt to avoid that purpose, and as I saw it not to be a victim of it. In school, I was an underachiever, never living 'up to my potential' as I was often told. Though I was lazy as is common today, most of this stemmed from a silent protest against conforming to the social norms. Even almost eight years in the U.S. Navy did not do much to break me of this. It is easy to see looking back that the extreme weight gain for which I was discharged stemmed from this rebellious nature. My love for the Navy way started to soured when I was recognized for going above and beyond. It was not that I scorned achievement or greatness, just the opposite. I just wanted to define greatness for myself. I wanted my purpose to be determined by my own will and not dictated from the outside.

Though my anti-social tendencies are stronger than most, this is the nature of the human condition in relation to God. The darkness and spirit of this world is basically open or hidden rebellion against the will of God. That is why I say and write that one must first be saved, first be united with God by Grace through Faith in Christ, before one can truly seek to be His knight, to seek to be heroic in their obedience and service. One may work many works, do great and noteworthy things, but when they are done by our will they are done outside of God's will. Without God's work of regeneration that Grace brings through Faith it is impossible to do His will for 'it is God who works in you both to will and to do for His good pleasure'. (Philippians 2)

When I was young in our Faith, I thought of righteousness only in terms of myself. It was how well I obeyed, how many vices I put away, how much virtue I gained. It would be some years before God would burn enough of this rebellious nature, until I gained a measure of humility to understand that key was not the purpose which God had for me, but that His purpose was important to me because it was His. It would take some time before I would shed my Gnostic views and know that obedience and submission to God was not about me, but about God. I spent some time seeking to do God's will from the view that my Honor is found in how well I obey. In short I was not fully 'submitted to the righteousness of God' and so ended up 'seeking to establish [my] own righteousness'. (Romans 10) But eventually I learned that our Honor is not found in our service, but in the Cross. Our Honor is not found in our righteousness, but in the righteousness of God. Our Honor is found in Jesus Christ who is the 'wisdom from God, and righteousness and sanctification and redemption' (1 Corinthians 1).

Neither those Christians who do not do the Will of the Father, nor those who seek to justify themselves by their works will be saved (Mathew 7.) God would express this again by stating that we are saved through Faith apart from works, and a Faith without works cannot save. (Romans 3, James 2) Traditionally this is reconciled by pointing out that if you have been regenerated, if you have a saving Faith then you will produce works. That was my view early in my Faith, very often I did not feel like I had a choice, but over the years I came to the view that our Faith produces works because we love God. 'whoever keeps His word, truly the love of God is perfected in them.' (1John 2). Obedience, our striving for righteousness, works of Charity, are a form of worship, an expression of our love for God.

We strive to live as much of God's righteousness as we can, not because the Law demands it, but because it is a way of thanking God and giving Him praise for our salvation, our regeneration. Through our Faith the righteousness of God, Jesus Christ, was revealed to us, and we who beheld 'as in a mirror the glory of the lord, are being transformed into that image from glory to glory, just as by the spirit of the Lord.' (2 Corinthians 3) By Grace through Faith in Christ we have gained a glimpse of what it will be like after our resurrection, the image of His glory and righteousness which we will share. So striving to obey God's word, striving for righteousness is a way of saying we want God and His righteousness. A way to declare that all our works, all of our own righteousness is nothing to us compared to the righteousness that is found in Christ. Obviously I have not always worked with such an attitude, which is just another example of why the Cross is such a praise worthy thing that we can rely on His righteousness instead of having to establish our own.

The Changing of the Guard

'Of all the dispositions and habits which lead to political prosperity, religion and morality are indispensable supports. In vain would that man claim the tribute of patriotism, who should labor to subvert these great pillars of human happiness, these firmest props of the duties of men and citizens. The mere politician, equally with the pious man, ought to respect and to cherish them. A volume could not trace all their connections with private and public felicity. Let it simply be asked: Where is the security for property, for reputation, for life, if the sense of religious obligation desert the oaths which are the instruments of investigation in courts of justice? And let us with caution indulge the supposition that morality can be maintained without religion. Whatever may be conceded to the influence of refined education on minds of peculiar structure, reason and experience both forbid us to expect that national morality can prevail in exclusion of religious principle

'It is substantially true that virtue or morality is a necessary spring of popular government. The rule, indeed, extends with more or less force to every species of free government. Who that is a sincere friend to it can look with indifference upon attempts to shake the foundation of the fabric?' - President Washington's Farewell Address

You said you were rich and had no need of anything. So, God sent those who were poor to say you had only dust and straw. You said you were strong and none could stand against you. So, God sent those who are weak to tell you there is no victory without the Cross. You said you were free and you would not be bound by anything. So, God sent those who are slaves to say that you are trapped by your desires. You said you are holy and belong only to Christ. So now God sends the Fire, so that may come true.

Did you think that God would retire the old guard without bringing forth a new one? We do not look like our fathers because our war is not the war of our fathers. Did you think that God would leave the wall undefended? Our war is not one of flesh and blood, nor of politics. Or did you expect us to defend you against God, like too many of our fathers did? Death is the nature of the Word. Either your carnal mind dies, or your Faith does. One is either destroyed or disciplined by God's Fire. The Cross either kills us or purifies us. God leaves room for no other choice. One must repent or that one perishes.

The Christians of the first century and the authors of the New Testament never made the mistake of thinking that their task was changing the culture. They drew a sharp line between the saints, those who belong to God, and those who do not. They did not protest government policies, create any revolution against Roman rule. They simply refused to do that which Faith forbids us to do. The Martyrs went to their death, not to change the culture, but in order to prevent the culture from changing them. And they changed the hearts of others, not by force of sword or politics, but by having hearts pure enough, an Honor great enough, a Love holy enough that it was better to die then to forsake God.

How petty we make their sacrifices. How petty we make the Cross when we complain about our rights. When we say that it is our right to have vice, to be immoral, to sin. Freedom, be it political or spiritual, lasts only as long as it is exercised with responsibly. Freedom, be it political or spiritual, has been bought at a price, been paid for by blood. Freedom, be it political or spiritual, continues to be paid for, by blood, by the sacrifice of those with Honor. Freedom, be it political or spiritual, is lost the moment in which there is not enough blood, not enough Honor to protect you from your own lawlessness. And when that time comes, when there are no heroes left to pay that price, you will cry out. It is just a matter of whether you cry out to God, or to the Tyrant.

Make no mistake, just as the excess of freedom found within a democracy hand that nation over to a tyrant, so does the excess of freedom found in Grace hands the church over to the Enemy. Gone are the days, if there were ever such days, that you could rely on another's light to carry you through the night. Gone are the days, if there were ever such days, that you could stumble around in the dark and expect to be safe. Gone are the days, if there were ever such days, that you could serve two masters, that you could be both of the World and of God. Just as a tyrant force everyone to be either for or against them, so to now is the time in which you are either for the enemies of God, or you are for God. Now is the time in which the lukewarm will know no peace, and those who will not run the race will not win the prize.

The Church was born in the Fire and the wise are refined by the Fire. A Fire hot enough to burn away the flesh, to burn away everything which is not gold. One does not fear the darkness when the sun is up, and when the sun goes down, we turn on the lights. One does not fear the Light, unless they love the darkness. And one cannot love the darkness unless they hate the Light. And one cannot hate the Light, without rejecting the Truth. Thus is the nature of the Fire. Thus is the nature of the Word, both the Holy Scriptures and the Spirit of God. One either accepts it or they reject it. God leaves us no choice. One must repent or that one perishes.

Nations are destroyed when they forsake that most ancient of laws; hospitality, the love of one's neighbors. God's People are cut down and thrown into the Fire when we forsake Him, when we fail to place God first. When 'mainstream' churches and denominations disregard the authority of Scripture. When 'mainstream' churches and denominations ignore the widow and the orphan. When the 'mainstream' churches and denominations are split to the extremes. When we are a house divided, a house that cannot stand, then there is no safety to be found, except in God. No force, neither sword nor politics, can bring you Faith. There is no one who is safe to follow except for Christ, no one worthy to listen to except the Word. How are you to know who speaks truth, if you yourself do not know the Truth?

God sends the Fire, so that you may know the Truth, so you may know Him. God sends the new guard so that you may know the Word, so you may know that God will give gold refined by Fire and the robes of purest white to those who endure to the end. We stand only as watchmen on the wall. We will not run the race for you, only share what we have learned from running our own race. We will not tickle your ears for the Word burns in our hearts. We will not condone your sin, any more than we condone our own. We will not pretend that your halfhearted faith is enough. God leaves us no choice. You must repent or you will perish.

Not in my lifetime

'In this situation of this Assembly, groping as it were in the dark to find political truth, and scarce able to distinguish it when presented to us, how has it happened, Sir, that we have not hitherto once thought of humbly applying to the Father of lights to illuminate our understandings?... All of us who were engaged in the struggle must have observed frequent instances of a superintending providence in our favor....And have we now forgotten that powerful friend? or do we imagine that we no longer need His assistance? I have lived, Sir, a long time, and the longer I live, the more convincing proofs I see of this truth- that God Governs in the affairs of men....We have been assured, Sir, in the sacred writings, that "except the Lord build the House they labor in vain that build it." I firmly believe this; and I also believe that without His concurring aid we shall succeed in this political building no better, than the Builders of Babel: We shall be divided by our little partial local interests; our projects will be confounded, and we ourselves shall become a reproach and bye word down to future ages. And what is worse, mankind may hereafter from this unfortunate instance, despair of establishing Governments by Human wisdom and leave it to chance, war and conquest.' - Benjamin Franklin (the Constitutional Convention Requests Prayer June 28th, 1787)

There have been times, though not in my lifetime, as a nation we understood that success was meaningless without Honor. We understood that our strength came, not from our wealth or our bombs, but our willingness to expend ourselves to do what is right. We understood that greatness could only be achieved, and maintained through the sacrifice which freedom demands. We understood that the bright tomorrow would not be won by the President, by Congress or by Wall Street, but by we, The People. When, with honest words we could 'Let every nation know, whether it wishes us well or ill, that we shall pay any price, bear any burden, meet any hardship, support any friend, oppose any foe, to assure the survival and the success of liberty.'

It is a story as old as history, freedom breeds prosperity, and as with the kings of old, prosperity breeds decadence. We may think of decadence only in the terms of vices, but to do so we simply excuse, justify our own decadence. The vices and sins of a decadent age are but a sign, a symptom of the decadence. The stench of decay comes not from sin but from a dead civilization who will no longer seek virtues. Long before our decadence leads us into a life of vices, we have already given up the will to do what is right. It is simply impossible to head down the wrong path, unless we have already quit the correct one, already forsaken the Way.

This is not about us, our society or even the age we live in, but is born out through history. We cannot blame living a decadent life simply on living in a decadent society. Neither society nor individual starts to decay until they are unwilling to face and bear even those mild discomforts in which civilization requires. When we are unwilling to face and bear those hardships it takes to succeed. One cannot choose the easy path of vices to distract us, unless they have already rejected the need to take the hard and narrow Path. Neither society nor individual starts to decay, fall into vice, until they stop striving for the perfection that patience works through our struggles. When we fail taking responsibility for our own Faith, our own lives, and give it to another.

It is time, well past time that we wake up, open our eyes to the fact our war is no longer about the culture, if it ever was. Our parents argued over whose orthodoxy is the purest, but now we debate over whether or not there is such a thing as orthodoxy. The fight is no longer over who has the best doctrine, but can there even be doctrine. Our parents fought over many things in which may have been important to them but in the light of what we must face today seems petty and a luxury. The war of this generation will not be over who can gather the most followers, bring in the most money, sell the most books. No, our fight is to safeguard our Life. Yes, indeed, our fight is to insure the very survival of the Church itself.

Think not that I am writing of persecution. Put out of your mind the lions and fiery stakes of tribulations. Such things may be, by and by, but if they are, they can only make us stronger, by and by. The real danger is the gangrene which was yesterday rotting the extremities of the Church has today advanced enough to threaten the entire Body. The disease that has gone unchecked for too long of ministers that preach anything but the Word. Ministers that preach the Gospel without the Cross. That preach revival without repentance. That preach sin as a good. Indeed, even those who preach that there can be justification and salvation without Christ. That your good is good enough so there is no need for the Cross in our lives.

With few exceptions, the heresies of old were from going too far in defining those mysteries which belong to God alone. The Trinity, the complete divinity/complete humanity of Christ, those things which can never be put fully into human words, or captured by human thought and reasoning. In essence, from the pride of pulling God down to the level of our own minds, instead of accepting that God is beyond and above us, completely.

The modern heresies are like the old in that way, in its pride. Yet, instead of trying to pull God down, it seeks to elevate man to the level of the Most-High. The post-modernism of our parent's generation combined with the cynicism of our own to create this desire. No longer is it enough for our pride to think that we can fully explain the Way of God, but we have grown so arrogant that we seek to bend His Will to our own. No longer is it enough for us to ignore the calling and commands which does not please us, God must now resend those decrees and Words in order to please us. Can you not see, that we are guilty, all of us to one degree or another are guilty of doing that which the antichrists have long claimed we have done. Forging God into our image, into what we want Him to be?

I am insane, indeed, to write such words. It is impossible to transform Him for He does not change. But we try none-the-less. How long did you think God would put up with this? Preachers go on television and teach that God is the way to wealth, and there was no uprising. Preachers stand in front of a crowd and give praise to other gods, and there is no uprising. Preachers openly endorse doctrines of demons, and there is no uprising. Pastors claim to be from God but live in the most base and sinful manner, and there is no uprising. Worry and pray for them no more, God tells me. Those who seek Him will be saved, as for the rest...

The heresies of today are not like those of yesterday, as they contain no bitter words. They come not in language offensive to our ears. The False prophets of today come preaching false gods, coating them in pious words. They sell their lies in the very dialect of the Truth. They come with words praising God, all the while setting themselves up as gods. And when ever someone questions them on their deviation from the Word they use strategy of the Serpent of Old. Asking 'did God really say...?' So devoid are we of even the most basic beliefs of our faith that many, unfortunately, bite into fruit.

What shall we do then? So many people have so many answers, and as they are so unlike the other they all cannot be from God. And that is, in fact, the entirety of the problem. We need to stop looking for our answers in the teachings of others, no mater how popular or titillating. We need to, to be blunt, grow up and stop looking for people to spoon feed us bits of truth. We need to; Seek our refuge in God, our Life in Christ, our comfort from the Spirit, and our answers from Scriptures. It might not be the easiest way, but it is the best way.

Preach the Gospel

People will often say that morality is subjective. What they are doing is mistaking abstract with subjective. Morality is no more subjective, and is only subjective in the same way that the colors lime green and tangerine are. (yes, the color of the devil in my dreams.) Each language has a different word for them, each of us are going to perceive them according to our rod and cone ratio, and not everyone is going to like their devils dressed in lime green and tangerine. Colors as subjective only because we experience them differently, and because they are a matter of taste.

Morality is subjective only the way we describe it, and in that we may or may not like them. Morality is an abstract in which we argue on what is the best foundation on which to order our lives. Moral arguments never rest on there is no morality, only on what it should be based. It is ultimately an argument on what is the perfect image or Ideal for which we should strive. Only the truly antisocial personality argues that there is no such thing as morality, that every whim should be satisfied. Whether by nature or the events of my early childhood I lack the emotional foundation to feel sympathy for the emotional distress of others. Before my conversion I still argued for morality, it was simply based on function, efficiency. I had a pragmatic moral philosophy. Others believe that it should be based on the evolution theory, either the biological instincts or those more extreme, the eugenics of creating a superman. For others it is the social norms, that whatever society says is correct is also moral. Still others, those not unlike ourselves, will argue that morality should be based on the Law.

So, we argue and have not found a solution. It is understandable of course. A democracy, with its cult of uniformity, its fetish of conformity, is directly opposed to true multiculturalism. And there is some question as to whether or not a democracy, even one guarded as a republic, can survive without a unifying morality. The philosopher I am finds it a bit exciting. To be alive, able to observe and maybe record while a democracy tries to adapt to the Philosophical Polytheism of multiculturalism. It almost makes me wish I had specialized in cultural philosophy…almost. I could make a case for the need of a unifying culture and morality, as no society has yet survived long without one. However, that would be a purely political argument. But as a Christian philosopher I am far more interested in arguing that Ideal for Christian morality is not the Law but the image of the glory of Christ. (2 Corinthians 3)

As I have pointed out several times it is not our place to judge those outside the Church. And it is illogical to expect them to live, or even understand our morality because they do not know Christ, lack the Grace of having a Life in Christ. How can we judge them for not living up to what the God demands of us, for we are in Christ so we know that it is only by having his Spirit that we are able to live according to that morality? They do not see that image of His Glory, cannot please God because they lack Faith, and as such any understanding we could part would purely be a human understanding. Any work they do, any living by our moral standard would be dead apart from Faith.

Indeed, why do we argue morality with one who lacks Faith? Can the Law save them? Can their morality, virtue and righteousness outside of Faith justify them? Striving for perfection, sanctification, purifying our hearts is something we can only do by the Grace we have through Faith. We desire, and can only desire to be pleasing to God through Faith. By our Love, our Charity we correct our fellow knights when they go astray, but it is only by Grace through their Faith that they are convicted. So, I ask again, why do we preach morality instead of the Gospel, the power of God to save us, to justify us and to sanctify us? Could it be that we preach morality to the unbeliever because we ourselves are trying to be sanctified by the Law apart from Faith? Could it be that we preach morality as a means of sanctification because we are catering to those who are Christians but are, in fact, not in Christ?

Mystic or not, convert or not, whether it there was a day you can point to when you were born-again or it happen in a more subtle way which seems to be common with the young, by the power of God we are regenerated, a new creation, born-again by the into Christ. Each of us, if we are truly in Christ, was given Christ's righteousness, and sanctification is the work the Spirit does on us to live up to it. We have the Law of Grace by virtue of being regenerated. We, through Faith, are able to 'see' the image of Christ's Glory as through a dark glass, we have Scripture to refine and give details of that image, and by the indwelling of the Spirit we overcome our sins to live up to, to be transformed and conformed to that image. (Galatians 3)

The Truth in Love

Unfortunately, at this time it up to the individual Christian to discern which teachers are from God and which was are deceiving them. Not that we can find much better times in Church history, but at least there were times when the obvious heresies were not so popular. Times such as these, in which people were irreligious rather than looking to have their ears tickled. So, in regard to that I have to ask how are people to know that I am not deceiving them? I am smart, have a way with words, and can use Scripture as well as anyone. So how is one to know if God has sent me, or I am just one of those who use sweet but empty words to corrupt people away from God in those subtle ways? Just as important, how do I know that I do not deceive myself? As it is just as important that I do not deceive myself, as it is I do not deceive you. I answer that, as I always have, with Charity, the Love I have for them. (1 John 2)

Indeed, mystics are known for being the preachers of Love, which may be the reason why we are so popular today. But…one must ask how are we to know that it is truly Love in which we are experiencing. And keep in mind that I am writing about Agape, that Grace of Charity which God gives us to love others, and not what passes as love for many today. How do I know that I truly have Charity and not simply deluding myself? An obsessed person may stalk and even kill another out of what they consider to be love. An enabler will, out of compassion, give an addict that which is destroying them. An abuser will call what burns in them love, saying they control the other for that person's own good.

As our natural, animalistic or carnal instinct is to judge what is good and what is evil on the grounds of whether or not we like it. So, our natural tendency, in showing love is to make a person feel better…this is not Charity, but affection. This obviously hinders us in knowing God's Will, as we are inclined to judge something as His for no other reason than it titillates us. We have all, in our ministries, run across those who have justified the most deviant of behaviors by saying that whatever the self wills, God wills. Those who will say and even teach that our carnal desires and behaviors are not sinful because they are natural. Ironic is it not, considering the natural state of a human is as a sinner, so those who say such deny the Gospel and deceive in their teachings

Love, even on a human level is not simply a desire to give comfort but to also give aid, to be a benefit. A doctor cannot be said to be giving aid if they give pain killers for a broken leg but leaves the bone unset. Before conversion, without the Spirit in us, we are incapable of Charity. I am not saying that the unsaved are incapable of love, only unable to have the kind of Love which is a Grace of God. For while the carnal mind may have a will in order to act in a loving manner, Love requires us to find our rest in the Lord. Charity requires us to find our strength in God. Something which a carnal mind cannot even understand, because Charity goes beyond simply the desire to give physical and emotional welfare. Charity requires of us to give aid to one another for their spiritual welfare as well.

It is even believed that one can stop loving. If we look at the greatest of the human love, between husband and wife, there are those who say that we can fall out of, just stop having this kind of love. While the saying that love is not always enough, this shows our tendency to think of love only as the pleasure we get from desires fulfilled. Desires rise and fall, come and go, and when it goes, when they are no longer feeling the high of pleasure, they say they are no longer in love. Beyond the fact that such people will never really know even human love, the linking of pleasure and love is dangerous as well. It is dangerous to judge people by how they make us feel. A true friend is dedicated to our betterment, not our pleasure.

If we are a mature adult we can easily understand if another loves us they will not only do things which are pleasing to us, but also things in which benefits us. My mother would not let me get a motorcycle when I was in high school. Though this irritated me to no end, and I reacted with those tantrums that teenagers are famous for, it was a act of love. She was correct that my lacking a sense of self-preservation, commanded by the youthful feeling of immortality I most likely would not have lived long. This is, of course, one of those 'eat your vegetable' kinds of love. Just as there are parents and spouses who lack love, who think only of their own pleasures in their relationships, there are those who claim to be Christians but do not have Charity.

While it is beneficial to know who loves us and who does not, who we can trust and who we cannot, as a Christian being loved is not as important as loving. As mystics of the Cross we cannot expect others to Love us, or at least not perfectly, but we should be striving to Love others perfectly, to the height of the Grace of Charity given us. If we are not living for the benefit of others, if we are not striving to Love more, to have Heroic Charity then we cannot rightly call ourselves a mystic. If they do not bring a greater Grace of Charity, all our mystical experiences no matter how grand are worthless (1 Corinthians 13).

This is might be the very reason why God has made me a mystic, given me the Grace of perceiving Him. As I said, without the new heart we receive at the Grace of Salvation one cannot have Charity, but I was without love even by human standards. I was filled with bitterness and anger, even by human standards. I could blame this on the pain of my heart, of being one of those sensitive souls coming to age in a dark culture. I could blame that, but I mostly did it to myself. I worshiped strength, and prided myself in having the apathy to accomplish any task. Having spent my youth in church, and with a hard heart, God had to hit me hard in order to get me to repent. Just as before my conversion experience I had no concept of sin, neither did I have any concept of love. I was in that group who thought that all the theories of love, and all religious stuff was simply a means of keeping the exceptional from controlling the mediocre.

Needless to say, just as my sense of sin became more acute, putting away old sins and learning of sins I have been ignorant of, as I matured so has my Charity increase. Indeed, Charity covers a multitude of sins for not only will you not count the sins against you, but you will strive not to sin against others because of your Love. True to the mystic's view, I found that all Christian morality is based on Agape. The more perfect is our Love the more perfect we keep the Law (Romans 13). Yet, Love demands more than simply fulfilling the Law, Charity demands that our morality is based on more than doing only what the Law requires (Mathew 5).

Just as the overcoming of sin has been a gradual process so has been increasing increase of Charity I have. Though I can honestly say that the change in me at the moment of conversion was a greater change then in the years following, I had to pursue Love. Indeed, the struggle to have Charity is very much a struggle against the carnal mind, and is only separated for ease of understanding.

Charity, if we pursue it, will take beyond the love carnal mind. Just as the carnal mind will try to tell us that we are righteousness enough, it will try to convince us that we love enough.

There is nowhere in Scripture which says that we shall know others belong to the Lord by the miracles they perform, by their wisdom, by their intelligence or by their mystical experiences. In fact, Scripture seems to say the exact opposite starting with the Lord Himself (Mathew 24). While this does deal with the End of the Age, the fact that false prophets will use great signs and wonders to deceive, and if possible, deceive even the elect, is an important thing to keep in mind. If our love for one another is how we and the world is to recognize that we belong to God, (John 13,) then the Charity we strive for must be greater than the world can know. While the love which says to do no harm may be sufficient for a heart which knows not God, we must pursue Love which says we will do good.

Those who dismiss Scripture, or at least disregard or twist the ones they do not like often do it in the in the name of Love. They may do it out of a great concern for the emotions of those that hear them, they may have great affection but they are not acting from Charity, at least the way the mystics of the Cross understand it. Which is why I say that we know those who are from God by their Love. In truth there must be Love, and in Love there must be Truth. Those who Love us will give us the truth of that Love, from that Love.

When I was young in the Faith, I could not see much point to theology. I read Holy Scriptures, I am studious by nature and there is no better devotional than the Bible. I often said you have theology, I have God, I have the better deal. A view I still hold, that God is more important than theology, that having Faith, truly being in Christ is by far more important than being orthodox. But it is a fine line, and fine lines can be most dangerous, deadly if one does not take it seriously. Yet, as the more God gave me a measure of that Grace which allowed me to Love, the more I saw the need for sound theology. The more I Love, the less my focus was on my own sanctification and more on aiding others in the sanctification of others the more important theology became.

I am a heretic to some simply because I am a mystic of the Cross. I can easily say that Love is enough to base all morality on. If by love we mean Agape, the Love in which God has given us. The kind of Love which we have for enemies (love your enemies) and allows one to forgive even while being nailed to a cross (Luke 6 and 23). There is no doubt in me that the Love brought by our Faith is only true and proper motivation and proof of our Salvation. (James 1 and 2). That the proof we know God is not that our theology is correct but that we Love one another. But if we are motivated by Charity, then we are going to want the aid we give to be true and not lead people astray.

To be sure, can anyone argue with that? Can anyone say that they are showing Christ's Love by turning them away from God. The more we Love, the more we want what we preach, teach or write to be true. That if we truly have Charity, if we truly Love each other in Christ, the more we want our lives and words to line up with what is true from God's view and not just our own. This is because the more we Love, the more we understand God's Love for us, the more we understand that God's Love for us, and God's Will for us is one in the same. I am just the latest in a long list of people to say this but the more one Loves and the more one wants to make sure that everything they preach or write is an aid to the souls of others, the more one understands the importance and predominance of Scriptures in forming theology.

Why would a mystic, such as myself, who has had so much of God's extraordinary Providence in his life say that Scripture is superior to raptures and visions? Is my Love perfect? The raptures and visions have taught me humility and Charity but am I not still a man? Am I not still in the flesh seeing through a dark glass? (1 Corinthians 13.) And not be rude by answering a question with questions, Scripture has always been the place I went, the guide I used to make sure I, myself, was not going astray. I did not go to seminary or a bible college, did not have anyone to guide me in the way I needed. All I had was the bible and my prayers. It was in fact, the study of Scripture for my own edification and sanctification that though they are grand, raptures and visions really did not teach me anything, they simply gave me to motivation learn, to Love, to live the Life I had been given by Grace through Faith in Christ.

I can easily involve myself in the war of the mystics as God told me directly that Scripture would be my basis for all doctrine. That even if it seems that I have wisdom and understanding that goes beyond Scripture I can only write on those things found within the

Bible. If any conclusion I derive seems, even if it only seems to go against Scripture, go with the Scripture and not what I am concluding. My wisdom and understanding of God and His Will are speck of sand in the universe compared to that which is found in the Bible. It is where my byline comes form, that I know nothing except for Christ, Him alive and in Him Life. That I know, we know God personally only as mystics. That is, we only know God by that direct revelation which comes with the Grace of being in Christ. That regeneration, that being born again, being saved is the only experience which is required, the only wisdom and understanding which you cannot derive from studying Scripture.

There are others, of course, that will say that God has told them differently. That Scripture no longer applies, or that it has been down-graded to outdated wisdom. That God has declared that in the name of Love that sin no longer matters. They say that God has inspired them to give their blessings to behavior of the sinful nature, as long as the sin is done in the name of Love. Which is really the point of all this, how do we know what is or is not derived from Charity, and what is derived from our carnal nature? I declare that God says one thing, another declares that God says the opposite. How can you tell which one of us, if either, is from God and which one is not? How are you to choose? I can only say when you are faced with such choice, reject us both.

I mean that most seriously, as there is no way you can tell if God has worked in me through his extraordinary Providences or if I am simply delusional (or worse), except for the same way there is to judge all teachers. I consider the very debate on who has authority to teach to be an invalid because one first has to ask why one needs authority to teach. What is the purpose of writing, preaching and teaching? Though I am, obviously, one who believes in the gift of discernment, how you answer that question really determines who it is you listen to. The teachers you gather to, the leaders you give authority to give you answers. If you think our purpose is simply to teach the data and information about Christianity then Love is unimportant and you will be impressed by the education of your pastor. If our goal is to get you to feel good about yourself, insure you that you are not that bad of a sinner than Truth is unimportant, then you obviously listen to those who can put on a good show, who talk well of warm affections or the sins of others. If you think that our purpose is to seek after God's extraordinary Providences, visions and raptures then you will listen to those who claim that they have found a way to force God to give them to you.

Yet, if you are like me than you believe that the purpose and goal of the clergy is to focus our time in aiding others in the maturing of their Faith. That it is our purpose to help you find those answers for yourself, to learn to know and do God's will for yourself. As our own goal is to mature in the Faith, one who teaches us must themselves be both mature in Charity and mature in Faith, in the Knowledge of our Jesus Christ, our Lord. (1 Peter 1.) We must first have removed the board from their own eye before we can be an aid to one another in removing the splinters. (Mathew 7). And a part of that board, for those who are called to write, preach or teach, is that spiritual pride which makes it any of it about defending our authority to write, to preach or to teach. Maybe it is just me but authority is not as important as whether or not I am being an aid to you maturing in your Faith. Maybe I am wrong, maybe I am projecting the way God has trained me onto others in saying that the role of the clergy is to be helpful to the Sanctification of others. But I am convinced in both my mind and spirit that I am not. (Ephesians 4.)

So, to answer the question on how do we know to whom to listen to, I can only say that we should listen to God. That we should feed our hearts with prayers, and our minds with Scripture. Any authority which is derived from God is not the kind which makes us the authority. It is not the authority to declare what is or is not true. But rather, it is the authority to urge your heart to prayer, and your mind towards Scripture. Indeed, I would go as far as to say that it is not authority at all, but a responsibility to be an aid in another's sanctification. A Sacred-Trust important enough to strive in both knowledge and Love. Or to put it plainly, those to whom we should listen, those who we should read, those who we appoint our teachers and preachers should be ones who go out of their way to make sure that they are writing and speaking the Truth from Love.

Feel the Yaboo

Galatians 3: Have you suffered so many things in vain – if indeed it was in vain.

What do I have to praise God about today? Absolutely nothing, so that means absolutely everything. At the moment I am working on understanding mortification as a vehicle of Grace, and how vehicles of Grace only work through Faith. So, I have been hunched over my Bible until my back hurts, and checking to see what others have had to say on the subject. And as I was doing the obsessive writer thing, I had one of those yaboo moments, you know when you have to sing that lumpy song and dance that lumpy dance. One of those moments when you have to stop what you are doing and simply praise God.

It happens, as least for me most of the time, as simply just a general feeling. This time however it was for *unio cum Christo,* for our union with Christ, so I figure I would share. I have been in that midlife crisis we are obliged to go through when we realize that we have already spent more days than we have left. For me, as I think with most of our generation, it has less to do with the fun we have missed out in life as it is with our lack of any real accomplishments. I was thinking about this in context of the contrast between self-mortification (self-putting Self to death) with God using the struggle of our life for mortification, to sanctify us. And for me, the part of the Self, the flesh, which has been and is being put to death is that part that has been looking for some sort of satisfaction in my work.

More than once people have voiced astonishment at what I have done during my life. I can only shrug my shoulders as they are bitter ash in my mouth. That is, that feeling of accomplishment on finishing something such as a book, or an article last at most five minutes, about as long as it takes me to figure out what to do next. And this has been rubbing me raw over the last few years. That is God was drawing out that writing was a something rather than the nothing it should be. Or for those not comfortable with mystic terminology, God was using the struggle to show me that I could not get any satisfaction from ministry precisely because I was looking for satisfaction from the work instead of from Christ.

Obviously, the details will be different, and we use different words to describe 'the joy of dire struggles' depending on our traditions. We all face hardships in life. When we ask what have we accomplished, as it seems like we have not done enough for the Lord. Or those thorns of Charity, in which you rip out your heart, giving it all you have and becoming frustrated because it seems that our work is pointless, not baring any fruit. Or just the normal hardship, such as when your body first starts falling apart showing you that you are not that young person anymore that can heal quickly. (I blew out my shoulder some months ago and I just got full motion back.) I am sure that I am not alone in this, but I always seem to forget that during the front-end of a struggle. That regardless of what we go through, because we are in Christ our suffering is not in vain.

What I am getting at is that I am not satisfied with this, because as always, I do not feel that I have expressed what I am trying to say well enough. Which would be horrible and unforgivable if this was a something. We cannot derive satisfaction from our works because even though they may be a something to us, they are really a nothing. I can write, I can edify, I can spout grand philosophical babble, I can take over the world, but none of it, no work I could do can bring you into that union with God. The only work that can do that is Christ's work upon the Cross. Can you see that freedom of having a union with Christ? That the most important work that needs to be done, the hardest trial, the impossible struggle of being brought into Christ was done for us. That by Grace though Faith in Christ I have been given a union with God. I mean really, give it some thought. We are able to be sanctified, mature in Faith form our struggles because we are in Christ, and we are only in Christ because He paid the price for that as well.

Come now, with that in mind is there anything to do at this moment but to stop reading this and feel the yaboo? I do not know about you but I am going to get back to singing that lumpy song and dancing that lumpy dance. That is, I am going to stop writing this and get back to praising God.

I'll Help You If I Can

There I was just sitting in the park
On a bench, alone, scared, and in the dark.

Along you came and sat next to me for awhile.
Then you turned toward me and put on a smile
Saying all that you dared "what's up man,
Don't be blue, I'll help you if I can"

I looked away, trying not to see
All the caring and love you had for me.
I thought long and hard for what to say.
I was sure that it would take me into the day.
Because whatever I said it had to be clever
But the only word that formed was "never."

I turned my head to look at your face.
Seeing the tears that formed in your eyes, I fell in disgrace.
I could never speak in a way to make it sound like art
Then the words flowed and came from deep within my heart
"I am sorry to hurt one such as you
But I'm in so much pain deep inside, what else could I do
I realize the error and evil in my ways
I did the wrong and you're the one that had to pay
I beg your forgiveness and ask you to leave"

Even to this day I still don't believe
What you said as you stood "I'm sure that you have a plan
And I hope it works, as I said before I'll help you if a can"

As you left, then also out of my life went the last spark,
So here I sit, hoping, in fear, alone and in the dark

The Rise and Fall of a Xristzen

The term Xristzen first started as a label for myself in my journal, and eventually in my fiction, because it represents well the paradox of my life. I am a Christian, and I am a Zen man, and these two are ultimately incompatible, though more from the nature of people than the nature of the two views. But there is a reason that I must clearly separating the two.

I read these modern books about mysticism and it always seems like the authors are simply masking their poor communication skills with pseudo-mystic language. They speak what is considered the proper language, but if they understood they would be seeking to help others understand. I know, they would say to me that all knowing must be humbled by unknowing, and assuming that they really understand I could only reply, 'yes, but unknowing must be expressed by knowing if we are to help another. After all, you are reading these words.' If you still do not understand then 'what does reading these words have to do with God?'

Which is my point about the language. If you do not already understand, you have no clue what I just wrote. If you do already understand, there is no point in saying it except to confuse and prove how enlightened I am, thus proving I am not enlightened. Why not just start by saying that language can only capture a small part of the reality of our lives so stop limiting yourself to a world created by words? Which I can say that this is true but we are limited by our communication when helping others in their lives. And then, while the artificial construct created by language does in fact hinder us, it has little to do with Christian spirituality if one has Faith. And I threw in the irony that writing and reading is limited completely to the matrix of our language-understanding.

Do not misunderstand me. I am not anti-enlightenment. I like enlightenment philosophy, as I like history, and Zen is the best of them. There are some good teachers out there that are enlightened in the Zen sense. But there are also a large number of them who are speaking nonsense, seeing only the concept that such words understand, and thus know only what words to say to sound enlightened to the unenlightened. But more the point though, the benefits enlightenment philosophy claimed to those who are in Christ is extremely exaggerated.

Enlightenment philosophy and its sister the philosophy of logic can be of limited benefit in the same way as exercise, and quickly becomes dangerous, very much so when we start seeing them as a method or practice of religion. That it is good to keep in shape because of how being out of shape affects our moods. It took me a while to understand that as well. I have the low view of our bodies, simply being vessels of our spirit. But I learned that keeping physically active gave me more energy to study, write and pray. It is good to practice logic to hone our reasoning as it is needed in the study of Scripture. And the self-awareness of enlightenment philosophy obviously is helpful for the same reason, so we accept Scripture for what it says instead of what we want it to say.

The problem I had was not the philosophy per se, it was that it had replaced Scripture as my instructions in sanctification. And because of that I started confusing enlightenment with sanctification. When that happened stopped being Xristzen and started being Zen Christian. That is, I started seeing Zen less and less as a means to better serve God and seeing the Spirit more and more as a means to reach Zen. Obviously, God would not, did not stand that for long. A Zen Buddhist can reach a point in Zen which they can easily jettison or give up Buddhism. This is because for some of them Buddhism is a means to reach Zen, that is enlightenment. When I reached that point, I had no choice but to jettison Zen. Enlightenment is a nothing to start off with, and compared to the Cross is a distraction at best. (1 Corinthians 2)

It is very easy to mistake enlightenment philosophy as a spiritual path. I had sat down to write a path to enlightenment, thinking that enlightenment and sanctification was the same thing. The more I wrote the more I realized that the only enlightenment that mattered was that Grace through Faith. I may someday finish that work, but upon reading it I realized that enlightenment was fine and all, but what I was writing was useless unless one was already in Christ. The only understanding I wanted people to 'get' was the Gospel, the only revelation I wanted people to have was Faith. If one is not in Christ then all the philosophy, no matter how well crafted, will not get them there, and if one is in Christ then the Spirit is our enlightenment. (Romans 8)

I can still claim to be Zen because I am no longer a Zen man. I can prove to be enlightened by saying that enlightenment is a disease. I could write in the paradoxes language which is meant to 'awake' you. But what it really comes down to is, we have only a limited amount of time in this life. You can do what I did and spend two decades chasing after enlightenment, which in the end did not come close in comparison to what I already have in Christ. Or you can do the enlightened thing and forget about enlightenment and seek sanctification according to the Spirit and Scriptures.

A Chaotic Twist

'The difference between the right word and the almost right word is the difference between lightning and a lightning bug'   – Mark Twain

Ugh, ugh and ugh again! Twenty-seven pages and I still do not know what I want to, what I need to write about. I have ideas, but am having trouble finding that balance between dry analytical thought which only I find interesting and poetic drivel which is fun to write but rather pointless...I am dreaming a dream of what the world could be when dreamers are free to dream of worlds which may be...it is an issue of motivation. The nature of genius is obsession, and the nature of obsession is to seek fulfillment. I have been no different, am a creature of obsession as any addict. Only that my dreams are of the gossamer understanding of the soul. Born of the struggle to survive the isolation created by my own mind, the desperate attempts to breach those walls and make contact.

Obviously, this has been the self-interest that has motivated me to start writing. The speech impediment of my youth caused by my mind working faster than my body can handle limited me to connecting only to those who had both the capability and inclination to understand me. In a way that is old news, after all I speak well enough that few even recognize my difficulty speaking now. But it is also the reality of my life. Though I am now able to express myself, and I believe I do so in a fine manner, I still can only connect to those who have both the capability and inclination to understand me. The truth is my inability to connect has nothing to do with my ability to express myself but in my complete incompetence in being able to think like an average person.

I have lost my obsession, or maybe I should say, have failed to recognize that my obsession has shifted. I just do not care about it anymore. My lack of connection, attachment, feeling like there is a place for me...all so...whatever. It is not because I am content with the attachments I have, and I will get to that, but that I no longer feel any need to explain my choices to the mediocre. Why I refused to live up to my protential as they see it. Why I turned my back on my abilities. Why I choose the path of an outcast and rebel instead

85

of conforming to the mold of the modern church culture. Maybe I have just grown tired of the pointless labor of trying to express why it was so important for me, for those like me to follow the classical death-of-self-will mystical tradition. That the greater the person, the greater the need for them to subjugate there will to the Will of God.

A bit of a twist there, I know. Not all that surprising as it is, more or less, what I have been expressing all these years. Greatness found in being the master of fate instead of its victims. To have, or not to have according to one's own will. To control tym, to hold the threads of fate in your hands and to create your world to your liking. Yes, the Will to Power, the power over one's own life. The Will to Choose, the freedom to choose what path your life takes and what you get out of it. And the question of what you will do with that freedom? Will you serve your own will and be a tyrant, or submit to God's will and be the hero that a knight is meant to be?

But to twist it back, the primarily problem, the reason I have been having difficulty holding an idea long enough to write about it, is that I am a stereotype. A genius getting into mischief because he is bored...so completely and utterly bored. Turmoil, hardships, struggles, while for the average person these may seem like things to avoid, but are these not just other words we use for excitement? Maybe not, maybe it is just me. Which is really what it is all about, these writings about giving up. I could shrug my shoulders and say that if you have never felt like giving up then you have never really tried. But it sounds a bit silly, as I am loosing the fight from having nothing to fight against. That everything sort'a makes sense now, no worries, no struggles just life...just life.

Boredom may not be the right word. I do not feel bored. I have not that anxiety, the feeling of needing something to do which boredom describes. Lazy would be a better description of what I feel, content to the point that there does not seem any on fighting. Satisfied to the point in which I am not hungry, or at least not hungry for the need to express myself. Obviously, that would account to why this has been a rather chaotic mess. But my new obsession will have to wait until next time.

Lent, Mortification and Hubris

Saw my first bug of the year, so that means only one thing. Lencten is upon us, or for those of more modern taste Lent, that is Spring-Time. Which it is also means the forty days, Quadragesima for you Latin types, or Tessarakoste if you prefer Greek, until the celebration of the Resurrection. Forgiveness Vespers/Ash Wednesday was a couple days ago, except for Tiny which it is next week if I am reading my Julian Calendar correctly. Observing the forty days leading up to Easter, as we call it in order to Christianize the celebration of an Old Germanic goddess, or if you prefer a bit of Polish, Wielkanoc or 'great night'. It, of course dates back to the early Church, and was recognized by the Council of Nicaea, though I have never looked up what they actually wrote on it.

As for what I am doing for this season of lent, well, nothing. I feel no inclination to do anything, and so in many ways it would simply be hubris to do so. Sort of like all the Latin and Greek words above. Obviously, some people oppose the observance of Lent, because for the equally obvious reason that it is not found in Scripture. It, undoubtedly, falls under the heading of new moon festivals. One of those things which are not wrong in the doing, or not doing. It is really more of a question of why you are doing it. But that is a question which can really be asked of anything.

Some things are considered duties, things which are done because they are done by the upstanding and good members of their group. To create a sense of community among the group. Obviously, Lent is like that in some traditions. Weddings are a more universal example. A marriage is a marriage, but the feast or celebration which we picture with the dress and the music, serves as a means in which to create a closer unity within the community. Public displays of linking families, and all that jazz. There is, of course, always the problem in communal religious observances that one does it only from the hubris of duty. Doing it simply because it is part of the image of what a 'good' person does.

But Lent has become popular outside the communal use of ceremonies, with those who are not part of a tradition with a liturgical calendar. Even within groups whose traditions have been historically against all such things. And that is fine, in that new moon festival kind of way. But again, one has to be careful about motivation. There is that tendency to look at those who we see as a 'good' member of the community and ask what their secret is. To look at one who is a 'good' example of a Christian, and emulate their practices. And while it is certainly good to be inspired by those who have lived the sanctification our Faith brings, there is a pride in thinking that you can be like them by doing the things they did.

The leading line right now is that those small sacrifices bring us closer to the Cross. Mortification is a vehicle of Grace, but as with all the vehicles the Grace works through Faith, not through sacrifice. The idea that our suffering, in and of itself, brings us closer to God, forms us more into the Image of Christ is hubris. Plain and simple, and very much counterproductive. It is pride and counterproductive to mortify with the attitude that because we suffer we are more like Christ, become more like Christ.

Mortification of the Flesh is not about suffering like Christ, so we can be like Him, but so that we may know better His suffering. Observing lent, fasting and the like is really only beneficial when it done in humility, or at least teaches humility. And this is really what you should understand about it, mortification is not really about our sacrifice and suffering. Fasting, and Lent, and all forms of mortification is a celebration and praise of Christ for His Sacrifice at Golgotha.

As I have commented many times, I do not fast because I am holy but fast because I am not. My suffering gains me no Grace, it is simply a reminder that the Grace I have, the Grace with overcomes, our very salvation was purchased through the Cross, through His suffering. And for all my fondness of the Catholic Tradition, this is why I am still a Protestant. My mortification has brought me Grace, has been a vehicle of Grace only because it has been done through Faith. Showing my old-school mysticism, the observing of Lent, fasting, or any outward or inner-work do not work Grace in us except when they are obedience to the prompting of the Spirit.

There is surely Grace to be had in mortification. I think teachings that you must mortify work only because they capture those who should be doing such but are not. But they do so by putting an unfounded guilt on those who need not. I have seen such guilt in the eyes of others when I have spoken of fasting, and if I had felt it was the Spirit convicting them, I would say so. Most often it is not, and simply that pride which equates mortification with holiness. I am not trying to talk anyone out of their observance, or giving a chance for excuses. I am simply pointing out that whether you mortify from the prompting of the Spirit, or for some other reason, it does not make you better or worse then anyone else. That we may do many great things, and strive our every waking moment to live our lives as God would have us live them, but our Grace, our justification and sanctification, the foundation of our very Lives is not found in our works but the work that Christ did for us. To think otherwise is simply hubris.

Our Glory in Christ

1 Thessalonians 2 and 3: For what is our hope, or joy, or crown of rejoicing? Is it not even you in the presence of our Lord Jesus Christ at his coming? For you are our glory and joy.

So, after the warrior and the poet spent the rest of the night in a slapping contest, they finally came terms. As it often happens with such inner-turmoil, well inner-questioning as it does not rise to the level which could properly be called turmoil now, I feel silly do to the obvious nature of the answer. It answers a lot of questions, indeed, that what I desire is to be inspired. This is not new, I have never been much of a taker, never been one to fight simply to gain, to have something. I have always needed to have something to fight for. This has always been so for me. My conversion, and the maturing since has not changed this, only shifted it from 'The Cause' to the individual.

I have spent the long hours sitting by myself pondering and writing, have spent those times I went hungry and cold, sacrificed my own interests in ways that have astonished. I have done so in part because it was needed at the time, but I have to admit now that I was able to do so because I had no real reason not to. Basically, being a writer, I have no inspiration, no motivation to engage the world socially beyond what is needed to keep writing. Though it is most complex, in simplest terms writing is not enough for me…and I do not know why.

As frustrating as it is, I have learned not to try to guess where the Spirit is guiding us, in what it will be the sanctification the Spirit is working on us will look like. Or maybe I have just learned that I do not have a good track record of predicting where God's will is leading my life. It might be, as John has contended for these past few years, that I need to be more socially engaged. That is what it seems like for the moment, but it could easily be the lesson that I need to be content with just being a writer. That is really the question in all of this, whether to come out of my cave, or learn to be content within its limits. Obviously, that is a question which will only be answered in time.

For now though, as I am on the topic, I should write about

that inspiration, ministry, of pride and our glory in Christ. Though only some of St. Paul's writing is directly on love, there is very little of it in which he was not declaring love. Such as that found in the second chapter, continuing onto the third of first the Thessalonians, the sentiment that 'you are our glory and joy' is found throughout his writings. I can explain that in humanistic terms, as I take no real pride, no sense of accomplishment in the things I have done. I have a far greater sense of satisfaction in what my pupils have done, the growth my disciples have experienced. There was a time, however, when this was also pride, as in hubris. That is, when I still saw the individual as 'the cause' then it was more the feeling of 'look what the person accomplished because of me' kind of thing.

I do not want to discount what I have done, or the affect that we have as individuals on other individuals. But as I wrote John a few years back, very often I feel like people grow in spite of me rather than because of me. There is obviously some humility in that, as pride is ultimately the ego-self, the part which glorifies in 'I have this' or 'I have done'. The part which values ourselves by how much we have, or how we are important to the cause, etc. But more to the point, humility is found in that 'our'. Paul did not write that you are my glory and joy, but that you are our glory and joy. Humility is first and foremost a submission to God's Will, but it is also a recognition that in that will is that our labors are communal rather than individualistic in nature.

Certainly, this applies to the pastor behind the pulpit or a writer such as myself in that hubris when we make too much of a thing out of our importance in the process. Indeed, this seems to be a common problem in where we think that the responsibility of another growth is dependent on how well we preach, or how well we write. But it is also found in that idea where we limit our source to one or few others. Or if you would, when we discount the fact that we are a source, to be a source for the growth of others. Again, I do not want to discount the role in which a minister plays, but am simply pointing out that it is only a single role, in which you have your own, not only in your own growth but the growth of others.

I am also pointing out that, while I find nothing wrong with that pride I feel for my pupils in their accomplishments, or that which you may find in the accomplishments of say your children, the glory, crown and joy which is referred to here is 'you in the presence of our Lord Jesus Christ at his coming.' It seems that is lost in much our ministry today. That the joy is not to be found in how many we can get to agree with us, or how many we can get to join our club. It is not a joy that is found in a culture which conforms to our morality. It is not a joy in which is found in making sure everyone is orthodox in their views, or making sure that they are loving enough. These are all important to one degree or another, but the joy is found that those who you have given your lives for, those that you have love for will be in the presence of the Lord when He comes again. It is the joy that we did not work in vain, not in that 'how dare you waste my time' kind of way, but the relief that our fear that you may not make it was in vain.

I put this in terms of inspiration because I am a firm believer that we are sanctified by the Spirit according to the Will of the Father. That there is a reason that we are inspired differently. A reason why someone such as myself was first inspired by how best to serve the Church, and then only now am inspired to start dealing with more practical matters. A reason that someone, such as John, was first inspired by practical matters, home and family if you would, and is only now starting to focus on how best to serve the Church. That reason being that it is not 'me' or 'mine' but the 'we' and the 'our'.

The Faith Divide

A while back I told a youth who wants to be a philosopher not to start reading philosophers but rather start with history. I think it is a mistake to start with philosophy, not in regard to the philosophical process, but with reading philosophers. History is more productive than the writings of philosophers because it creates a wider view point than ideology. Or if you would, one gains a perspective on ideas relevant to their times. For example, it helps understanding that Marx's statement that religion is the opium of the masses, was at a time when all the major denominations were declaring that democracy was of the devil. That is, when reading philosophers out of time, not taking into account what they were actually arguing against, one naturally forms a lopsided view. As a general rule, I find it dangerous to read a philosopher without knowing the times that they lived in, and the culture which they were rebelling against. Or if you would, one easily falls prey to the rhetoric.

For example, was Nietzsche anti-Christian? In a way, to be sure, he wrote many things which shows that he was not a Christian, that he did not have Faith. But the way I read him, he was far more anti-Humanism then anti-Christian. Or if you would, he took his atheism seriously, and since he had the view there is no God he was asking why do Humanist still act like there is a God. He simply considered Christianity to be nothing, no more than we would regard the worship of the old Greek gods. So, if you would, his attack on Christianity was really an attack on Humanist who shares the same concept of morality as us. I consider Nietzsche to have simply brought the atheistic argument of morality to its natural conclusion. That is, post-modernism where there is nothing outside the individual on which to base morality. Or if you would, Humanism is also a religion, which can do nothing else but also die, for the rejection of God rejects any moral authority outside the individual. Human nature and human desires vary too much to derive any absolute morality from it.

In philosophy class you have to read the philosophers, but mostly what you learn is what someone else says what philosophers means by what they wrote. Which is what I just did. My understanding of Nietzsche was formed after I already knew that by the time of his writing Humanism had replaced Christianity as the dominate religion. And as for the twist I am about to pull, it became the dominate religion inside the Church. Proof? Can you say democracy? Humanism gets its name because it is primarily concerned with human needs and abilities. That is, meeting human needs through human abilities. I am rather fond of it as a political philosophy. After all, I do not sit here praying that God will plant my garden, but rather go out with a shovel and plant it.

As with all modern democracy America has always been a humanistic country. It has at times appeared to be a Christian country only because, and to the degree in which it started with the presupposition of God as the Law-Giver. I have no problem with, and am rather fond of Humanism as a political philosophy. That is, convincing through argument instead of force of arms, or idea that humans can control their destiny through reason. But when this becomes, a religion is completely opposed to the Gospel. And what I mean by this is when humanism is used to determine what is good and evil, instead of simply how to act on what we know to be good and evil, it has replaced the Cross with our own work.

I favor Nietzsche, not so much that he wrote with an understanding of the four percent or so of us who have a Will to Power. Some people consider Nietzsche as nihilistic, because they see that as the final conclusion of secular humanism. I disagree, in that I think he was preaching the postmodern philosophy. If there is not Law, no absolute morality, then I am the only one which can determine what is good, what is evil. The fact that one lacks the need to justify their behavior is enough to justify their behavior. My actions are limited only by what I desire, and what you will let me get away with. The same view I had, and why I am glad I did not read him prior to my conversion. He was brave enough to bring secular humanism to its logical end. That is, ultimately morality, what is good and evil is determined by those who have the power to exercise their will.

Obviously, there are having been some good attempts to replace God with some other absolute, or foundational truth. Utilitarianism is founded on the principle of maximizing happiness to the largest number of people. Situational ethics is the most popular, the love found in that golden rule. Anarchism and Libertarianism are founded on the freedom of the individual. And so on. That is, Nietzsche and true postmodernism really only applies to the four percent who as anti-social tendencies. Our society is postmodern only in the since that people choose which humanistic philosophy, they belong according to what they like. That if you follow regress argument logically, it shows those areas in which one accepts an assertion on faith.

A short description of what the regress argument is simply to challenge the assertions on which an argument is being made. Any assertion must be based on a defendable position, but that position is also relying on assertions which can be challenged. Though the regress argument is abused in debates, it is important in analytical philosophy for determining your preconceptions, or presupposition. When you run your logic through enough regress arguments you discover that all positions trace back either to themselves, or to an assertion that must be accepted without it being proved. The dignity of every single individual human person is defendable only on religious grounds. Obviously, we all want to be treated with dignity, but on what grounds do we prove that we deserve equal respect.

All of this I pointed out before. Asked, as a Christian, what is the foundational truth in which we are to base our morality? And made a point that what makes us different is that the presupposition, the foundational truth in which we order our lives is God. But today I am really pointing out that it is not so much that one believes, but how important that belief is in our lives, or if you would the Faith Divide. Faith which does not produce works is dead, because faith which does not place God as the foundational truth is not really Faith. That is, a foundational truth is one which literally all others are founded. Therefore, it affects all other truths in the thread. As a Christian our foundational truth is God, not our Faith, but God Himself. Our Faith would be meaningless if there was no God. As I have written and said many times our Faith is not simply believing that there is a God but that we put our belief and trust in Him.

Obviously, one must believe or they could not trust, but our morality as Christian is not found in the Law. Not simply that God exists and gave us some rules to live by but is found in union with God. My byline is 'Knowing Nothing except Christ, Him alive, and in Him life', because it is the progression of our morality. Christ that we know God, united in Christ is to be united with God. This is only so because of the work that Christ did on the Cross. In humanism we consider ourselves a good person if we do those things which we reason a good person would do, in Christianity we consider ourselves a good person only because of what Christ did for us. Because of Christ, we have Life. That all moral philosophy is useless for salvation for it does not bring Life outside of Christ.

Which is why I call it the Faith Divide. There are those who are humanistic and simply have belief in God as part of their morality, and there are those who the trust in God is the foundation of our morality. Or let me put it a different way, the Faith Divide is between those who put their trust in what they believe, and those who put their trust first in God Himself. I think the best example of what I mean is the Bible, the how and why we go to Scripture. There are those who believe in God but put their Faith in Scripture. That is, they read Scripture because they believe that if they believe and do what it says then they will be saved. They put their faith in humanism, in the ability for them to reason out of Scripture what they must do to be saved. If they just believe the right things, do the right things then they will be justified. It is a bit of a fine line, but it reveals itself in the position that if your theology or your views on morality is not the same as theirs then you are really not saved.

How much Faith, how much trust must you place in God before you are saved? What must you believe? How moral must you be? All these questions start from the preconception that salvation is based on you, on what you believe or on what you do. Or if you would, that we seek to be moral, seek to be orthodox in order to be saved. But the other side of the line, the side I am a proponent of is that, we start with being saved. That is, our morality starts with regeneration, with justification. We seek to be orthodox because we want to know the truth about God, we want to know Him who saved us. We seek to be moral because we want to live up according to that nature we now have in Christ, the righteousness we share with and derive from Him.

Or if you would, the first point in Christian analytical philosophy is the belief in God, the first point in Christian moral philosophy is putting our trust in God. Belief and trust together make Faith.

Moral Philosophy

I should start by explaining that my need for inspiration comes from the fact that I have explored analytical philosophy about as far as I can and so it is time to start exploring moral philosophy. By moral philosophy I mean actions determined by reason, and that means limiting the field of study. For example, I know just enough physics to know that I would have to focus on physics to the exclusion of other disciplines, in order to determine if there is any validity to my wild ideas or if it is simply good science-fiction. Or in sociology, my Central Populace idea has some merit, but I have not worked on it in years because for the most part it is really a trick of mathematics. That and if it has any use at all it would be in social engineering, of which I am no longer a fan.

If you would, analytical philosophy is concerned with orthodoxy, or correct belief, moral philosophy is focused on orthopraxis, or proper behavior. Analytical philosophy is governed primarily by data, the outcome depends on the measure gives to individual points of data. One who considers Scripture as being what God would have us know is going to come to a different conclusion then one who gives a greater weight to current culture in determining truths about God. Moral philosophy, however, is driven mostly by need, by desire, by motivation. Or if you would, reasonable conclusions cannot, or at least should not be influenced by what we want, but our behavior is guided by the goals we wish to achieve.

While people have considerable trouble with analytical philosophy, and usually neglect observational philosophy all together, moral philosophy seems to come naturally to humans, but is also far more complex. As I have pointed out before, our minds naturally will give weight to our desires, and balance them without much direct thought. In fact, I would go as far to say that the strength of our desire is determined by how many other desires our minds are holding at the same time.

Wealth for example. Even someone like myself would find having a measure of wealth attractive. We want to be rich. The reason that we are not is simply we do not want it enough. Or in context, it is not the only thing we want. If money was the only thing you wanted, you would do anything, and everything in order to get it. Make and sell drugs, prostitute yourself, your wife and children, etc. That is, other desires are present, and compete with the goal of making money. Avoiding jail, not being an antisocial person, or not being perceived as one, love of other people, wanting to play that video game right now, and of course, the desire to do God's will instead of our own.

Obviously, God's will is a big one for us, which makes Christian moral philosophy both easier and harder. At regeneration came that desire for the Perfect, conform to the image of Christ. Though it manifests differently, in many ways we can say that is the mark of conversion, that longing for the Perfect, to live inwardly and outwardly according to God's will. It is how a considerably number of false prophets and false teachers gain their following, by promising that the Perfect can be had in this age. That is, while it is true that as we grow, mature, are sanctified, we are better able to live up to the Image of Christ, but it also comes the understanding that we will never see the Perfect in this age, we will never see God so clearly as to be perfect in this age. That the line as to where the person we want to be is always just out of reach. This is, in fact, what makes it easier.

We may at times desire a sin more then we desire to be that person, but as the Spirit works on us we become that person. Sometime kicking and screaming like the children we are. We can avoid it, we can fight it to our determent but because the change is the work of the Spirit of God rather than our own work we do not have to study philosophy or spend a great number of hours analyzing ever tidbit of data we collect in order to know how we are suppose to be growing. We simply have to place our trust in God and live our lives the best we can. That is, I disagree with those who say that one must be orthodox in their beliefs in order for us to be either justified or sanctified. However, I must be quick to add that we are hindered in our growth when we are not. Scripture has been given to us precisely because false teachings will divert us, having us chasing rabbits if you would, placing our trust in the wrong things instead of in God.

To put it in terms of moral philosophy, I will still do good if the desire for my heart is good, even if my mind does not understand it is good. But when my mind does not understand what is good, there is nothing to hinder my heart when it desires that which is evil.

We study Scripture not only analytically, to discern what is true, but morally, to discern what is good. We study the Law not because we are bound by it, but because it reveals that we are not yet perfect. That as we once stood condemned, so too would we now still stand unjustified without the Cross. Which also what makes Christian moral philosophy harder, in that that it is not about the Law. If it was simply a matter of doing this or thou shall not do that then it would be a simple computation. But Christian morality is not based on the Law, but on Love.

I know, the much maligned and much abused Situational Ethics position: Love is the guiding principle for Christian morality. I have not been able to find any fault, either philosophically or theologically, in that view. The problem is not in the proposition but in how one defines Love. Or more aptly, how we determine what is or is not an act of Love. For in theory Love is easy to define as simply carrying more for the needs and welfare of another than we do for our own. That Perfect Love means a willingness to sacrifice one's self, completely and in all ways for another. Would you not, if it was possible, give even your very salvation to one to whom you Love? It is the ideal which we strive for, but one which we will not know in this age. In this age, as with the example of the desire of wealth above, our Love is limited by what desires and even needs we may have for other things. And our ability to express Love limited by the desires limiting others in their Love.

Faith, virtue, enlightenment, love, all the noble ideas are easy to hold when one is isolated from the world. As I have often told you, it is easy to be enlightened when you live in a cave. In this age, in a world which we not only yet have the Perfect but where Love seems to be lacking terribly, moral philosophy starts with the question to determine which needs are to be met. One thing I have learned in all these years is that you can quickly be devoured by those who will not limit their appetite to what you are capable to give. In fact, it is for that reason that Scripture limits the command of Charity to fellow Christians. We are certainly to love others, all others, as ourselves, but command to Love applies only those whom are commanded to Love in return. We are commanded to Love, to see the needs of others in the Church as not only equal but greater than our own, so that we may be a light, and example of the ideal of Love for the world...a task in which we are certainly failing in.

My near-tirade aside, as you well know the primary vice which has hounded me in my drive for the Perfect we may have in this age has been pride. I had to focus mostly on humility before chastity, before I could even think in terms of romance, was because of my boundless pride. My detachment, my depressive fits, my much preferring criticism to praise, indeed most if not all of my struggles have been based on that prideful foundation, on an ego-self which says, even demands that 'I do not need.' Better to give up all desires than to admit weakness. The need for Love, to have someone look out for our welfare is a weakness. But one which I can admit now is a fundamental aspect of being human. One of our absurdity, if can forgive the expression. It is funny that we do not consider eating a weakness. It is, of course, but one which shows that we are not perfect, as God is perfect. And in many ways, I feel I did years ago when I first started the practice of fasting, when most of the time was spent just trying not to get distracted by the fantasies, thoughts about food brought on by the hunger.

Tired would be a better word, so very tired. You know, when you are tired and are at the same time fighting not to go to sleep. Which is to say, I have no idea what I am writing about beyond the theoretical, the abstract. Except that my view is unabashedly self-centered at the moment. What I need is someone who knows me, who can confirm and convict me in the way only a spouse can. I can say that what I need is reason to break out of my own mind, to go beyond the analytical in my own life. That I have a good handle on the inner-life, I might even be able to call myself an expert, but that focus robbed me of any real understanding of the outer-life of our faith. That, as a pointed out in a twisted bit of chaos, I am simply incompetent in what most people consider life. I focused on my genius and fell into that trap which specialists fall into, unable to relate outside of their field. And a symbol of all of this, it is like the question on whether I can keep my hippie-rags or should ninety percent of my wardrobe go in the trash.

A request for aid

I came to age during the Devil Scare, and so my default position is people are just being paranoid. I do think that anti-theists whine too much, thinking them a bit intolerant or just wimps for being offended because someone says a prayer during a graduation speech, or that there is a Cross on some government seal (assuming that it has been there for a long time.) but that aside, much of the time I agree with them because in a polytheistic and polyphilospical culture, either all prayers need to be allowed, or none at all. That someone praying to Shiva for a swift and total destruction of everything is as valid as any other. Or things like the Ten Commandment in courthouses, or nativity scenes on courtyard lawns are simply not conducive to a society which desires to be free in their practice of religion. In many ways we can blame those nativity scenes for the loss of religious liberties.

Jesus junk, Christian nick-knacks, bracelets with WWJD on them, pencils with Scriptures on them, Protestant icons with verses on the front and 'made in China' on the back. I am not an iconoclast in the sense I would promote the teaching to throw them all into the fire. Such things, I suppose, can be beneficial as a daily reminder of our Faith. Footprints in the Sand giving comfort, the wisdom to know the difference to remind us of patience. But on the other hand, they have become big business, have taken over much of what used to be book stores. And their commonalty, and the shallowness of their nature does nothing to promote a sense of the Sacred. They are made to make money, made to give comfort, to remind us to be good, but they are not made to promote the fear of God.

I really do not care about nativity scenes or cheep nick-knacks. They are only a means of introducing the topic, more of a symptom than the illness. In fact, being a writer what prompted this was reading what people write, and what they write or preach with seemingly no sense of the Sacred. No fear, no awe, no respect and no regard for the authority of God. Indeed, I adopted the use of the term Sacred-Trust during my study of Native American cultures because it captures the importance of duty, and the drive to make sure what I write is true far better than the modern use of the term calling. I spend considerable amount of time in study to make sure what I write is as factually correct as possible. Spend time in prayer so that I write in the correct spirit, with the attitude it needs to be written in. and I work to put away my sins, to become Nothing, to mature in the Faith and understanding what that means in the hopes of being able to write in a way which helps people with their own sanctification. And I continue to do this even still because of fear and because of love.

Remember in the youth of your Faith during those times when God would have you go right, but you decided to go left because that is the way you wanted to go? Remember those times when you remained going left because you were afraid, afraid of the disappointment you thought God must have for you choosing poorly. Afraid to turn and face God again? Much of the fear was unfounded, for there is not condemnation for those who are in Christ. But we learned about conviction, and we learned that we do fear God and that fear is indeed the beginning of wisdom. We fear God because we know that it is God who sets the standard, and we know that we cannot live by that standard. We fear God because He is the King, our Lord, so He can demand any price, set any course that He chooses for our lives. And we gain wisdom for we learn that the prices he demands, and the courses He sets are the wiser choices.

It starts with fear, it starts with concern for our own souls. Will not a teacher be judged more harshly? Even though we are saved from God's wrath, will we not still be judged according to our works? We feared to face God again when we went left because we were ashamed. Is that not so? That we start wanting nothing else than to be able to say that we gave it our all. We sort of get used to being stupid, it is the human condition, but in the beginning, we desire to be right, desire to write or preach what is true, desire to be moral because that is what is best for us. But also with that fear caused from our concern for others. Do we not want to be wise for sake of our spouse, our children, for those who listen to us? Do we not all experience, all who are regenerated feel that Sacred-Trust in one way or another? Are not all who are saved have that Sacred, because we are knights and God is our Lord, our King. We are on friendly terms with God, to be sure, but none the less it is because we know God to be, well God. That God is so far beyond us that we are awed by it.

Pastors 'called' to bless same-gender unions, open theism,

Christian universalism, Word-Faith and a hundred other heresies are the product of one thing, a lack of respect for God. The lack of a sense of the Sacred, a lack of that Sacred-Trust which I see even in the earliest converts. I see this even among those who I theological agree with. A pride in which it is more about them being right than it is about God being right. But this is too easy for me to write, been there, done that. It is easy for me to throw the first stone because I have outgrown the desire to be the Lord of my own life. But I have also learned that I have a tendency to hit myself in the back of the head with the rocks I throw. Which is more or less the point I think.

We cannot comprehend not being Knights. We just cannot see how one can have Faith and not have Christ as our Lord and King. Oh, we can understand how one can run from it, we can understand why one would avoid obedience, but we really have no understanding how one can be saved and not understand that God has the authority in our Faith, in our Lives. It is possible, very possible that they are not saved at all, those who use human reasoning and human standards to decide what is or is not a sin. I think such questions, doubting another's salvation is something that we should not do. But certainly, we must judge who we listen to, decide who are teachers will be. That in this time when there is so much disagreement, we must apply some sort of measure to the teachers we gather around us.

Or more to the point, as we are of the age in which we are the teachers and preachers now, we need to understand that we need to be that which we did not have. What did we need, but did not get from the old guard? Was it not aid in living according to that Sacred-Trust? We talked of that inner desire to follow Christ, that union with God of our hearts that drives us towards righteousness, and we got only blank stares in return. We wanted to know Scripture in a way to help us be perfect knights, instead we got pep rallies and shallow Bible studies. And so, the question I guess, for those of us who are teachers, preachers or simply writers, are we going to pass on the dysfunctions of the Church?

I feel like I am being incoherent, trying to get too fancy, or maybe I am just distracted by wanting to get back to work on the Traveler's Guide to the Colonies so I will put it bluntly and revisit the sense of the Sacred latter. Over the last fifteen years I have been hungry, cold, been abused. I have given everything I could manage and asked very little in return. That now changes. Now I ask, no, demand support. Not support for me, but for the Church. Not for church culture, or the social clubs that go by a name that is alive but are dead, but for the Church, for our younger siblings in Christ. What form this support takes, I cannot really say. Most of you are mature enough to know what God would have of you, and that is really what is important. God's will and not our own desires. Maybe you are already doing it, and so I am just saying to give it some more prayer. Maybe this is just all about me, as that is the direction I am heading, the rock hitting me in the back of the head. I have been worrying about my own life, about my own shortcomings and what I lack, so I just need to get back to what I can give.

Moral Exhibitionists Need Not Apply

My computer broke, managed to fix it, then it died. Been borrowing one as old as my nephew, but then I left, I have been gone for awhile, obviously. Been up in Dallas helping out, building, repairing and spending time just being Lumpy. While it is always tempting to remain in that philosopher's bliss of continual pondering, my compulsion to communicate pushes me once again into the thoughts of words, so that by expressing the idea I can learn if it is genius or simply insane. That is all I have to say about that except maybe that I surrendered in my long war with the framing gun. It bit me and nailed one of my fingers to the one next to it…good times. In one of those flashbacks to my childhood I looked around embarrassed. Not by the accident, but because my first thought was regret for leaving my camera behind because it would have made a cool pic, and then, as I pulled it out it reminded me a lot of cutting up chicken for dinner. After letting it bleed out for a while, I made a bandage from tissue and duct tape, which ironically did not embarrass me at all, and then went and put that last nail in. because, course, it was the last nail of the job that bit me. alas…that is life.

Back in the day I spent six years as a vegetarian. My reasons were personal, and I came from a school in which it was a personal choice rather than a moral choice. I am sensitive to the individuality of animals, and for a time could not be the cause of the end of that individuality. A phase of my life, if you would, in which I was haunted by the squeals of pigs being slaughtered. At the time I never got along well with other vegetarians, and it took me awhile to understand why. It was those who considered it a moral choice in which I had trouble with. Those who considered eating animal products immoral had a way about them that grated me. I horrified one poor girl by siding with the evil meat eater by giving philosophical justification for eating meat. Needless to say, she lost interest in my romantic protentional as I had become a devil. In her view God had ordained that we should be vegetarians (Daniel's giving up of rich foods) so I was preaching sin. But looking at it twenty years later, what bothered her was without being a vegetarian she would have nothing to feel morally justified. She would have nothing to which she could point to and say 'I am a good person because...'

Biblically it is that pride of the Pharisee that was happy not being that sinner over there. We call it being holier-then-thou, and in more modern terms it is called Moral Exhibitionism. It is found in our treatment of others, but I am more concerned with the pride which motivates our behavior for no other reason than to feel moral, to feel just and justified. That is, we can be motivated to Moral Exhibitionism by not wanting to have Moral Exhibitionism. Or if you would, humility is not humility if we are proud that we are not prideful like that prideful person over there. That is, I have observed in others and in myself a holier-then-thou attitude towards those who have a holier-then-thou attitude. For a most part I write and speak of being a sinner because I feel like a sinner, my own imperfections are grotesque and hideous to me. And for a large part in an attempt to disillusion those, my sister included, who see me as a Saint because my behavior and attitudes are as those they see as some Holy Man of a by gone time. But in that, I have noticed a feeling in me of a pride of my awareness of my sin keeping me humble. A pride in what I have in my self that keeps me humble...do you see my point?

Most recently up in Dallas. A group of church people invaded one of the neighborhoods I was at. I was expecting some sort of church-membership drive and I was not disappointed. I was expecting it to be a straightforward invitation or some sort of evangelizing effort. I am often annoyed by such people but I can understand those who want to 'get people saved and churched.' This was more a bait and switch, as their flyers were a sign up for a request for aid. Yard work, minor repairs etc. I said I do the same thing, mostly from family while I quickly read the paper. Having known and worked with many ministers I was fully expecting that question. you know 'would you think about volunteering?' or something to that manner. Instead, he missed the opening and commented about how some people do not have family. True enough, but as we were standing in an upper-class neighborhood people mostly likely would not be living there unless they could afford repairs and a gardener if need be. So, I looked up and examined him in that sociopathic way I have of reading people. He looked at me blinking, obviously knowing that what he said perked my interest in deeper matters. He opened his mouth to say something, but I said thank you and walked away in that sociopathic dismissive way I have sometimes.

At some point I might feel bad about it in that kinda-sorta-not really kind of way. I was born a king, born to command and I am not pleased at those times when it comes out. Those times in which I treat people like subjects rather than people. Not in the dismissing, as an honest look around shows that commoners want to be commanded, but rather the proof that my tyrant is not yet dead. The virtue of nobility is service to the People, and is maintained by seeing others as people and not simply tools or objects used to achieve a goal. Or to put it more plainly, I was not bothered because I dismissed the fellow as irrelevant but that I did not start the argument in which I was prompted.

Charity is a lifestyle. Moral exhibitionist need not apply.

A life of Charity is an everyday thing, not a once a year lets show that we care so you will like our church thing. That is, I read in the man's eye that the argument would have been taken as an attack and accomplished nothing. But should I have not at least tried? I have enough talent in reading people that I have been asked if I am physic more than once, but I am not perfect. Was there not the slightest chance that I was wrong and he would have understood? Been helped by my preaching…the probability was against, but should I not be a gambling man.

These are the things I was thinking about as I went back to digging the trench that would drain the swamp of a back yard. I am sure of my observations. The probability that my assessment was correct was well over ninety percent. I am usually good at such judgments, they are, after all a large part of how I do what I do. And much of my experience has been in that aspect of the Church. I was raised as a child of church leadership, done work for two national para-churches both before and after my conversion. I have seen…and read enough to see the Purpose-Driven movement in church culture as an adapted form of the Market-Driven movement in business culture. That is, once upon a time I was an insider and could easily been considered an up-and-comer…until my conversion. All in all, the facts that they only did this once a year and that they were targeting a well-off neighborhood (low class believers are oh so much work) was pretty suggestive that it was a membership drive instead a real outreach ministry. I have seen it played out enough times that I could script it for you. It starts off with good intentions most of the time, to show some Charity, some Christian Love. You get to help make both someone's life and Life better. I mean really, can there be a greater life than that. Oh, now I remember, the greater life is to fulfill the reason, the purpose if you would God gave you your Life.

See now, I know nothing of that specific church, they may be wonderful, perfect and oh so lovely. Their appearance was just a trigger for my thoughts on the matter. After examining my data points, as is my habit when making an observation of others, I look eternally and see how that observation also applies to me. How much of my own work, from the striving to virtue to the aid I give to others at the expense of myself, has been rooted in a kind of Moral Exhibitionism. I am not one to care much for the opinions of others of me, so how much of it was so I could feel good about myself? How much of my struggle against pride was so I could feel good, take pride in my humility? More than I care to admit, and obviously there is a progression. But it also explains the struggles I have had lately, the frustrations I have had. Why I have been struggling with having satisfaction with God's will.

I have never been one to care much about money. Even in my investing days it was more about manipulation and making the right choices. The first time I went hungry because I gave away my grocery money only bothered me because no one really seems to care. And when ministry brought me a time when I was hungry and cold, well that part was an adventure, as it was other aspects of that time which made it hard. I am a looser by choice. Not that I choose to be a nothing only that I choose to follow Christ regardless of where He took me. It was all part of cost…and of course also the Moral Exhibitionism…nothing is worth doing unless it is hard, nothing is worth writing if it is not worth writing it in your own blood…sound familiar. It is a subtle piece of pride, in that it is not the boast in what I have given up, or given to others but only the subtle satisfaction of having something to point to in order to 'prove' my Faith. The dissatisfaction started, as vice always leads to dissatisfaction, when I realized that I have nothing more to give, or I should put it, I am already giving all that I have to give. And everything I give I have been given.

Putting it thus makes me realize that it is a fulfillment of my third vow; whatever He gives me I will give to others. I have no wealth, but I have something rarer than gold for I am rich with friends and family who adore me. Most of them would argue against me being a loser, because I give them Hope. When I am with them they feel, regardless of how bad things are, everything will be alright. My dad spent a considerable amount of time watching me to figure out how I do it and why people listen when I talk. I know from his Gnostic spirituality that he was trying to discover my secret. Ironically, I told him, as I try to get across to everyone that they are simply responding to the Hope I have in Christ. That is, I have learned that no matter how hard life is, no matter how hungry or cold we are, if we hold on to our Faith, hold on to our trust in God everything is alright. Not everything will be alright, but it is already alright. By most standards my life sucks, but what is that as this is where God would have me at the moment.

My current problem is that by my standards my life is not all that hard. I have food and shelter, there is a computer I can borrow to write on, and most days I even have coffee and tobacco for my pipe. Life could be better of course, and that is always a temptation. After all, dreamers dream of what the world may be when dreamers are free to dream of what worlds could be. That is, it is just, and right and good to work on a better tomorrow, but wrong to be dissatisfied when tomorrow is not today. This is not the first time for this struggle. I went through the same thing with ministry. It is just in a different, personal context of romance. Pride how it relates to lust, if you would. But I could easily point to the past and look at the sacrifices I have made. But there is nothing now, at least from my view, which I can point to and see that I am making a sacrifice. Others see and say that I do, which is sort of the point of all this.

These outreach ministries, and the membership drives are based on a concept that I believe in. People see your theology in your actions, people want you to show them what you believe. It boils down to that famous biblical text of being a doer of the Word and just not a hearer. I could stand up and give a sermon about the sacrifices I make, the work I do, all that all-so-wonderful ways that I help people...and if you are a Christian than you do the same thing. You know what? I do all-so-wonderful things to help people and if you are a Christian than you do the same thing. We are called to a life of Charity, are we not? That is not in question, but rather the question is in how are you to express that Love. The answer to that question is always right in front of us. Family and friend, spouses and children, people at work, the single-serving friends we meet in the Life of High Adventure. Charity, Love that flows from our Faith, is not found in the works themselves but is the motivation for the works. Or will we do not have to work to show our Love because we are working because we Love.

This is not really about membership drives disguised as outreach ministries, though in many minds there is not a difference between the two in the first place. It is about that line between doing something because we feel like doing it, and doing something because we want a feeling from the doing. It is as like our Faith. The whole Reform mantra, for if we are working to prove we have Faith, so we have works to point out to ourselves so that we may feel saved then that is not Faith. For our Faith is placing our trust in God, first most trust in Jesus Christ for our salvation. When we work in order to have something to 'prove' to ourselves that we are saved then we are placing our trust in our works instead of in Him. It is the same problem I had with my mystical experiences early in my Life. I looked at them when I wanted to be reassured, to have proof that I am united with God through Christ. But just as placing our trusts in works or mystical experiences hinders the maturing of our Faith, so to placing our trust in works for proof of our love hinders Charity. Or in context of me, as it is always about me, is Charity any less grand if it is not given with great sacrifice to the giver? Is a parent any less loving if they do not have to go hungry in order to feed their children? Or it is like being a genius, if you go around trying to prove to everyone you are a genius chances are you are not one.

This goes beyond just Faith and Charity, but to virtue as well. If it was simply a mater of gaining a feeling then that would be easy enough. I could feel humble just by focusing on the motivation of this that is not about me, and ignoring the part of the motivation that is. That is, if all I wanted was to feel humble then all I would have to focus on is my humility and ignore my arrogance. I would simply ignore that it is in my rambling that I come to understand what I am writing (and I would ignore that my thoughts ramble much more than my written). But then…I guess I am concluding that for us feeling virtuous is not enough, we actually want to be virtuous. So for us striving for the feeling of virtue gets in the way of striving for the virtue itself. I am, of course not saying that we are not allowed to feel a virtue. Just because I lack such feelings does not mean that there are not emotions linked to them. But, the problem with feeling virtue is that then we fail in that virtue when we are not 'feeling it'.

All virtue, like Faith and Charity is a lifestyle, it is in our (new) nature and not momentary events. Has this not yet been proven to you in your Faith. We all face those times in which we can not 'feel' God. Terrible times when it felt like God left us and took our very Life from us. Dark nights of the soul as the Catholics call them, dry seasons as I most often heard them called. and what do we learn form such times? Was God punishing us for some sin, as one book I read put it? Is it that we need to do more as another book put it? pray this prayer, pray this way? Give all your money to me, as many preachers on TV seem to answer? But as unpleasant as those times are did we not learn that they were necessary? Obviously most people are not philosophers, or obsessed with finding words to express what they have learned. But one day after going through such a time, you wake up and see how you have changed. How god has used them. That God used them, and other things to grow our Faith, to change our character to one who trusts Him, and keeps on with the service even when we are not feeling it, feeling rewarded for our service. That is, we learn that the Spirit really does work changes in us. He forges us into what He wants us to be. And then, if you are like me, we start stressing and worrying about what God would have us become.

Without a doubt we should strive for virtue, and even surer there will be hardships, dire temptations along the way. And it is helpful along the way to keep in mind that it is God who works in and on us. That though God works on us through the struggles, the dry periods and hardships that the change is a Grace, a gift from God given according to His will. Not that it helps much when we are in such times. This is nothing new. Indeed, how many times have I preached for you pray for virtue, for God's will to be done instead of falling into that trap of praying for God to take the struggle away from you? As many time as I feel into the trap of praying for God to take away the struggle, the hardship. As many times as I found myself tired of that inner-fight, tired of the struggle against the flesh. To be sure, if it was simply a matter of knowledge, then I would have learned my lesson with all those years of pride. I would not find myself, instead of praying for the strength to do God's will, praying for God to take way my lust. Praying to return to those days in which I did not feel my desire, did not feel my loneliness…and thus everything fell into place…I am a spoiled brat.

There…I said it, yes I did. Some of you will understand, some of you will not seeing I do not live the life of the rich and famous. God has spoiled me in my Life. Looking back over my Faith, who I was, who I am, everything I have wanted, everything I have earnestly and diligently sought for myself from God He has given me. That is not to say every prayer I have ever uttered in momentary desires has been answered, but all the ones in which I returned again and again God has given to me. I missed it because since my conversion my life has been marked by one failure after the next. I went from an up-and-coming to a middle-age could-have-been. And as my lust has brought that in focus, and my pride is going Whisky Tango Foxtrot for some time, I have to laugh now and ask 'is that not what I have been praying for all these years.' I have been sitting here actually complaining about God giving me a Life of Faith, Hope and Charity I wanted so much. I have been making much ado about nothing, don't ya think?

Let me conclude this with something that those of you who have gotten this far might find helpful. In the Life of High Adventure, our goal as knights is not only to live but to be of character which brings glory to Chirst. In all my years with my struggle with pride I learned that there is no room in that for seeking glory for ourselves. That we have to give up our birthright as kings, give up our inheritance in this world. I am not saying that it is wrong to build empires, only that it is wrong to build them as monuments of our own accomplishments. Or if you would, should not we be working to show the greatness of Christ rather than proving our own greatness?

So far with lust, I have learned that it is what you desire to take from another, while love is what you desire to give them. And the purpose of hormones is to make you stupid, though I am not sure if that is at all relevant. What is relevant is that our relationships with one another, whether romantic or not, are really the monuments in which the glory is written. That pride hinders us by trying to hog the spotlight, while lust hinders us because we are seeking our own gratification. My pride wanted to be counted a great servant, instead of simply serving greatly. My lust keeps asking what do I get out of all this. Being a starving artist never really bothered me, as I really did not want anything. At any rate, did not desire anything that would tempt me to give up writing for it. I went through hardships and trials, been mistreated, misused and abused, and only thought about giving up on individuals, but with lust I have found myself, more than once thinking about giving up on ministry. There are moments in which I would gladly trade writing for a wife.

Ok, not so helpful, but this is what I am getting at. Pride, lust, greed, whatever we struggle with, we are struggling with them precisely because they are conflicting with our true desire. That whole regenerated heart verses the flesh, the knight verses the dragon thing. We struggle because it is our nature to struggle, and could not give up the struggle any more than we could breath water. We struggle only because we do not like those aspects of ourselves that seek for ourselves rather than to glorify Christ. We struggle because the Spirit of God is working in and on us to subdue the flesh. And we have learned…you have learned from prior struggles that if you keep your Faith, if you keep your trust in God He will complete the work. In this moment the struggle is hard, tomorrow you will wonder why you were so worried, and the next day will bring a new struggle…thus is the Life of High Adventure.

Shadows of a Midlife Hangover

There comes that time in life when that ache you had every once in a while, becomes a daily pain. There comes that time when the calf muscle you pulled in your workout, the joint you blew out in your labors takes weeks, or even longer to heal instead of just a few days. There comes that time, of course, when you realize that you have less days to count on than you have already spent. Midlife, obviously, that time stereotyped by fast cars and romance with the young. A time for John to lament that he has not had as many adventures, and me to complain I have no one to share my adventures with (ok, I think that was a movie, or tv show rather than real life. but anyway...) But generally, it is a time when we are sensitive to the work we have done with our lives and what we have to show for it, or what we lack to show for it. A time when life is not as titillating as it used to be, not even as exciting as the word titillating. And whether it is something biological or psychological it is just another one of those times time when you are not really enjoying, not really feeling it.

The nihilism of youth cannot compare to the despair possible when the shadow of midlife passes over you. For when we are young we question the point and purpose of struggling because of our lack of power. We rebel, those of us who rebelled, did so from an apathy to a world in which we had no control. We lived in a world in which the freedoms of our actions and the results those actions could achieve were curtailed by our lack of experience. But that lack of experience also limits our apathy, for we still hold out hope that our will, talent and hard work could, in fact, give us that life that popular culture has promised it would. But given time we learn that while luck may favor the bold, the nature of our world favors the privilege of birth. While we are young, we can hope to defy the odds, to deny the percentages, for everyone who achieves their goals there are thousands who have failed. That in youth we could celebrate with the movie, rock or sports star. We could honor the business moguls. We could salute the victor. We ignore the piles of the broken bodies of those who had contended for the prize, because we never thought we would end up like them. But today we wake up the shadow of midlife, like a hangover from our youth. Today we wake up with the realization that the work and struggles, the pain and hardships, our talents and genius has only purchased the life we have today.

I have written about this before, from a younger man's view. I have spent literally half of my life, twenty-three years now, in study and contemplation. In the irony of my existence, I have spent time analyzing the lamenting the lonely life of the philosopher driven to analyze all the data and experiences that come our way. Pondered about why the melancholy tone comes so easily to my writing but I can rarely bring it forth from my lips. Indeed, I have wasted much time meditating on the waste of time meditating on an idea can be. Contemplated on what I have gotten from all my contemplation, and how best to put it to use and pondering on how to overcome the obstacles which prevents me from doing so. And most of all, I have sought to answer that most puzzling question of all. Should I 'suffer the slings and arrows of outrageous fortune or take up arms against them, and by opposing, end them?'....oh...you know...like whatever.

I write now from the view of a middle-aged philosopher who has wasted half his life in contemplation. Most of us are not experiencing that midlife crisis in the stereotypical way. We do not lament the fun we missed out of when we were young. John has had his own adventures, and I have more people wanting to share my life than I can handle. We enjoyed our fun and our freedom in your youth. In taking stock of what we have done so far, it is hardly play that we missed out on. Rather, looking back, we lament the lack of stability and accomplishments that a serious and sober life creates. Most of us are not in danger of loosing ourselves in drunken orgies, but rather being crushed under the weight and restrictions of striving to have some achievement, to have something, anything so that our entire lives was not the waist of time our youth was. That no matter the details of the lacking, or how we look at it, or how we are reacting, our focus are on those things in our life in which we have failed. Those areas in which we feel like we have not achieved and accomplished that which we could have, or want.

It is, of course, our reactions to the shadow of midlife, the temptations that unachieved goals can be which is the most concern for me. It obviously does not need to be said that we cannot exchange the Life we have in Christ for the illusions of this world. That is, the warning seems unnecessary for our honor as Knights of the Sacred Rose, is bound to that Life, and in doing the will of God. Yet, more than a few knights have fallen precisely for this reason. Nor can I advise to simply give up on the dream and settle for a life of mediocrity, for without our goal we have no Honor. In those times in which we are drowning in the deepest waters of our souls, desperately trying to find the way to escape the prison of our own mind, we need a reason to make the suffering of an unfair and dark world bearable. In the Shakespearian tragedy of our lives it is not enough to fight, one must have something to fight for.

Pride, greed, lust, anger, living for those momentary pleasures or sacrifices for the image and substance of success, all the vices which we have focusing on what we can gain for ourselves. That we have learned, or are learning that the very things we have lamented or lamenting are in those areas in which we have fought and struggled for our own gain Obviously, these times of lamination are what we call conviction. Times in which God is showing us the affect our sins have had on our lives. Times when we are being called to repentance, to put aside our selfish desires and to live that noble purpose revealed to us in the Cross. That the question is not whether or how well you fight, but for whom are you fighting.

Philippians 1: For me, to live is Christ, and to die is gain. But if I live on in the flesh, this will mean fruit from my labor; yet what I shall choose I cannot tell. For I am hard pressed between the two, having a desire to depart and be with Christ, which is far better. Nevertheless to remain in the flesh is more needful for you. And being confident of this, I know that I shall remain and continue with you all for your progress and joy of faith.

I know, I know, that is why I have never been a good preachers, I cannot even make our very salvation, our justification and sanctification about us. Is that all there is to our Faith, so that we may escape hell? For me, the awareness of sin and our worthiness of condemnation is the beginning of repentance, the beginning of the Gospel not its conclusion. I fully understanding the temptation that heaven can be. The comfort that can be found in that no matter how horrid this life is it is finite, will end someday. I know better than most, even before conversion, what it is like to look forward to that end. suicidal tendencies, self-destructive behavior, ruled much of my life. I longed for, ached for death, even more now considering that death is not simply the end of the suffering but a gain. To put it most bluntly, viewed through the lenses of personal gain and loss the most logical thing would to end my suffering and put a bullet in my head. The Catholics answered that by making suicide a mortal sin, but that just makes things worse. That is, it gives a selfish reason not to kill yourself, but not a reason to live. That is to say, a reason not give up on life, a reason to make it worth continuing fight and struggle.

While needing something to live for was for me literal and more likely figurative for you, it still applies nonetheless. Though more extreme in the possibilities, in the depression I knew most of my life I have learned that personal goals are meaningless. When you make a habit of going above and beyond, giving all you can, there are many times when you have nothing left for yourself. When you have nothing to gain from your struggles, you need a reason to struggle other than your own gain. With my skill with words, I could be most popularly indeed if I would just give up and cater to those who see, who want a religion of self-help. Prayers as a means to health and wealth, God as merely a tool for our own satisfaction.

But the shadow of midlife, as with all such times is the temptation to give up what we have been given, for the sake of what we could gain. In the irony of our lives, these temptations are at their worse because of the awareness, either acute or abstract, that there is no gain for ourselves, nothing we can do to increase what God has given us, to add to what Christ has done for us. The nihilism of our Faith, for in the end, measured by what we have gained for ourselves, our lives have been nothing but shadows and dust. When we die, all the things we have gathered for ourselves, the wealth or respect, those moments of pleasure or empires we ruled, has not done us a bit of good. At the White Throne when we all shall be judged by our works, the only works that will have merit are those which have been done by Christ. All that we may acquire for ourselves in this life is meaningless because it does us no good once we are dead. But…yet as we live we are a gain to others.

I brought up John at the beginning because I know him well enough to know the specifics of his laminations. Because I was thinking of the loneliness of responsibility, he brought up the last time we spoke. That struggle between pride which strives to claim that place in which should be ours by right, and the proper and just drive to succeed for the sake of his family. And I know him well enough that I am sure he is doing better than I am with my lust, which I will write more specifically next time. But also because he is alone, in that way we all are. That is, there are things, aspects of our life in which we have no one to look to for support, except for God. There are times when He brings us when we struggle with our Faith, struggle to keep that peace and joy found in trusting Him and His will. That in those dark days of our past or in the now, when we cannot see any point in the struggle, when we cannot see past the pain, it was a daily struggle to trust in Christ that we do not fight in vain.

That is what it is really about, from beginning to end, is it not? Having Faith, placing our trust in God. It is the easiest, and the hardest thing to do, is it not? Easy, very easy because of the Nature of God, hard because of our own nature. See now, we know full well that God's will is always better than our own, we would not call ourselves knights if we did not. But this is where I must ask if we are fighting in vain. Are we fighting in the vanities of our own gain, so that we may say that we have fought, or are we justly and honorably fighting to be a gain to others? I ask that question of you a lot, I know, but only because I ask it of myself a lot. That in the youth of our faith we lament because we are weak. We lament because in our weakness we are still sinners, and for the harm our sin causes us. But as we mature into the midlife lamentations of our faith, we lament because we are weak, because the harm our sins cause others. In our youth we struggled with trusting that God's will for our lives is a gain to us, and once that is settled, we struggle with trusting that God's will for our lives is a gain to others.

I can write easily about the dark days of my past because my depression are years behind me. I can admit freely now that I have contemplated suicide more than once because I am no longer at risk of doing it. I can write about the laminations of both youth and middle age because they are laminations I have had. I have struggled with that doubt that there is any gain in God's will, for myself or for others. I have struggled with trusting God that there is any purpose in any of this. Starting some time again with who am I to say such things, and recently, most recently in trusting God that the gain for you is worth what it cost me. Now I can write that it is, but not because of some great example I can point to. No rapture or vision, no parting of the clouds of a glorious day. It was more like...you know...what ever. It was more of a shrug of the shoulders because when you have Faith, when you put your trust in God and His will it is not the struggle and the fight but the laminations which are in vain.

Beauty in the Eye of the Mystic

'When you shall these unlucky deeds relate,
Speak of me as I am; nothing extenuate,
Nor set down aught in malice: then must you speak
Of one that loved not wisely but too well.'
-    Othello by the Dead Bard

I said I would write about my lust and so I shall. You will forgive me, of course, if I am poetically philosophical about it, or even philosophically poetic. I cannot help but to write with an ironic smile on my face...and a glimmer of a tear in my eye. For mine is the tragic but typical story of a cynical romantic. Well, maybe not typical, as I hardly look the part, or even act the part. That there are many reasons to be a romantic, to believe in true love, that one can find happiness in love. And many, many more reasons to be cynical, to believe one will never have happiness in love. As you well know, the distance between artistic and insane is measured by success, and as I am not successful insanity is all I have left. For dreamers can dream of impossible dreams unfettered and unhindered by what could be, and even go beyond, dreaming of a mind free even of restrictions placed on us by our dreams. A mind without limits, without boundaries...a mind in chaos, a mind insane...and in that endless ocean of a mind where you can find no land to rest upon it is not a question of if you swim, to do otherwise is to drown like the rest.

Sanity is really nothing more than the minds tendency to limit our choices within manageable levels, and as it is judged, within acceptable and functioning limits. It is a function of reason to limit possibilities by giving parameters to variables. That is, we know that we cannot role a 12 on a 10-sided die as it is not within the parameters of the variable (V= 1-10). Likewise, reality can be defined by only even or odd numbers (Ve = 2,4,6,8,10; Vo=1,3.5,7,9) or say by prime numbers (Vp = 1,2,3,5,7). Now, we spend a lot of time on defining the variable, trying to predict which number will be rolled, to gain some edge in life. But what happens when we ask that hidden question, those questions we never ask because to ask them is insanity. Why are we rolling a ten-sided dice in the first place? Why do we define reality as having only ten sides? How does one go about being 12 or even 20 sided in a 10-sided world? How does one keep their sanity even with only ten sides when most see the world only with 8 or even 6 sides? When even reality goes beyond what is considered sane? I mean, after all there are only 10 types of people in the world; those who can read binary and those who cannot.

The most obvious point I am making there is more to life than we sometimes perceive, and there is also less than perceive. Genius, and not simply being intelligent, it is a mind balanced on a razor's edge The greater the mind the greater the ability to see the possibilities, the greater the heart the greater the ability to imagine the impossibilities. There is no line between genius and madness except the work one is willing to do to see if there is any possibilities in the impossible. How many digits you are willing calculate to see if there is truly not an end to pi.

But as you know, I rarely go for the most obvious thread, and am rather pointing to the mind which dreams impossible dreams, which sees not only possibilities but impossibilities as well. That mind that has no choice but to spend energy on examining every idea, on defining variables, on remaining sane. The very nature of genius requires a specialization in order for the sixteen-bit analytical part of our brain to give meaning and order to the workings of the chaotic and abstract subconscious which can be measured in the gigabytes. Focus determines our reality, because we define the variables of reality by the variables we are focused on.

That is why along with the fine line nonsense there is also the idea that a genius in one discipline is often rather stupid in another. An idea important enough to be found in logic, with the Appeal to Authority fallacy, as the definitions of variables in one discipline rarely caries over to another. While I will most likely return to concept of defining life by constants and variables, it is the concept of the Appeal to Authority fallacy which is most relevant to the current thread. It is the nature of mind to be intolerant of undefined variables, to experience stress from what we do not know. In general terms we call curiosity, and like all stress-motivations there are different means of dealing with it. And as with all stress-motivations we are looking for ways to alleviate the stress. We handle this stress mostly by deciding that lack of knowledge is irrelevant. Why does it not bother you that you do not know what the yen to dollar exchange rate was today? Why does it not bother me that I do not know how to spell words I have typed thousands of time. Focus determines our reality, because we are focused on what is important to us.

You may not understand how this is related to lust, but that is only because you cannot see my white board. Not that you would understand if you saw it, as lumpy script has become even more unreadable since I taught myself to type. But there is a reason why I did not experience lust in any great amount until my pride broke like a bad fever. That is, pride manifests differently deepening on personality, but generally the desire to be the center of the universe, or at least the center of the universe we are focused on. In many ways it is living the Appeal to Authority fallacy, where we think because we have mastered one area of our life we are or at least should be seen as a master in another. When a biologist writes a book on historical sociology or a preacher writes a book on biology. A movie star making political statements or a model making theological ones.

As I wrote years ago, pride is what drives pastors to become politicians and saints to become crusaders. A more subtle as aspect of this, however, is to be the one, not only defining the variables, but to be the one who decides which variables and constant are most important. This pride is common in our culture, and is the fundamental paradox of post-modern philosophies. But more to the point, lust was not much of problem from my pride, because romance was unnecessary, even counterproductive to the universe that circles around me. That is the philosopher-genius finds the whole concept rather vulgar, common, and irrelevant to the intellect's work to understand.

But more to the point, the variables and calculations that were so helpful for humility, and the fires of the turmoil which burn away my pride, have little use as a weapon against lust. Pride is primarily a vice of the mind, the intellect, and can be dealt with by redefining the variables. Ultimately, humility is discarding ourselves as the authority of our own lives, and instead accepting God's authority. It is defining the variable of success not by social standards or by what we hope to accomplish, but instead by what God would have us do. Pride is making ourselves our own god, and idol. Lust, however, is a vice of the heart, of the will, a temptation of passion instead of reason, making something outside of ourselves a god, an idol...

While as knights we live according to the Mind of Christ, but our carnal mind seeks to be our own masters. While as knights we live according to the Spirit of Christ, but our carnal hearts seek to fulfill our own desires. That ultimately our goal is to have our own intellect and will transformed to reflect those of God. And on their most primitive level all vices are desires to replace God, and all temptations are distractions from His Will. Temptations are those things outside ourselves that is pleasurable to look upon while vice is that inside us which sees the desirable object outside of what God had willed it to be used for. Metaphorically, using a hammer to pound in a screw. More to the point, that woman I met once and will never see again.

The other day I went to the doc for my skin cancer, and the PA who examined me was the most attractive woman I had met in a very long time. And typical me, I did not even notice this until I got home. In fact, I did not notice it until I realized my sister did not ask me if I found her attractive. Anyway, I spent a day or so trying not to drown in the impossibilities, struggling against the fantasies of possibilities. The struggle was short lived because the whole episode, from beginning to end, was surreal. I never felt an attraction that way before, or I should say that quickly. I mean physical attraction, sexual attraction sometime comes very quickly, epically with that certain curve of the hips that beckons the barbarian and sets my teeth on edge. But such attraction is obviously lust, and being obvious, rises my defenses quickly. That is, neither sexy or beautiful sparks my interest long because I instantly start calculating probabilities, checking variables. Met a woman about a year ago with those come-hither hips, but the attraction only lasted until she turned around and I assessed her age in the mid-twenties. But I was

I was literally stunned for the entire time when our eyes met when the PA entered the room. So much so I missed her name entirely when she introduced herself.

Even odder was my reaction, or I should say lack of reaction to her putting her hand on my shoulder. Obviously, she was just doing her job well, consoling someone she told they have cancer. She obviously knew nothing about me either. How I look forward to death as an end to the struggle and work or my background in which I already knew what she told me. That it is cancer and there is only a slim, very slim chance that it is of a kind that will turn deadly before I can afford to have it cut out. As she was standing behind me, and my sister was freaking out, the hand on the shoulder seems like the empathetic thing to do. The event itself was not odd, but the oddity was that I did not cringe from the contact. She was beautiful and smart, my attraction was to whatever quality she had that bypassed my defenses and my dislike of physical contact. I do not have a name for that quality, but it is one calms instead of agitates me. It gentles the hurricane of my thoughts. While most artist, maybe even most people look for muses to spark the flames of creativity, look for titillation, I find what I treasure most would be a muse to damper the fire of my mind.

Let me rephrase that, for I do desire a muse to inspire me, but inspired towards what? The main reason I have never dealt with lust the way most have is because of Beethoven's 4th symphony. It playing at the moment, and is a good representative of intellectual pleasure. If I do nothing but listen, a sensation forms around and behind my eyes comparable to the physical pleasure of sex. That pleasure that goes just beyond the word pleasure, pleasure to almost a kind of pain, where you jerk back from it at times, where nothing is left but the sensation, that moment just before the release of climax. That music, good music anyway, can very well be seen as a form of mental masturbation. Thus is my life, my daily life. My mind always racing forward, chasing that next idea, that next turn of phrase, those moments when all the data comes together into something beautiful enough to struggle, strive and do all the work requires to limit my expression by those variables considered sane. And though it is a necessary part of being a writer, it can also be very much a mental masturbation. Though it produces a sensation comparable to the physical pleasure of sex, and some say releases sexual energy, it does not produce the unity, a connection with another.

Pride is primarily an intellectual vice. It is an appeal to authority fallacy, in that it makes our reason the authority instead of God. Lust is a vice of the will as it makes an idol of our passion. It is unavoidable to talk about lust without talking about sex. But the issue is far more complicated than simply sexual desire. Sex is just an idol, an abstract in which we place our hopes and dreams. Is it not so in our culture? Having sex is the solution. Uptight, get laid. Popular adult culture teaches that our hang-ups completely or in part come from not having sex. But sex is simply the symbol of what we lust after, the fulfillment of the obsession. While lust is the word used when the vice is focused on sex, it is ultimately just like any other vice of the will. That is, it is not about the stimulating of the genitalia, pleasure of the act, but rather the stimulating of the will, about the pleasure of the passion in it all. In lust it is chasing that hormonal high, that biological excitement, but with all vices of the will it is about that passion that gives the will the power to overcome the intellect. A desire to live insanely, unshackled from the variables of the reality of our lives. To live as an artist and dreamer, dreaming dreams free of even of restrictions placed on us by our dreams.

This is where the threads come together, for vice, any vice is truly a desire for insanity. Surely an atheist, one who does not know God, must disagree. For God does not exist in their reality, and so we are the insane ones. How much of our culture, indeed how much of church culture agrees that we are insane, because we know God and is known by God, and take that knowledge into account in the variables of our lives. But it is insanity to know God and then live as if He did not exist. Which is the nature vice, is it not? The desires we have to live as if there is no God. All vices regardless of how they manifest, whether they are of the intellect, will or a combination of the two, and regardless of the sins they bring, is the looking for an idol, and excuse to ignore the will of God in determining the path of our own lives. To be a knight, but to live as if we are unaware of the Sacred Rose. To call ourselves servants, but act like masters…for me, it is very much that selfishness that screams 'what about me?!'

There is a line in all this, though I know not what it is. It might have been different if I had not specialized on the inner-life.

If I had not focused my genius on understanding sanctification, focused it on that maturing the Spirit works in us, I might not have lost my ability to function in the outer-life. Then again, maybe I would have just with less understanding, as it is obvious even from my earliest writings this is where God was bringing me. Is not the third vow that whatever God gives to us we will give to others? If you have a loaf of bread… it goes to your children when you are a parent. It goes to your spouse when you are married. When you are a pastor, it goes to those in your care. When you are me…it goes to the next hungry person you run across. That is, just as reason the variables of possibilities into hopefully practical limits, gives structure to our thoughts, so to does relationships limit the possibilities of Love, gives the structure to how to express charity. Relationships form the logic tree in which we process who has the highest claim on our bread.

Being specialized in the inner-life I made the appeal to authority fallacy by applying this to the outer-life. Or, by judging by the variables of the inner-life I am a rather awesome dude, but by the variables of the outer-life I a loser, rather stupid in fact. And that is more or less, what all this lust has been about. That is, being a looser by such standards does not bother me. After all, as a general rule neither great philosophers or great writers have ever done well with the outer-life. Indeed, for all the boasting we make about the importance of art I must once again agree with Voltaire's father that 'literature is the profession of a man who wishes to be useless to society, a burden to his relatives and to die of hunger.' (Ironic because Voltaire was both recognized in his own time and did well with money.) But what is that to us classic art is timeless art, speaking to only a few in every generation.

Obviously when it comes to sharing understanding is not like finite commodities. Rare, maybe, but it cost one little to share those things they have learned. Long hours spent coming up with the right word combination, metaphors that work well, hyperboles that titillate. But once something is written, it is multiplied rather than consumed. Once we come to the fullness of the knowledge of the Bread of Life, our souls are never hungry again…but our belly still is. Knowing God in Christ means never again worrying about or striving to know God, but we still hunger to come to come to the full understanding, that Perfect which will come when we finally get to see Him face to face. That while we still live, we still hunger and are driven by our hungers. We still desire and will our desires. That in the variables of the inner-life, once understanding is acquired it is never lost. Forgotten at times, failed to be applied occasionally, but there is no loss by passing it along. Truly, understanding is increased in the sharing. In the variables of the inner-life gain is found in giving everything away, having nothing for yourself, being nothing for yourself.

Obviously the outer-life does not work on the same variables as the inner-life. And as I wrote, vice is nothing but our desires for that which is not God's will. This means not only desiring to achieve our will by unlawful means, as the desire to fulfill our lust in a drunken orgy, but also using good and just desires to avoid what God would have us do. The desire for romance, not to be alone, to be sociable is good. The desire for sex, for food, entertainment, physical comforts, the desire to create, to achieve to succeed, putting a little whip cream on your hot chocolate, all these things are good and just desires. If it was simply the matter of the desires themselves it would be easy. I am skilled well enough in my inner process that I could easily turn off my sexual desire, suppress my loneliness by simply not allowing myself to experience it. But I have learned, the hard way that while the suppression of sinful desires is helpful in controlling behavior, it also creates the illusion that we have virtue. That it is easy to ignore the question of what we are avoiding with our vice, what is it we are trying to achieve which differs from what God would have us do.

It is really a silly question of why I lust. Obviously, I am lonely and middle-aged loser, it would be far stranger if I did not make an idol of romance in my thoughts. When one is unlucky in love, they either become bitter towards the opposite sex, or makes an idol from romance. Which is how idols work, of course. The obsession that our life would be better if we but appease our passion, if we are but willing to appease the object of our desire. Or the obsession that if we but destroy and rid ourselves of the object of our hate. Either way obsession is an idol of our will, being driven by the agitations of something outside ourselves. Like I say, I am atypical, not in placing hope and dreams in the idol of romance but only in the awareness in that is what I have done. That I am practical enough to understand that romance will not solve my problems, but still, I place far too much hope in the idea. But in our struggles for virtue, the question of why we have vice is rarely as helpful as the question of what we are trying to avoid. What cost are we not wanting to pay? Very often, I have found, we run from God for reason that have nothing to do with the vice or sin we are running towards. We fear that we will have to give up the very thing which we are desiring. Why? Because we are knights, and that was precisely what He did at our conversion.

The youth of our Faith was marked with giving up that which we had desired before our conversion. That before our hearts were regenerated, we had hopes and dreams founded in the darkness, ones which we had to cast aside. An image of what the world and our life should look like that did not include God. It differs for each of us, for we it was a world ruled by the mind of a logician, practical, pragmatic and apathetic even to my own emotions. As efficiently barbaric as only reason can be. I wanted my world to be dictated by that southing and sane song of mathematical philosophy of the intellect, while God has wanted me to live in that insane and abstract world of my will. To live by my heart of a poet, fierce as it is sensitive, infinite as it is nothing, as strong as it is fragile. To weep from the darkness of this world, and giggle from the excitement of a blooming dandelion. But along the way I came to understand that I have become venerable to those who will take everything you have and then hate you because you have nothing more to give. That there are those, indeed that the majority of people abuse the gentle things in life, and as it has turned out I have become one of those gentle things. So as God wants me to become even more gentle, to give even more...I need an excuse to say I need to collect for myself. After all, it is not very practical to expect romance when all you have to offer is a heart of gold.

In the youth of our Faith, it is easy to think that God is asking us to forsake things, to give up what we desire. There is truth in that, but it is an issue of choosing between conflicting desires. At regeneration, in our new heart we have the desire to do God's will. The classic struggle between the flesh and spirit. Between our carnal nature, our dragon in the metaphoric language of the knight, and the new creation we are in Christ. And though this thread of thought seems to have no end, the point of all of it is the dealing with our carnal desires. That in my pride I thought it would be possible to put the flesh to death completely, to achieve the Perfect in the here and now. But I am older and hopefully humbler now, and I think I know the point of all the fasting. Hunger is a carnal desire, a desire is tied to being in this body. Is there anything wrong with hunger, with the desire to eat? Obviously not, unless we center our lives on food, chefs excluded of course. That the subduing of the flesh, is not so much the death of our will, of our passions as it is the subjugating it to the will of God.

A Suicide Note (Version 1)

I spend my days alone
Not a friend around
I would not mind a friend or two
But there are none to be found
Loneliness is my playmate
We play through the night

Loneliness turns to anger
Raging like a bonfire
Burning a hole in my gut
Burning me up from the inside out
Lighting the fuse that will explode
The bomb of rage that my fist can deliver

Anger turns to confusion
All thoughts of logic leave my head
Leaving only emptiness of being alone
Knowing only no one cares for me
Knowing that no one will ever care for me

Confusion turns to depression
Sorrow darker and colder then the deepest cave
Sadness as heavy as a mountain
Depression of which the only way out

Is death by my own hands (Or)

The love of another

Outcasts of the Tyrannies of our Churches.

'Fanaticism is to superstition what delirium is to fever and rage to anger. The man visited by ecstasies and visions, who takes dreams for realities and his fancies for prophecies, is an enthusiast; the man who supports his madness with murder is a fanatic.' From the *Philosophical Dictionary* by Voltaire (François–Marie Arouet)

The Enlightenment has come to an end, having died from a heart attack brought on by laziness and fast food. The Reformation is over, or at least has gone into hiding to escape the disarray, chaos and wolves which prowls the halls of our churches. Both, of course, follows that natural law which states that any extreme social pressure in one direction will eventually cause an equal pressure in the opposite direction, which will then have the strength to go to the opposing extreme once the original pressure is lifted. I think Machiavelli said something about it, but it was first proposed by Plato in The Republic.

In this case it goes back some eight hundred years to an argument between the Franciscans and the Dominicans on what was the highest power of the soul. The question, which is one of the first for a philosopher; is it intellect (reason) or will (passion) that is the highest power of the soul, the driving force of human behavior? Should the intellect rule over the will, or is it simply a tool to get what one desires? The answer one gives on the highest power of the soul determines one's approach to life, philosophy, politics and even theology. Indeed, I would go as far as to say that which is culturally held as the highest power is a major factor in creating the nature of that culture.

It is no accident that the Enlightenment and Reformation are decaying at the same time. In spite of Martian Luther's rant against reason, the Reformation gave birth to the Age of Reason, which gave birth to the Enlightenment. The Reformed children of the Reformation apply reason to religion, and the Enlightened children of the Enlightenment make reason their religion. And while Western Culture held in theory that intellect was the highest power of the soul, we had a unity of a family which could afford to be dysfunctional. Through the bond of reason shared between the

Reformed and Enlightened, we could be unreasonable one with the other. We were free to hate each other, as siblings often do, because we were safe with one another, neither could risk shaking the foundation of reason that Western Civilization rests upon. But now we find that we are living in the world that Nietzsche predicted, the Age of Reason is coming to an end and the will once again dominates.

In truth, the Enlightenment and Reformations were but myths created by men to give importance to their own actions. Or, as nearer to the case, the Age of Reason only existed in the mind of those few who took their reform or their enlightenment seriously. Mere illusions created by the way we handle history because the great masses have experienced neither. In the end, they have always preferred the will of Rousseau to the intellect of Voltaire. Utopian dreams and every attempt to make them come to pass have failed, sometimes with horrific affect, because of the fundamental truth that the masses can neither be reformed nor enlightened. An individual can, any individual can be, but groups and organizations, nations and cultures cannot be. As even a passing glance at history shows that group dynamics prevents any formation of any form of utopian style culture. It does not take long in talking with people to realize that many, if not the great majority have the views that they have only because they are the views that the enlightened or reformed are supposed to have. And…as this is about us…look how quick we are to declare someone as ignorant, unenlightened, and in need of reforming because they do not place the same importance on individuality as we do. The contempt we have for those who conform to the image of being a Nonconformist while lacking even the basic understanding of what forces us to be Nonconformist.

I read some the works of the pagan philosopher J. Krishnamurti while I was I high school, or maybe junior high. He did not hold my interest for long because I understood what I read. As opposed to my three-year obsession with the works of Plato for no other reason than it hurt my head the first time I read them. That is, I have always chased what I do not understand. Obviously as a Christian mystic I do not agree with Krishnamurti on a lot of points now, but none-the-less, the passing read I did give shape to many of the views I had in my youth. About myself, about being an individual, and the need to rebel against the expectation of those who look upon you as a messiah. Maybe it was not his works but being able to relate to his story that inspired me then. He was raised in one of those messiah cults that were common back then. He was raised and educated specifically to be the savior of the world who would bring us into a new age. He would teach his cult, and the whole world what we would need to know. The expectations placed on me were not so grand, but as many of you know the expectation places on us because we are gifted feel very much like that when we are young. Anyway, when he came to age and the leadership of the group passed to him, he stood up and…disbanded the group.

I laughed when I read it, laughed when I just wrote it, and laughed because of it many times through my life. Maybe I should be more sympathetic to the anger of those who had set him up to be the god, to those whose feelings were hurt because he refused. I cannot because they looked to him to enlighten them, and he did that in the speech he gave casting them away. That if you truly want enlightenment, to know the truth about yourself, about the world, about God, you cannot look for others to give it to you but rather must seek it for yourself. Now that I think about it, Krishnamurti could be seen as one of the grandfathers of the neo-mystics today, except they believe that there is some special method or secret which propels us into God.

This is just one of many examples of the masses following a leader because they think that the leader will bring them into enlightenment. Whether they define this as some form of social utopia, or some kind of nirvana (a personal-living heaven). But those of us who are ministers, who are actually capable of guiding others know that ultimately you have to figure things out for yourself. I can be an enemy and longing for the superman to you, but at the end of the day the quality of your Faith does not come from me, which pastors you followed, how much you donated, but your wiliness to allow God to take you where He would.

This I have pressed on you from the start of all this, fifteen years now. That the condition of your soul does not depend on whether or not you understand what I write, or that you take my advice, but whether or not you seek God. There has been method to my madness, even if at times all I could see was my own insanity. The purpose that we have trained to seek for ourselves, to seek God and His will not dependent on what others have told us what it should be has become evident since the Storm did its damage, has it not? We may be distracted by the economic down turn, but pause in your worries for a moment and see the chaos and darkness that has befallen the Church.

Now, as I have pointed out previously our culture has become philosophically polytheistic, and as such has been fighting a philosophical religious war. It is somewhat understandable. While the US was focused on becoming a great nation that was our only metaphysical guiding principle, our only philosophical god. I know, I know, but you know I have never ascribed to the idea that God was our nation's god, that we have ever been a Christian nation. There is simply no way to escape that Manifest Destiny was our god, for how else can on explain the horrors that are in our past if it was not excused by what was good for the country. If we have learned anything over the years it is that we cannot sin just because it is an easy and convenient way to get the job done. That is, I can accept that it was God's will for us to become a great nation, but cannot except that it was God's will in how we went about doing that. That comes into play in a little while, but to keep the thread relevant, after WWII and the decade that followed, it was obvious that we had reached that destiny, that we had become that great nation. So then, what has become our god, our metaphysical guiding principle as a nation? And more important what are we, as individuals, to do?

Oh, I am such a naughty boy to lead you into a trap of words, but then I gave you the way out before I laid the trap. We all know our nation is in trouble, and it is patriotic to want to enlighten it. We all know that the Church is in even worse trouble and it is charity that wants to reform it. Both of these are honorable and noble desires, but they are also the path to tyranny. It is, in fact, how a tyranny is formed, whether in a nation or in a church. In politics I am apathetic. Tyranny is simply the natural progression of democracy. As a classical liberal I look upon the eroding of our individual rights with some trepidation, but as a as a philosopher I find more interest in noting and documenting the changes than preventing it. What does it matter to the poor if we are devoured by a lion or by a thousand rats? If the political left has their way, we will morally free, but economic slaves. If the right has their way, we will be economically free but moral slaves. Of course, the worst of these, such as in Nazi Germany or the USSR, is when the left and right combine and the individual is completely subjugated to the State. The nature of tyranny the individual is secondary to the State, to the vision, or to the goal. Whether by decree of a dictator or by a vote of the masses, anyone who does not go along is dealt with harshly. As a minister, political tyrannies do not concern me, but rather charismatic tyrannies, the tyrannies inside the Church.

When a State passes a law, which forbids us from doing something that our conscience or the Spirit bids us to do, we are still free to choose not to do or become a criminal. When a State passes a law, which compels us to do something that our conscience or the Spirit forbids to us, we still are free to choose to submit to the state or become a criminal. Political laws have only the strength to compel us equal to the fear we have of worldly force, whether the confiscation of your popularity, your property, your freedom or your life.

But religious laws, doctrines and dogmas, carry a much heavier weight, do they not? For the punishment for violating them is not limited to the temporal but echoes into eternity. Indeed, the *homo religiosus,* the human religious impulse across cultural boundaries is founded on that feeling that what we do in this life continue to affect us after we are dead. How religious one is, is in direct proportion to the strength of their *homo religious.* How important eternity is to them. This is true even for individuals who follow a religion that does not have an afterlife but believe our lives simply fuels the future. Such as the view of the' religious atheist' who sees their lives as serving the progression, or at least themselves and their views as a product of such progression.

Some atheist voices a fear that of a religious tyranny. We might find this humorous as our society is not only decadent but glorifies in its decadence. But as I pointed out at the beginning of this, any extreme social pressure in one direction will eventually cause an equal pressure in the opposite direction. The chaos and turmoil caused by the democracy, eventually leads to the need to take harsh measures to control it. While you and I may enjoy a glass of wine or brandy from time to time, and alcoholic must ban such drinks from his life. When the people as a whole are unrestrained in their morality, a tyrant must rise to force them to…feed the poor, take care of the sick, do those things which are impossible to do when we are seeking to fulfill all our desires. Indeed, a tyrant rises to power by promising to the people what they want. That is, if only you give the tyrant the power to do what must be done, then you can keep your decadence and have order as well. You, of course, will not have to sacrifice because the problem is…that thing over there, that opposing idea or concept…those people over there that are holding up the progress. Those who are hindering our creation of an enlightened and utopian society. The atheist fears a religious tyranny because it will not create a utopia to their liking, but should we not fear it more because it removes the individual's seeking of the Righteousness of God? More than that, as Christians, does not it run counter to the very basics of our Faith. If the Law given by God cannot save us, then how can we support, and not fear a teaching in which places hope for salvation in the laws created by men.

We are not there yet as a nation, and there are too many undetermined variables to calculate what the American tyranny will look like. And as I said, I am apolitical, and it is the tyrannies we already have in the Church which is the most concern to me. Though I fear a religious tyranny, maybe even more so, one has to wonder at the capability to reason of the Free-thinkers who continue to fiercely attack the Sacred Texts of the religious. (But, just as many people do not take the religion seriously enough to seek truth so to do many who claim reason as a god do not take seriously the High Art of Reason.)

To disregard Scripture is the fastest path to that religious tyranny. I understand that they think if they can get you to disregard the authority of the Bible then there will be no Christianity. If you get rid of the Vedas you get rid of Hinduism. If you destroy the Koran then there are no Islam. While it is understandable for the atheist to desire all to worship the god of their reason, but reason should show us that when we remove the safeguards of the Sacred Text then religion restrictions and obligations become whatever I can convince you they are. Again, it is understandable, as they believe the *homo religiosus* as a vice, and religion as a sin and an evil. But if you take a close look at every cult that turned evil, every time a religion became destructive you will find that first there was a leader who was given greater authority than the Sacred Texts. A leader who said that it was acceptable to sin in fulfilling God's Will, and usually that sinning was God's will.

The atheist's view is understandable at least, in that it is consistent with their view. If there is no God or gods there cannot be any Sacred Texts. But it is hardly understandable, or reasonable to those who claim to have Faith to disregard Scripture. Even more so for a mystic. But on the moment focused on the social aspect rather than on us as individuals. That first, pragmatically, is that the Bible is a safeguard against the tyranny of false prophets and teachers. Or rather, submission to the authority of Scripture is a safeguard, as the bible can be used to by tyrants to enforce their will. But in such cases, the pastor-tyrant is not submitting to Scripture but have placed themselves above and judge of Scripture, have they not? You have to accept what they say because it is Biblical, and we all know it is Biblical because they said it was. Questioning them is seen as questioning the Bible or God Himself. To doubt the what the pastor says, is doubting God.

I was reading an article in Relevant Magazine titled *Elephant in the Church* about restoring fallen pastors. Early on there is this: The H_____ 'may be a well-known story of sin and recovery, but there are many other Christians in ministry struggling under the same weight of sin issues and leadership responsibility. And the question then becomes: How can the Church reach and restore them?' I read the article, and read it a second time in case I missed it, because question for me becomes: Restore them to what? While the article does touch on restoring them to communion and fellowship with the Church, it is obviously more about returning them to their position as an idol. I know, I was supposed to say leadership position, but as the two most often mean the same thing in today's churches, I will let it stand.

It does focus a bit on how people feel betrayed and are unforgiving, but in it, and the real elephant in the church is why they feel that way. I went through it as a child. John went through it shortly after his conversion. All of us, at one point or another have felt the pain of having an idol fall. As children we learn that our parents are not gods. It is a natural part of maturing, though for many of us it happened at an unnaturally young age. It seems natural, a normal reaction to make an idol out of a pastor, mentor, church, denomination or ministry. After all, when we are young in the Faith such people and groups seem so mature, so larger than life. And it seems, at least to me, that it is simply one of those dire struggles along the path of maturing when those idols come crashing down.

That is, if we learn that it was not the sins of the pastor, the hypocrisy or hyper-conformity of the church, or in my case no one could answer my questions, which was the problem but that our pain was caused by the fact that we were following and worshiping them instead of God. That we know, full well, that it is not pleasing to see as illusion those things in which we have placed our trust, our hopes and dreams. And by that, we learn to see people as people and place our Faith only in God.

Philippians 3: Not that I have already attained, or am already perfected; but I press on, that I may lay hold of that which Christ Jesus has also laid hold of me. Brethren, I do not count myself to have apprehended; but one thing I do, forgetting those thing which are behind and reaching forward to those things which are ahead. I press toward the goal for the prize of the upward call of God in Christ Jesus.

We can be forgiving to the congregation for being unforgiving because we understand that this growth takes time. We have less sympathy, if any, for the minister because ultimately it was not the failing to be perfect, but rather a failing in their calling. The purpose of a minister is not to stand up and be an idol, but rather to aid in the tearing down of the idols in your life, so that your Faith and worship can be in Truth and in Spirit. A teacher teaches not so everyone will know that they know a lot, but so that you may understand what is true. A preacher preaches, a writer writes not so that you may be amazed by how I can turn a phrase, but so that you may be helped in you 'upward call of God in Christ Jesus.' Minister or not, we strive to be knights, perfect knights not so we can say that we are perfect so that we can be testaments of the Perfect Knight. We are mystics because we know that our *nisus*, our perfective urge, our desire for the Perfect cannot be fulfilled in this world, but in Christ.

Of course, one has to wonder what someone sitting in church for ten, twenty or more years was doing if they had not learned the most basic of Christian doctrines, everyone is a sinner. Where do these hurt feelings come from if not the elevating of pastors to a position of a god, to an idol or living oracle of God? While it is somewhat understandable to think that that pastor who is capable of preaching so well is not also capable of masturbating like a monkey watching supermodels. (Ya matt, inspired by that part in your book, but also some monkeys at a photo shoot I was at in my youth. Basically, the same story, just a bit more pandemonium. But anyway…) Or the Teacher that knows Scripture so well may actually fail to apply it sometimes. Or that a mystic like myself that seems to always understand and know what to say may…actually be wrong sometimes. None-the-less, these things happen, do they not? Far worse things, in fact. But not to us, we say. Not our pastor. Our preacher, our church, our mission is safe to make an idol out of.

I cut my last entry short because my tapestry of thoughts started to unravel, which is a clear sign that there was something I did not understand. While I am not Gnostic in my views, do not believe that understanding and maturity is the same thing, God restricted my writing long ago to those things I do understand. Those things which I have experienced, I have struggled with. While most of it was irrelevant to the case at hand, having to do emotions and father issues, but the topic of vices as idols opened up my thoughts to the problems the Church is having. That as individuals we struggle against vice because they are distractions from the Will of God. That when my primary struggle shifted from humility to chastity, from against pride to against lust, it started first by denying there was a struggle. That it was just a momentary obsession, the tantalization of a rather charming woman I met. You know, when the hormone went away so would the desire, like it had the times before. I lost interest but the lust remained, and had to face that my loneliness was no longer manifesting in poetry but in physical desire. There were times in which I grew tired of the struggle and masturbate like a monkey watching supermodels. I tried to put the genie back in the bottle, which God would not allow. Which was sort of the point of the last rambling. That there is nothing wrong with the desire for sex, or the desire of romance, but I was looking to romance to solve my lust problem instead of looking to God. That I consider mortification, our struggle against vice as a vehicle of Grace because God uses it to teach us that our righteousness is found in Christ and not in our own solutions to our struggles.

But I am a mystic and have never been able to ignore that irritation the Spirit brings when we are avoiding the struggle, avoiding His working in our hearts. I try, of course. I run from God just like everyone else. And like everyone else I avoid those things that have a chance of bringing us back, of reminding us, or making us aware that we are running. I misplace my bible. I do not listen to music. Most of all I avoid writing anything because I cannot do hypocrisy well, cannot write of the inner-life while avoiding it. Others, such as my best-enemy and closest friend John, avoids me when he is running, as I am his minister as well as friend. I have never given that much thought until recently because the issues that have to be worked out is not me and others, but between me and God, him and God, you and God. Obviously avoiding God is not the way to work out relationship problems with Him, but that is not the point here. But rather, as I have noted before, idols are simply the metaphor for those things which we use to distract ourselves from God, that we use as a self-medication to avoid awareness of our sin, avoid God's will.

To be sure God holds us to a higher standard. For when we presume to teach of Him and His will, we are judged not only by what we do but also by what we say, or write. I am responsible for every word, every idea expressed, precisely because of the trust you place in me and my views. Indeed, what can we think of a minister, and especially a pastor who violates their Sacred Trust and has allowed themselves to become an idol. Those who have so thoroughly forgotten the Reformation that they would stand up as an idol to replace Christ as the mediator between you and God instead of doing their job by helping you destroy the idols that prevent you from going to Him? Would not it be justified to be upset with a mechanic that filled your car with sand instead of oil? Or a doctor that cut off your arm in order to remove a splinter? As such, what does it say about a church culture in which they will not accept a minster, especially a pastor, who will not allow themselves to be made into an idol? That not only condones, but expects them to violate their Sacred Trust to give them bread and circuses?

All religious tyrannies in church history starts by replacing Scripture as the Oracle of God, with a person. Sometimes a group of people, a board of elders, a tyrannical oligarchy. It was bad enough when we had the fundamentalist and charismatic cults on the fringes, but this has moved into the Church Body as a whole. Now again, I am simply documenting the shift, the choice of the people is up to them as it always is. Just giving a warning, that in their attempt to escape the tyranny of the Bible, they are delivering themselves into the hands of a tyranny of the man. Do not like something Scripture says, then find yourself a preacher that will tell you it does not say that, not really. Or that Scripture is wrong or outdated.

But having given a person such authority, to say that they are wise enough in the ways of God to overthrow every Saint for two thousand years, also gives them the authority to decree what they will. And the day comes, the day has come in which they will have the authority to cast out of their church whoever does not agree with what their will is. That when you disagree with them, with their vision, the vision, the purpose or goal, you suddenly find yourself among us, among the ones you never thought you would be. You become just more of the scum among the outcasts of the religious tyrannies of our Churches. So, the real question becomes: what are we going to do now? Should you seek to go along, to knell to the idols of the pastor or church, purpose or vision? Should you make an idol out of your outcast status and raise a fist against the church of hypocrisy? Are we to be angry at God because we were rejected by those who claims His Name? Or should we continue on the path of casting away all idols which distract us from Him.

I have been an Outcast for a long time now, over ten years. I cannot even really say I have ever belonged to a church since my conversion. God would not let me take the traditional 'career path' of ministry. I had always figure that this was personal, a maturing thing. I have always had a way with words, dynamic ways of expressing myself, which makes people listen. Which is a good thing, but is bad when you are immature in the Faith and very arrogant. Or, up until recently I have never completely agreed with Jim that God is calling people out of the churches. I mean, I agreed as an individual, but not as a group. I still do not believe in a general call, that is, if you are a 'real Christian' you will have nothing to do with our church culture kind of stuff. But I doubt that is what Jim means either. Or, what I believe is that more and more God is making us choose between Him and the idols we have made of our pastors and churches. Choose between Him and the visions and purposes. As noble and correct as they might be, they are not God.

This is one of those threads of thoughts I hate. I have come to the end and still have found no conclusions. Where I can offer no advice except for those among the Outcast to examine their own motivation. In avoiding church are you also avoiding God? In church, our out of it, our goal is that 'upward call of God in Christ Jesus', and as such have you used the pain and suffering inflicted upon you as an excuse to avoid that calling? There may be some grand reason we are Outcasts, God never fails to awe me in such ways, but on an individual level, on a personal level, was it not because we turn the fight to 'save church culture' had become our idol? Had distracted us from Him? Maybe, maybe not, but it was such for me. That before we could and can fight the good fight, we must mature so we can do it according to God's will and not our own. That coming to understand that many pastors fall because they did not have time to mature in the Faith before being thrust into ministry, we also have to seek maturity, to lay hold of that which Christ Jesus has also laid hold of us, before we could take up the mantel of reformation. So, we may reform church culture into the image of Christ instead of transforming it into the image of our idol of reformation.

Ethics and social collapse.

So here we are…at another Teotwawki (the end of the world as we know it)…but as I am just a handful of hours away of finishing the Saint at Spears End, the first RPG book for Yon'o'wari, which is a name I derived from the Japanese for the end of the world… and I feel fine. Except, of course, I wish people would stop predicting the end of the world because it does get tiresome to have use my awesome and amazing imaginary powers to save you all once again.

In this case, I will just give you another 144,000 days, so we will not have worried the Mayans killing us off until 2410 or there about (I just woke up so my brain has not gotten enough caffeine to care about precision, which is a learned skill for me. Division was never my strong point, and besides if it matters pull out a frak'en calculator… I also get cranky when I first wake up, until I eat something…any way ill attempts at humor aside, I think I forgot the point of my rambling. Which is sort of funny as rambling does not have a point…but anyway…)

I make fun only because I am a prepper which is woefully unprepared. I need an ax, and a new shovel as mine is not going to last the season. A hoe would be nice but I do not really need one (no jokes on that one please.) All and all, if the zombies attack today, I am going to need a new shovel. So, whoever is in charge of releasing the flesh-eating zombies hold off into I get the chance to get to the store for a shovel, two, hey might as well grab all of them they have in the store as they will make a good Teotwawki investment. At least those who know about long term verses short term investing. So, I thought I would talk about investment philosophy, in Teotwawki terms but also how they apply to life.

The Teotwawki in the past we now count as the beginnings. And I am inclined for a total collapse, with zombies roaming free, simply because it is fun. Probability factors makes me more inclined to a collapse more like the Great Depression, with a shift in our views of government, each other, etc, rather than a complete collapse with pockets of humanity protecting themselves from roaming gangs of barbarians. That would require, only really require, a destruction of the entire electrical grid. No electricity and we have no society, but that requires a unpredictable complex event. A massive solar flare, bombardment by aliens with some EM pulse bombs, etc.….but besides being fun, the 'start over' scenario is also useful in examine our own social views.

Food is the best example of long-term verse short term investing, as we all need to eat. Not as much as we currently eat, but we still have to eat. So short term, one needs to have a stock pile of food. How much, of course depends on its availability. We live in a world of cars and supermarkets so we do not need to keep any food in reserve. Anytime we are out of something, we simply go to the store and get it. Of course, we do not want to go shopping every day, so we buy food for a week to a month deepening on your shopping habits. Living in places where it is difficult to get to the store, or the power can be out in wide areas means that we buy just a little extra to give us a few extra days leeway in when have to go shopping. Some people keep a larger cushion, from a few months to a year, depending on their reasons. Or they buy a stockpile of something because it is on sale, and the price will be higher when the time comes that they will 'need it'

This is short-term investments. We are exchanging our money for something we would use but once used has no lasting value. That is, its purpose is to get us something which we will use. A stockpile of food will get us through a hard time when food is not available, and can be used as a hedge against inflation. But it does not increase, does not get us 'more' food. Like an emergency cash reserve kept in a savings account its purpose is to be their 'in case' as a buffer so we do not screw up our credit report if we lose our job. It is not so we to make us more money. Short term investments generally have direct value because they are something we can use, or they are 'prepaid'. A year's worth of food is worth a year's worth of food regardless of the monetary changes in the cost food. That is, you have prepaid a year's cost of food, whether you use it over the next year or keep it stored (rotating so it does not go bad) for some latter use, you still have prepaid for a year of food. But while the mice trying to eat your food multiply the food itself does not.

Short term investments are also marked by little risk. True, prices could drop incredibly of food so the monetary worth of the stored food decreases.…but it still is a year's worth of food. Inflation can go through the roof, and your money stored becomes worth less, but the numbers of dollars will not decrease. Long-term investments, however, always caries risk because it requires one to basically bet on predictions. Those who expect high inflation bet by borrowing money. During the Great-depression, the inflation Germany experienced was so high that after only a few years a farmer could pay off the debt from buying the farm with the price of a single egg. Inflation is what makes a home a good long-term investment. You will, of course, end up paying 3x the price of the house but after the 30 years that it takes to pay it off, it will generally be worth what you paid for it. But not really to the point, and only indirectly relevant to shovels being a Teotwawki investment.

So let us look at the traditional hedge against inflation, gold. It is way down on my list of Teotwawki investments because it has no real value. You cannot eat it, or dig with it, or live in it, or wear it...well you can wear it but it will not keep you warm or dry. A good investment for a recession or depression but not Teotwawki because when you are hungry, truly hungry, you will trade me that gold coin for a loaf of bread. And tomorrow when you are hungry again, well that is where the shovel comes in. Most preppers are unrealistic, in my opinion, in that they focus on the gangs of zombies that will come and try to grab all their stuff. But if it gets so bad that hordes from the city are rampaging through the country side looking for food, there are first going to be those who fled the city because they were not mean enough to fight for the limited supplies that where left. That is, 'the civilized' are the first to flee, or at least attempt to flee, any collapse into anarchy. So, the first people to reach your country estate will not be the barbarians bent of rape and pillage, but the huddled masses looking for a place to settle, to live in safety.

A year's worth of food for 4 becomes 6 months for 8, three months for 16, and 45 days for 32 and and 22 days for 64 people, the same number of days that it takes some radishes to grow. Which is why is say that community is actually the number one Teotwawki investment. A year's worth of food for 64 people, becomes six months at 128 people, and three months at 256, which is a frak'en city in a Teotwawki scenario. But that food will run out, so...crops have to be planted.

As most of you know I have an experiment garden. While most gardeners focus on better quality and quantity, my focus is on all natural. I do not mean organic, but getting the garden producing without any outside input, and in this latest round no machines either. That is, just digging the soil under with a pick and shovel. Without adding fertilizer or top soil I produced barely enough for the next years seeds. The second year, was better, and the third (this year) I expect to be actually 'worth' it. That is, both times here in the South, it has taken me three years to go from barely getting seeds for next year to the expectation that I could live on it. More to the point, it takes a lot of work to dig it all up by hand. Ideally there would be a horse and plow. But negotiations are based on two things, your ability to prevent the other side from taking what you have, and your ability to have something the other side wants.

As the first, got to have a hoard of guns to keep those zombies from taking all your stuff, right? No, what you need is a stinger, the ability to give the impression that if they try to take what you have, they will be hurt. Why are we afraid of wasps even though they cannot kill most of us? Because we know if we grab it, they will sting us. So, we negotiate with them, try to wave them away rather than trying to grab them. In truth, most people even with a gun could not force me to negotiate, beyond the fact that I am more than a bit suicidal, believe that the power is found in the gun and not the hand that holds it. That is, a threat of violence is pointless if one is not willing to do violence, a gun may be used to intimidate, but eventually you run across those whom it only matters whether or not you can pull the trigger. And those who are willing to pull the trigger, do not use guns to intimidate, or rather for them when the gun comes out it is time to pull the trigger. But anyway, the ethical question is a stockpile of guns for fighting of the barbarians which come to raid, or as a means of intimidating that hungry family coming for aid.

People who do not think they are a sinner have obviously never been hungry. When you are starving, moral questions go out the window. So obviously the presence of fire arms will prevent them from acting like barbarians...until they are hungry enough. The problem is that you have something they want (food) and the means in which to prevent them from simply taking it (gun), but they do not have anything you want. They need food, but have nothing to trade so, at some point their fear of the gun will be overridden by their hunger. So, they sneak back at night, or their own guns come out, and there is fighting, pain, maybe even death, all because you did not have a shovel. That is, the shovel, the axe, extra tools have incredible value in a Teotwawki scenario because they give the other person a value to you. Suddenly they have something to trade, their labor. Labor is just about worthless today because we have machines. A farmer with one of those multi-million dolor tractors can plant and harvest thousands of acres, a farmer with horse and plows a hundred (this is a guess), and a person with a shovel maybe five.

That is, the obsession on Teotwawki is generally a selfish impulse. A fear of the unknown and how am I to survive in the 'what if.' This is why few people are actual preppers, as they are more concerned with getting the latest gadget then they are about Teotwawki. I do not mean selfish as in greedy, but selfish as in viewing it only in terms of the self. Viewing their preparations in terms of protecting what they have instead of investing in the future. Just because society collapses, does not mean there is no society. I am a free-market anarchist, so it is all about spontaneous order for me. We build communities, societies naturally, without it having to be forced from the top. Which is why any attempt at government is eventually prone to tyranny. As it will eventually try to force an order opposed that we are forming together. Communisms fail because most people want a free market, they are going to trade with one another no matter what you do. They banned cigarettes in federal prisons because they were being used as money, so the inmates started using sardines instead. In a Teotwawki scenario, the cultures that form are going to be the ones decided by the preppers. Simply chasing off anyone in need will create a society in which one has to grab and protect.

When I talk with John with that, I make it clear, and he reluctantly agrees, that I would be in charge. Not because I am smarter, or wiser than him, it is because he will be the one focused on keeping the barbarians away. Most preppers I know do not agree with me, but I find not use for guns because I have people who can pull the trigger. They point out that John could take over because he had the guns. That would be true except for two reasons. It would be true if by being in charge meant being a tyrant, a cult leader that everyone has to do everything I say. But if that is the case then on his Honor, John has to take over, or at least depose me from being in charge. That is, John is not a bully but a warrior, a military man. And the purpose of a society's military is not to be a stinger to the masses, but to be a threat to those who would sting the society...all enemies both foreign and domestic...secondly, and more importantly, then he would have to start worrying about crop rotations, and resource allocation, housing, and all those other things that goes into a Teotwawki community. That is, I would trust John with being the stinger of the community because he understands that there are threats to a community that cannot be shot.

There is a paranoia, a lack of trust, among Teotwawki preppers which I cannot share. Yes, there are evil people who would grab everything you have and leave you to starve. So should we, in our preparation be evil ourselves. Let the grasshoppers starve is what I hear. To be sure, there would be too many grasshoppers to feed, but how many potential ants will die from that attitude. That is many of our preparations, our investments are focused on what others might do. Trying to prepare for all the evil which may come to us, rather than preparing for the good we might do. Thoughts on how we can protect our food, instead of means in which we can share it. That is, can we call it good to prepare with the notion that we are Noah building an ark and everyone else deserves to die? But as Christian should not our focus of preparing for a collapse of society be on charity rather than our own survival. To die is gain, to live is Christ, yes?

More to the point, as it seems my ramblings do have points after all, does living in a world in which material welfare comes cheap mean that spiritual welfare is also cheap. We have, as the old guards pointed out, have already experienced spiritual Teotwawki. Those happy and innocent days of the 50s were long gone before I was born, even if they existed at all outside the islands of suburbia. They had their culture wars to try to bring back the world that existed just as with our economics collapsing there are those who are trying to keep it alive. It might not be too late in economics, though I doubt it, but it is too late culturally. That is, our culture is in chaos and everyone is fighting over who is going to be the tyrant. Being a philosopher, I have a tendency to look at root causes rather than manifestations. In this case, we live in a dark, cold and cruel world. It was no different then, the only difference is our attitude about pain has changed. I do not believe that there is more pain now, it is simply we are allowed to talk about it, and use it as an excuse.

See now the mixed blessing of Teotwawki. Using our pain

as an excuse for our behavior is bad, but the fact that we talk about it now is good. That is, back then only an artist or looser would talk about how hard they find life. Arguably because we artist do find life really hard, at least conforming to social life, but I do not believe it is more painful. Anyway, this was a bad thing to the old-old-guard, I think, because they viewed Faith through the lens of belief and law. You are a Christian, you behave like a Christian, there is nothing else to worry about. Even better, I think it was a philosophical misunderstanding that only sinners, only really-really bad sinners have spiritual pain. Surely no Christian would, no real Christians anyway. Even better than that, it was an indication that there is something missing from the Church if so many people are still in pain. While the culture war is out outside of the Church, in the world of politics, I care little for that, because the war within the Church centers on how we find comfort in this life.

And this is who all this applies to us. Should we be selfish in preparing spiritually? I have my food, go get your own kind of thing. Or, try to stockpile enough food so that we can dispense it to everyone who comes along? Feed a man a fish kind of thing. Indeed, you will be popular indeed handing out bread, but they will get hungry again and eventually you will have no more bread to give. That is, when we are young in the Faith our focus is on our own pain, overcoming our own sin. As a minister it is geared towards eventually helping people in that struggle. Maturity before ministry as I oft say, for too often ministers use ministry as a means of ignoring their pain.

So, I can cut this off, and get back to work. In preparing, our focus should not only be on making sure that we have enough, but also on how to have extra for others. Can one truly say that they have matured in Faith if all they have done is fed themselves, have an easier time avoiding sin? For that matter, if they are motivated only for their own 'righteousness', opposed to one, say, that seeks righteousness, does what God commands for the sake of others. I have observed that Charity, if we truly love, we are motivated to righteousness so that we may better serve the ones we love. As a spouse, a parent, a minister, a teacher, a whatever, we strive for perfection because our love desires to give more than we have right now, more than we are right now.

Age of Accountability

The doctrine of the Age of accountability would be an easy topic if it was not such a touchy subject. It is one of those areas that I have sympathy for these who ministries require them to be pastors. That, it is one of those topics we only discuss seriously when a child dies, and so there are obviously the need to give comfort. In such times it is difficult to tell people that we do not really know and thus have to trust in the Will of God. Or, it is one of those areas in which the Bible does not teach or imply directly and so we have to simply put our trust in God, and His will. The question for the free-will sects is: what happens to those who are unable to make that choice, either through the lack of knowledge or ability. The doctrine age of accountability makes sense and is necessary, if our justification depends on making that choice. The age of accountability does not make since from the view of the predestination doctrine because we do not hold that our salvation depends on our ability to choose Christ, but rather we choose Christ because God has shown mercy on us. So, for us the question is: does God give that grace, show that mercy to children who die.

The age of accountability is a strong doctrine (logically required) within the free-will doctrine, as they teach one must choose to be saved and so must answer for those who are unable to make that choice. And there is no 'original sin' doctrine within the free-will doctrine. In so much as it teaches that we are not born condemned but rather choose to be condemned by rejecting the offer of salvation found in Christ. And as the majority of the Church hold that our will if free to choose God (in practice if not in doctrine) without first being saved, and as such the doctrine of age of accountability is used as a loophole for those who have yet to develop the intellect to make a rational choice. This of course gets expanded to those who have not heard the Gospel, and then to those with compulsions (such as an addict or homosexual), and then generally everyone depending on how liberal they are with their theology. I bring this up, because the majority of defense of the age of accountability doctrine is in line with the free-will doctrine. And as it is commonly understood is false. In so much as it teaches that everyone is born saved, and at some point, we decide to give up this salvation.

The Scriptures used to support the doctrine (the ones that are not taken out of context) refer to children being innocent. Such as Christ saying we must become like those children if we are to enter the Kingdom, or the numerous references of the innocent children in the Old Testament. Basically, the logic is that children are innocent, already holy and therefore already saved. This understanding of the doctrine is false as it makes the case that children are not in need of God for their salvation. That is, it makes salvation dependent on who we are, instead of who Christ is. Which, not to be preachy, is a popular error in church as a whole anyway. The age of accountability is a protestant doctrine, precisely because we believe that salvation is given according to God's will, He shows mercy on who He chooses to show mercy on. Saved by Grace through Faith, and though the modern church has forgotten, Faith is a gift given by God and has nothing to do with our own ability to reason or understand.

Me being a genius is helpful in explaining matters of Faith, but is irrelevant to my having or maturing in Faith. I would have reached the age of accountability at six or so because that was when my reasoning ability reached an adult level. But if we are not condemned until we are able to reason, make a knowledgeable choice, then no one is condemned. Because human reasoning cannot take into account God. The Gospel is foolishness, unreasonable to those who are perishing, because they lack Godly reasoning. Human reasoning cannot accept that our salvation or condemnation has nothing to do with our own guilt or innocence, but rather completely on Christ and His innocence. (ok, preaching over…I think)

Reform theology has a hard-doctrine of the age of accountability as well, as a primary argument against infant baptism. That is, against the teaching of original sin as us being guilty of Adam's sin, rather than inheriting the sinful nature. It is not a declaration that children are already saved but that they cannot truly consent to being part of the Church, truly make a declaration of their Faith, until they have the ability to give reasonable consent. As the child is not guilty of the sins of their parents, they cannot be saved by the faith of their parents. But as our position we are not able to choose God until we are born of the Spirit, we do not hold that children are not automatically saved. As the human reason, regardless of age, cannot choose Christ until He is revealed to them by the Spirit, we do not reach that age of accountability until we are saved. As I noted at the start of this, the Bible does not give an answer to the question directly. Much of the doctrine of the age of accountability is based on wishful thinking, and the same kind of logic that has God saving everyone except the very-very bad. After all, if God will save children by virtue of them being innocent then why will He not save that simple person who spends their lives doing good work unless they have Faith? That is, I personally reject teachings that are based on us judging God on the basis of our sense of fairness.

However, unlike the salvation of the 'good person' there are hints in Scripture that God shows favor to children. Hints that God will show mercy on children who die. That is, while the Scriptures people present in favor of the doctrine does not prove it enough that we can consider it a doctrine, the Scripture does give us enough evidence that we can place our Hope and place our trust in God that He will show mercy on the children who die.

I am stressing here is that there is ample reason that Christ will justify children, who die, there is not enough to make it a doctrine, or more aptly dogma because of the implications. We can have hope because of our own Faith, our own knowledge of God allows us to be able to place our trust in Him. But also, I have heard the age of accountability to justify abortion, and is the reason I did a study on this some years ago. That, as the argument goes, if all children are atomically saved, then abortion is the greatest evangelizing tool. After all, how many of those children would grow up and not be saved? The age of accountability makes sense according to our reasoning, but our reasoning is not always Godly. Or, as we do not know for sure, as the Bible does not clearly state that God will justify all children who die, abortion and any child's death remains a tragedy for us.

Also, much of youth ministry philosophy is based on the idea that we are 'born saved' and so is focused on keeping the youth from losing that salvation. A glorified babysitting services, focused more on giving them a temptation-free zone then being a ministry. Or if you would, focused on them keeping the youths like children than nurturing the inner-life we have in Christ, if they are in Christ. That is, in a real way the age of accountability, or the application of it to all children and not just those who die as children, is one of the main reasons that the Church is in the dire straits that it is in. That, if all children are saved, then all children are in Christ, and so anyone who is not a Christian as an adult is simply fallen away from the Faith. We see this attitude in apologetics, in where it is assumed that all atheists know God and are simply in rebellion from the knowledge. But as any convert can tell you, that is not true. In spite of growing up in church, before my conversion I knew of God, but did not know God.

More important to me, are those who are in the visible church, but are not in Christ. And in my view, this is the continuation of the doctrine of the age of accountability being applied to all children, or how the transition is handled in youth ministries. They made that declaration and was baptized when they were young, as I did and was, and so their view of being a Christian is keeping their nose clean. Of being a good person like children are. Basing their view on who they are instead of who Christ is. And this circles back, for we do base our own salvation on the power and mercy of God. He saved us even though we were most unworthy, according to His will and not according to ours. That there remains that slight doubt of the salvation of children, because we have to trust in God's will, as well as His mercy. That we know firsthand that God shows mercy on some, and not on others. We know that He has a reason, a plan that is beyond us. Beyond us to understand, or to judge. That even though there is ample evidence for the Hope of God's mercy, we also have to trust God's will is for the best, whatever that turns out to be.

The Object of Faith

One does not have to debate much before they hear the charge that Christians are trying to make a theocracy out of America. Before you dismiss those charges as paranoia, look around a bit more and see it for yourself. From those with the Kingdom Theology to those trying to redeem culture there are many who confuse the duties they have as a Christian with those they have as a citizen. While the former is clearly heretical the fight for a Christian culture is at best a distraction. As your study of history leading up to the Reformation should have showed you, when you make a Christian culture, you end up with a lot of cultural Christians, a lot of people who do not know that it is Faith into Christ which saves (1 Corinthians 15).

You do not even have to be well traveled for I am sure you have heard that we are, or at least were a Christian nation. I can agree with that if by it one means that the civil religion of the nation has shared the same name as our own. But none-the-less it has been a civil religion in which our nation has held, or do you really believe that our nation has been His Body. A cultural Christian believes what they do because they have to in order to belong to that culture, we believe because we have Faith. The clergy of a civil religion preaches the truths, mores and norms of their culture, we preach the Gospel.

That contrast between the Christianity of Faith, and civil religion of Christianity is one I always keep in mind proceeding into the future. We cannot speak ill of those of the old guard for their focus on the culture war. After all, 'evil company corrupts good habits', and Christian morality is good for a person even if it will not save if they have not Faith. However, we must keep in mind that preaching the Gospel is not simply trying to change a person's mind as if marketing a new kind of deodorant. We are sharing a revelation, a Grace no human hand can give, one which no work of our flesh or mind can produce.

In this context you will find that most of the heresies and the other problems facing the Church really belongs not to us but to the civil religion. Our obsessive drive to try to prove the Gospel is completely unnecessary for us. Indeed, the Cross is foolishness to the atheist. The Gospel is most illogical and unreasonable unless one has Faith. Even more is it offensive to the those who are pious and honest in their civil religion. While you and I may argue whether hell is eternal destruction or eternal torture the civil religion must put out its fires. While you and I by Grace through Faith in Christ is transformed into a new creation, the civil religion must teach there is nothing needed beyond simply being good. While you and I struggle against our sinful nature, the civil religion must teach there is no need to repent, you are holy, godlike as long as you believe the right things, vote for the right candidate.

It is not that I do not long for the whole world to know the Truth, it is just that I have to wonder if we not asking too much when we expect an atheist or pagan to believe when they do not have Faith. That can it not, in fact, be considered that we are asking them to be dishonest to believe something they for which they have no proof? Maybe it is because we forget that Faith is our evidence of things we have not seen, and without Faith it is impossible to live a life pleasing to God (Hebrew 11). In our vain and often arrogant attempts to prove that we are right we often fail to preach our Faith, as if we are ashamed that the only reason we believe is because God reveled Himself to us in the person of Jesus the Christ.

We should never forget that Faith is not simply giving an intellectual consent to the Gospel but also the surrendering of our will. Our intellect, as it guides our will, has its place within our Life, but it cannot produce the kind of belief required to save. While Faith will certainly produce belief in the Gospel, belief itself is not enough for salvation (James 2). Regardless of what you call it, or how you experienced it, whether it was a boom-bang or a gradual awakening, Faith is a revelation. At some point we were given the revelation that the Gospel is true. It is that Faith which produces in us works which pleases God (Galatians 5) and fuels our prayers (1 John 5). Faith is the knowledge which gives us certainty in our beliefs. It is Faith which allows us to know that Scripture is not simply a philosophical work in which we can create an ideological framework but the very words of God (2 timothy 3). It is Faith which is the dividing line between saved and unsaved, between the Church and the civil religion.

It is dangerous, however, to think of Faith in terms of the Gnostic's revealed knowledge. To think that we gain salvation because of the belief instead of it coming from God. We are in Christ because of our Faith, and it is in Christ we have Life, salvation. The Gospel is the Faith by which we are saved, without it we believe in vain. Otherwise, we turn our belief into a work, an attitude in which we can create and earn ourselves forgiveness. Above all, Faith is not just the knowledge of God but a love for Him as well. No one can diligently seek Him without loving Him.

Because of this we should we make the mistake the fundamentalists did in the nineteen twenties and go on a crusade to rid the Church of all those with a 'false' Faith. Indeed, Faith produces so many outwards affects with the desire for God and His ways to various degrees through one's Life that rightly God reserves such judgments for Himself (Mathew 13). One can even say that what is unfolding with the Church, now and into the future is God doing just that. While we should, and have a duty to correct poor theology or moral misconduct, including expelling from our fellowship those who lead others into such things, any attempt to separate those who have Faith from those who 'only believe' is to invite injustice. Our responsibility is not to punish the wicked, or the lukewarm but to present them with the Gospel of Jesus the Christ (Ezekiel 33).

Indeed, one in Faith may be satisfied and forever trust and believe that God is faithful, another in Faith is inspired with many questions and seeks to learn how God answers them. In Faith one may care little for the prophecies found in Scriptures, while another in Faith finds edification with their fulfillment in Christ. In Faith one may be inspired to preach, another in Faith inspired to sweep up after the service. We each experience Faith according to their purpose, and so too is the weaknesses and strengths of our Faith according to that purpose. We differ outwardly, but these differences are for our edification as there is only one Gospel, only one Faith, Faith in Christ (1 Corinthians 12)

Faith as a Mystery

If you have not figured it out by what I have written so far, I am one of those who define the mystical tradition not as the means of gaining extraordinary experiences but diving directly into the mysteries of our Faith. The mysteries, such as Charity, which cannot be understood unless we live them. Embracing whole heartily the paradoxes created in part by theology but mostly from simply having our Life in Christ. This obviously puts me at odds with the neo-mystics which make it about how to gain those experiences. I can only wonder about the reasons they never bring up the difference between a mystical experience in which we generate ourselves and those which come from God, but regardless, the desire for such experiences come from a lack of Faith, not from it.

I have generally kept my mystical experiences to myself, or within a small group of people. It was hardly those who doubt my sanity with such talk who bother me. I, in fact, usually prefer such people. It was that I became tired of those who think that because of my extraordinary experiences my Faith was somehow special, somehow better than others. My irritation was from my pride, or I should say that it was that they were offering temptation to my pride. I was used to being superior to others before my conversion. It was easy to see those things which makes me better than others, and easy to overlook those things in which I am, for a lack of better word, incompetent. Indeed, even I saw my lack of empathy not as a weakness but a strength.

While people admired me for my experiences, I came to admire them for how they could hold onto the Faith without them. In truth, I had to ask what did it say about my own Faith that I needed reminders to place my trust in God. Was it only because of my pride in which God had to use extraordinary experiences to teach me that trust instead of just the ordinary means which are common to all with Faith. I am not saying that I did not benefit greatly from them, or they were without purpose, only that to seek them is very much akin to an atheist asking for proof of God. Saying that we will not have Faith until God reveals Himself to us in some extraordinary way. (Philippians 1)

Faith being not simply intellectual agreement that there is a God, or even belief in the Gospel. It is the placing of our trust in God, and that we saved in Christ. Not just that God exists, but He is worthy of our trust. A part of that is to trust God that the Spirit will guide us into understanding and He has and will give us what we need to grow in that trust. That it produces Hope, a limitless trust that we have mercy from the Father through the mediation of the Son. And also, Charity as we come to rely not on the works of our hands or minds but the Cross for our sanctification we come to understand mercy. (Ephesians 1)

Though the neo-mystics have a Gnostic view of mysticism, Christian mysticism has been defined as seeking to perfect our union with God in Christ so we are separated from our carnal desires and worldly concerns. Basically, we want to be holy as God is holy, perfect as God is perfect. In short, we work for that impossible goal of being perfectly sanctified. That is, we see the Poor Knight paradox, that we are both saint and sinner, and only want to be saints. We seek to do God's will perfectly and know that is impossible while we are still in this flesh. So, we seek to unite with Christ on the Cross, to die to self, to kill and beat down our flesh which prevents us from loving Him, prevents us from doing what He would have us do. We seek to live a Life which flows from our Faith. (1 John 3)

Obviously, such a definition is not popular because it takes the elitism out of Christian mysticism. It makes mysticism nothing more than different words, a different language, a different viewpoint of seeing the sanctification process which is common for all those with Faith. Indeed, that is precisely how I see it in myself, simply different experiences or awareness of the process which all who have Faith goes through, or should go through anyway. But pride aside, the differences we see in Christian mystics is for the same reason we see differences between all Christians. That is, how we experience and define Faith in Christ. Indeed, by what how we experience and define being a Christian.

Undoubtedly there are many times many today who call themselves Christians who do not believe, just as sure as there are those who are very devote and pious individuals who believe but do not have Faith. Indeed, it is a question of justification, for to say that we are saved only by belief is to have Faith in our belief and not in

God. Am I saved by my belief? No, I am justified and sanctified by Christ. It is Faith which allows me to believe, to know, to trust. (James 2)

Faith is more than belief, and it is more than trust. We are in Christ, are saved by Grace through Faith. Being in Christ we are a new creature, one who wants to be obedient. Faith is also that desire to be perfect as God is perfect, to do His will perfectly. A longing for that perfect union, to know God in that we will in the next age in when there will be no sin, no rebellion on our part. A desire to carry a cross of our works, and to cast aside those things which burden us in those works. Indeed, it is understanding that though there is a struggle, it is far more burdensome to sin then to keep God's commandments (1 John 5)

And we should not forget that Faith is a Grace, a working of the Spirit of God. To have Faith is not simply to have a new life, but Life in the Spirit. While there are too many who focus on the Gifts as if they were superpowers, our Faith focuses us on Christ as Life. We are justified and sanctified, but we are still in this flesh. Faith, along with belief is also trusting the Spirit to work on in our sanctification. As Faith is a longing for that perfect union with God we will have in the next age, so too is it having the Spirit to guide us in this age. (2 Corinthians 3)

I Like to Sin

I like to Sin! Oh, I know I am supposed to write about how I am all holy and righteous. I am so holy that I fast every week and so righteous that I no longer sin. Yet I fast because to remind me that it is not I but Christ in me who is Holy and, well, the truth is I like to sin. I hate sin, which is true, but the fact is I still like to sin. If I did not like to sin, if there was not some satisfaction derived from the sin would there even be a struggle to overcome, any temptation to sin? If we were not barbarians at heart, if we did not like our sins, there would be no need for the Cross. Well…even then we would still need salvation but there would be no need to preach the Gospel for all would have come to Christ long ago. Indeed, if there was no love of sin, I could be sitting in a cave right now spending all my time praising God.

But alas there is. This fact, the reality of sin, and our love for it needs to be brought out in the open more. When we actually hate a sin, we would not do that sin. This is true, even of those without Faith, for none has a behavior in which they truly hate. One never acts in a way which does not, in some way, fulfill their desires. The difference is that with the Grace of Life, by our Faith in Christ we love God more than we love our sin (Romans 6). We love God and become a slave to His righteousness, and thus hate that about ourselves which desires to serve another master. We hate the sin which dwells in us, the flesh which desires to sin, the Self-will which is opposed to God's will. (Romans 7)

I struggle with my weight because I like to eat, a lot. I struggle with lust because I like the sensations lust produces, a lot. I struggle with pride because I like the satisfaction of thinking that what I have done has been from my own greatness rather than the Grace of God. We fight and struggle against the flesh, against the darkness within because we are a new creation, a new person in who the old person must be put to death by conforming to the will of God. (Romans 12).   The death-to-Self, emptying ourselves, becoming nothing are only the hyperboles we use in perceiving that struggle in sanctification which comes from having both Christ's Righteousness and sin dwelling within us. From clearly seeing that war in us between what we would desire to do, and pressing on towards perfection (Philippians 3).

I am a slave to tobacco as I smoke a pipe. Smoking is such a natural part of my life I simply do not notice it except during those times in which I do without. As with other addictions it is smoking that seems right to me and the times in which I cannot afford the luxury which seem unnatural. Likewise, the natural state of humanity is to be in sin. While it is true that an individual is born with a conscience to one degree or another, morality is based on the culture in which they are socialized to. Their guilt based on how they perceived living up to the expectations, norms and mores of their society. Such a person can only judge sin in terms what it is natural them to do, only according to what they could do naturally. Such a person sees sin only as feeling bad about themselves. (Mathew 15)

You know of your sinful nature because this is the first knowledge of Faith. For me it came in a flash, but for some it is a slow angst as the knowledge builds. The knowledge of our sin is necessary for without it one simply cannot see the need for the Cross. Faith, the Gospel, the entirety of the Christian Faith is insanity without sin. So, what are we to make of these preachers who say there is no sin beyond the most horrid, the ones which any reasonable mind would? Nothing good to be sure, but they do not concern us for we are mystics of the Cross, knowing that since the beginning of time whenever God is present we are always called to struggle against our sinful nature (Genesis 4).

One may fight against an addiction, they must first see it as an addiction. This why those without Faith do not struggle against a sin unless it is in some way causing them pain. An adulterer may honestly fight against adultery, but only in terms of not losing what they have in life. While we struggle with sin because we are no longer its slave, and would not be in its chains again. We are freed from that slavery because we have Faith, been renewed in the Spirit. We do not fight against our sinful nature in order to save us but because we are saved (Romans 6, Romans 8). We grow in sanctification because that is what happens when one lives a life of Faith (Galatians 5)

We must be on guard for the pride which can grow in this. Without a doubt there is a pride in which we think that we are better, more pure or faithful in our Faith. That is easy to say it is pride. The pride which is more subtle is the one in which you say to yourself that you should do better. It is subtle because it is true but it might also may be in the eagerness for perfection you have grown impatient and want it now. I must remind you that we cannot become perfect in this present world, and we need Christ in our sanctification as much as in our justification. As in Christ we are saved, we seek to have hearts and minds purified from of all things not pleasing to God…and by the Grace of God through Faith into Christ is the only means in which we can do it. While other mystics must surely disagree, there really is no other view for a Christian, for repentance without the Cross is meaningless in our sanctification.

While one may have great desire to please God, without Faith one can only use their own standard of righteousness rather than the Righteousness of Christ (Romans 2, Romans 10). Indeed, without Faith our desire to please God comes from a vain attempt to appease God, rather than an obedience born from love. This is why we must guard against any attitude in which removes the Cross and Christ's work upon it from our sanctification. As we were made holy by His sacrifice, so too are we refined by that Grace (Hebrew 10, Jude).   Forsaking this, one comes to lament over those imperfections that our Lord has not removed from us. Displeased with the struggle in being renewed in this age, we want to be resurrected. In our desire for perfection and our impatience of the pace in which God is working on us, we stray from Him into practices which are of no avail. This may happen many times until we learn that it is not by our works but by His Grace in which we are sanctified. (2 Corinthians 12).

Moral Sanctification

A person can only die once. Justification is something which occurs when we are saved. Birth can only happen once. Sanctification is something which occurs only when we are saved. The struggles and hardships of Faith do not make us more holy, more sanctified. One is either saved or they are not. One is either part of the Church, His Body or they are not. Justification and sanctification are acts which God performs by Grace through Faith into Christ.

If the death and rebirth happen only once, when we are saved, why is so many of the pages of my writing, and those of the mystics of old, filled with death to Self-will? Of becoming nothing to the existent that all that is left of our inner-self is what God has put there? Why are there so many books written in the past about self-discipline. What is the purpose of this work? (For that matter, what then is the purpose of a church, or any religious activity?) Why all this talk of sanctification, of growth, of purification and work to mature in the Faith if it does not justify or sanctify us?

It is one of those fine hairs, between the sanctification of the rebirth and the sanctification we improve over the years of our Faith. Between sanctification of being set aside to do God's purpose, and the sanctification of growth and purification that happens to us when we are doing His Will. From a mystic's view, or at least from the view of this mystic of the Cross, the sanctification or growth which happens after conversion is not about making us holier. Most of what we call sanctification is not really that but simply trying to live up to the holiness we have been given. That the work we do to purify ourselves is not to become sanctified, but to better live that sanctified life. Not to perfect our union with God through Christ, but so that we may better live according to that union. We just lack a separate word in our common language for all the work, all the hardship and struggle of Faith for that sanctification which is simply trying to live a life which is sanctified.

It should be remembered that even though we are saved from God's wrath, we will still be judged. We remain justified, and the nature of the judgment is of reward instead of punishment (1 Cor. 3) we will still have to face Christ for what we have done, or have not done with the Life we were given (Rom. 14, 2 Cor. 5). But it is not in regard to those rewards in which we work on our moral or virtue sanctification. Though we may speculate, those rewards are unknown to us and are not given in this lifetime. The rewards of this life time are to know love, joy and peace, the fruits of the crucifixion of our carnal desires the Spirit works in us (gal 5, 1 John 4).

I will start with moral sanctification, for it seems to be where the Spirit works in us first. I write 'seems' because when we are young in the Faith we first come to see sanctification related to our behavior. We see how we have violated the law as sinners, and so do not always notice that our heart is the cause. That is not to say that God does not start preparing our hearts, our character from the very beginning for the work He has us to do. It is not enough that we simply do the work for which we were called, we must also do it in a way which is according to God's moral will.

As a reminder, we do not have a Life, we have Life. To say that we have a Life is the same as saying we have a Christ for He is Life, our Life. The Life I have is the same Life as you have, just as we have the same righteousness, the same justification and sanctification, for we have the same Christ. For we are saved not only by Christ but in Christ, and our Life is in Christ and not in ourselves (Romans 8, Ephesians 2). Moral sanctification follows salvation, for sin while no longer deadly is an affront to our Honor in that Life. That being in Christ, and Christ in us through the workings of His Spirit, we cannot find peace unless we are living according to Life.

There are countless examples of those who abandon moral sanctification, and even the pretense of such. They find themselves floating into and out of church. At one time living according to Life, the next living for the pursuit of worldly pleasures. It is obvious that such people have no peace. But there is another which can find no peace because they avoid moral sanctification. These I know, having been one myself. By all outward appearances we are the most righteous, and are often driven to rid even the smallest sin from our lives. But not because we desire to live the Honor of Life, or not only because of that. There is also the motivation to be righteous so that we do not have to repent. Both these types do not truly live moral sanctification, even when overcoming sins, because they want their salvation, but they do not want Christ as their savior. We want Life, we want to be saved when we are in the fire, but we do not want to admit that our very Life, our very salvation has nothing to do with our own nature.

We all struggle with sin. Completed purification, perfect moral and virtue sanctification is simply not attainable in this life. Anyone who thinks that they have reached a point in which they are not sinning is simply fooling themselves (1 John 1). I may be sinless compared to the mediocre concept of modern morality, but compared to God? Compared to the ideal of perfection found in Christ? As time goes on, sins shift from what we do, to what we are not doing, and thus until we are resurrected, we see perfection as through a stained glass window. In fact, and the reason I link moral sanctification with the accepting not only salvation from Christ but accepting Christ as our savior, is because as we become more sanctified in that maturing kind of way, the more we are going to realize that we need Christ. At conversion we are saved from God's wraith once and for all, but we need God ever day to save us from ourselves. We need Him as savior, to be saved every single moment of every single day.

Moral sanctification in the early years is a time marked with avoiding God. We avoid God during that time because we are acutely aware that we, even the strongest among us, are weak. The knowledge bears down on us that we, even the best among us, are horrid sinners worthy of death. It is a time when we are ashamed of our weakness. We are embarrassed that we struggle. We are not yet comfortable going to God beating our chest with those famous words; "have mercy on me". There are a hundred different ways this manifests, and a thousand different excuses for it. Some will hide in their caves, or churches, so as not to face those dire temptations. Some go to such lengths to live an outward righteousness so they do not feel like a sinner. One might obsess on some small aspect of the Faith, or seek after only those mystical experiences. Others will avoid fellowship, and anything which reminds them of God. Still others will go further and join the ranks of the antichrists and mock the Faith. And the list goes on and on, the ways we attempt to avoid God is endless, but all in this regard comes from wanting to avoid that acute awareness of our sin in which God's presence provokes.

For the knights, such is the meaning and condition of sanctification. It is the awareness that we are sinner, awareness of the sin in our life. We struggle with sin in a way in which those without Faith cannot understand not simply because it is the Law, but because the Law is now written on our hearts. That from the mystical view, with saving Faith we are giving the righteousness and holiness of Christ. Our hearts have been replaced with the Heart of Christ, with His Honor. That Honor resides in us, creating our image of perfection.

The dream and drive to perfect ourselves is not, should not be about revelations and experiences. The dream of keeping the law, to keep it perfectly is born not from legalism, or from an emotional sense of gratitude, but because we share in Christ nature of righteousness and holiness. With Faith it has become our nature to live without sin. Of course, not sharing in the Godhood, being only His Body and not Him, we lack the ability to live up to our new nature without Him. The only thing which separates us from those without Faith is the Grace of God. It is God's Nature that saved us, and not our own.

The Ruby in The Dark

Like a ruby in the dark
I'm the friend you'll never meet
Loneliness is my trademark
Leaving gifts of pain at your feet

Like a lover in deceit
I'll never be truly yours
Like a roman solder in defeat
Out of those beautiful eyes of yours, the tears will pour

You came with the hope for peace and love
But you're a fool with a heart I'll break
For I never listen to the wings of the dove
So you see, you should, you must, me, forsake.

Hold onto Faith

I have always been both light and soft on my pre-conversion theology. I am soft, not willing to argue on it beyond that we cannot force God to give us Grace, because I am light on its study. I always take a soft position, and sometimes agnostic view on subjects in which I lack enough personal studies to be satisfied with my own advice. As my studies have followed the questions of my life and ministry, I have focused on our Life, our becoming saved instead of our being saved, our continued sanctification. It was not until I noticed how our view of justification affects our view of sanctification, did I gather my notes to look at the details of how we are saved and compared them to what others were saying.

Though I have the scholar's tendency to study I do not have a head for all the small distinctions theologians make. I have not found Scripture all that clear on the subject. We have created complex views by reading them by our own biases. Those whose gifting is in evangelizing are obviously biased by their desire to see everyone saved. From that desire they more likely to see Grace of salvation as a fruit hanging on a tree which we only have to decide to take hold of it. My experience and focus on what to do with that fruit inclines me to view it as something which God gives to us as individuals, according to His will, and we must choose whether or not to cooperate with the Grace. As it is not possible to see sin truly as sin unless God first gives us the Grace to see that our light is darkness compared to Him, our only option or choice in what to do with that Grace once we have it. This applies to our sanctification after conversion, but does that apply to the conversion itself?

That is the reason, the unanswered questions which prevents me from taking a hard position of the question of predestination verse free will. As Grace is something which God gives according to His will, rather than us first having to do something for it, are we then capable to reject that Grace? Could I have refused to submit to God when He asked? Though I believe that when we come into Christ, we have no choice but to repent, to have Faith and the like, I cannot say I know whether or not we can refuse to come to Christ when God is calling.

I am biased not by my own conversion but because sanctification in this life is very much a cooperation with the Spirit of Christ. Without a doubt after the Grace of salvation is planted in us, we can very much resist our sanctification, put up walls with our religious practices or even dive into decadence in order to the ignore the work the Spirit is doing with and to use. With lust, an unlawful desire for pleasure, some will go to great lengths in resisting the Spirit in an attempt to try to keep both their sin and their Faith. In my pride, making myself an idol, I have resisted God many times because He wanted me to rest and know that only my works which were dependent on Him bore proper fruit. But does this apply to justification, or just sanctification? Are there those who are unsaved but also haunted by God, or is it only for those with Faith who cannot escape conviction? Is it simply that for the unsaved the call to repentance comes from without while for those with Faith it comes from the Spirit dwelling within? (1 Corinthians 1)

It is undoubtedly that time which we come face to face with the poor knight paradox. That we are saints, separated and holy, but at the same time sinners, still in a flesh which is tempted. For me it came when I adjusted to the Light of conversion. The person I became was so radically different then who I was just days before was very much night and day. I was justified. I was sanctified. I was holy, and then came the Spirit's conviction of my pride. Then came the awareness that though I am holy I am still a sinner, still in need of the Cross. (1 John 2).

To truly be nothing. To truly be dead to ourselves, to our flesh, to our carnal nature. To be saved as we will be, united with God as we will be so there is nothing left but His will...having gained a taste, a pale-moon shadow view of what it would be like made it hard for me to balance a striving for that sanctification now, and being content with the sanctification I have. The paradox which has defined me more than any other. And one which I think is rather common, become overzealous for sanctification.

Though it manifests differently it is definitively the time when we learn that Christ is not only our Savior but is to be the Lord over all areas of our lives. It is that time in which we learn the importance of obedience. Works, while useless for justification, is a requirement of sanctification. As we are saved through Faith, we are sanctified by our obedience, not by the works themselves but in the process of our works. Just as belief itself does not have the ability to save without Grace, so to it is not our works which sanctify us but through works we live that Grace. Faith is us seeing our relationship with God in its proper context, so works flow from a Faith in which we know Christ as our Lord.

As there are those who believe without the Grace which gives them Faith, so too are there those who work, and do great deeds, without Faith. For them their drive to works is because they think through them they are saved, or are offering proof of their salvation. We do not have to worry about our salvation because we have Faith, we have trust in God, and not ourselves, for our salvation. But we may even experience such times when our love grows cold. When we work and strive just to prove we are not running from God. Those times when were become overzealous not for what the Lord would have of us, but to recapture a feeling we once had. These times, while harsh are not as dangerous for they burn themselves out. One with Faith cannot keep up such duplicity for there will come to a time in which God makes it clear that we are avoiding Him.

We may, for a time, refuse to admit when our love has grown cold but eventually we can no longer bare the lack of warmth. We ask what we did wrong, and sometimes spend some time, too long looking for answers when really all we have to do is repent, return to Him. Eventually learn that our love grows cold because we are not trusting Him for our sanctification, for our continued growth. This is why mystics often talk of pride, for it is our pride which wants to be in control of the process, who wants us to be our own god. It is nothing but pride which thinks that by our fasting, prayers, studies, mediations etc can we force God to work upon us faster than He wills. It is in our pride which we make ourselves slave to rituals, to methods and practices all in a vain attempt not to be a slave of God. (Galatians 5)

In the same way, in our longing and love for God we sometimes seek to strive past where He is taking us. We, in some fit of frustration over our lack of holiness, will do extreme things in a desire to break-free or break-through. Indeed, I have just heard recently (again), of one teaching that it is up to us not to experience a 'dry-season' again. Just another one of those countless teachers who would make us our own gods, and lack any understanding except in the world. It is only those works which are prompted by the Spirit which benefits us.

As I have written our real work is holding on to our Faith, and a large part of that is trusting that God knows what He is doing in our lives. That the Spirit will train us, will sanctify us to live in greater accordance to the Grace we have been given. It is one of those paradoxes that even though we know this, even though we know that it is the Spirit which sanctifies us, matures us in Faith, we have to be sanctified and matured by the Spirit in order to learn how to apply it constantly. It is only when we have gone through many 'dry seasons', only when God has taught us that we can sanctified enough not to have to learn the lesson again. (James 1)

The Now of God's Will

I do not really have a full understanding why the seeking of mystical experiences are so popular today. Or at least I do not fully understand why people with Faith fall into this. I know why I did. My faith started off with a mystical awareness of God, a clear and constant sense that God is with me, with us. So the first time He stripped this from me, where I could not feel His presence I spent some time making the feeling an idol. I did it again with revelations, and again with God's will, or being told His will in a direct way. So I fully understand why one would turn their experiences into an idol, but I was trying to get back something that God was just using in my immaturity. For whatever reason God wanted me and I was simply too arrogant and hard hearted to listen to anyone but Him. Though it runs counter to popular view, the more mature I have become in my Faith the less I have needed visions. And as for mystical experiences, all that remain is Life in Him.

Basically, I understand why I turned them into an idol, I just have a hard time understanding why one who lacks my past would discard Scripture for a promise of some experience. I know it is because they believe the lie that Faith is easier or somehow grander for someone like me, I just do not know why they believe it. Maybe it is a short coming in their education. That they have never been told that the problem is not that they lack a sign but that they lack Faith. Or if they have Faith, they should not be looking for a sign but putting that Faith to work. Or maybe that is what God is trying to teach them.

It is, of course, easy for me not to turn such things into an idol because I have matured enough in the Faith to see them as idols, distractions and temptations. I try to be patient, after all, it is a common misconception that a Life of Faith would be easier if we just had a sign. Is it not a misconception that our Faith, that sanctification should be easy? Or maybe I should say that we do not have to struggle and strive until we realize that it is easy. Maybe my Life has been easier because of my experiences. But then again, I doubt the average person has as much cause to doubt their sanity as often as I have. or had to struggle with the temptation of letting go of the physical world entirely and slipping into a world of the contemplative.

My first novel was a metaphor for my life to that point and the radical changed caused by the reality of God as more then up there, out there. The shadow world, the spirit realm I could accept because it was something I could examine, could analyze. Though it was mystical as some use the word, I could approach it with my analytical mind. It could be manipulated and controlled. The same could not be said of Faith, or of God. Even after all these years, after gaining so much wisdom God is still far beyond my understanding, and He is never controlled or manipulated.

Which is exactly what we are trying to do when we do some work in order to get something from God. When we pray trying to get a mystical experience, a sign or even for God to 'show us His will'. While it is proper to want to know God's will, what we end up doing too often is basically saying that we are not going to do anything until God does what we want. We will not live our Faith until we have a mystical experience, we will not act unless God gives us a vision. Though God does deal with us in such ways from time to time, we do not need them. Though Scripture does not reveal what God's individual will is for you, it does tell us how you can know it.

The problem we have in knowing God's will is that we think only in terms of what He is preparing us to go and do, of going there and doing this. Without a doubt God prepares us for the work we will do in maturity of the Faith. Though it is often forgotten in today's culture, there is character which God develops before one should become a minister. Or simply, maturity comes before ministry. Being able to speak or write well is a good skill to have, but if you do not have humility, you will use it to be worshiped instead of glorifying God. Theology is good, but without Hope you will use your knowledge of Scripture to soothe the popular mind rather than to convict sins. And without Charity one is simply too weak to preach the Word, to care for the poor and sick, or do anything which we refer to as a calling.

I knew since shortly after my conversion that I was going to be a preacher. In my imagination I dreamed of crowds and masses hanging onto my every word, my pride conjured all sorts of pleasing thoughts. I have preach but never formally, I have yet to step behind a pulpit. Most of my preaching has been done in the form of writing.

But whether in speaking or in writing I can hardly do anything without preaching. I really have nothing in this life except for my Faith. I am one of those losers who, if you do not care about your Faith, has nothing to offer. Not only worthless but a hindrance to those who want to hold onto their idols.

The point is that we should not so concerned about where God wants us to go, or what work God wants us to do, in so much as we should be more concerned about being and acting according to His holiness which we have in Christ. Part of this, part of our sanctification is learning to trust God. Having Faith is having trust in the faithfulness of God. To trust God to correct us if we head down the wrong path, or if we run from the place He wants you to be. And if it is important, He will make sure we know (Jonah 1, Acts 8).

Maturity of the Faith

Among the neo-mystics there is the problem of judging maturity of Faith by extraordinary manifestations. The charismatic mistakenly judge by the Gifts. Evangelists by their passion or skill with words, the fundamentalist by righteousness, and the religious judges by how many Scripture one has memorized or how often one attends church. The classical mystic, such as myself, too often sees the measure of maturity as being able to bare any hardship or pain with joy and praise for God, being able to keep our connection with God even during the most dire of temptations. The problem is that extraordinary manifestations are for babes if Christ. Gifts are a Grace, given by God according to His plan and not based on our nature. We can seek righteousness in a vain attempt not to have to rely on God. Neither Holy Scripture nor church services can save us without Christ, and a smile can hide a bitter heart or a martyr complex, even from ourselves.

There are other, more obviously worldly ways in which we judge maturity. By how much money people donate to our ministries, or how much we donate, how many people show up to listen to us, how much praise we receive, the size of the alter call, how many days of the week we spend at church. The problem with such judgments is that we judge according to our own tradition, and in this age navigate to a tradition which judges by what we find easy. Worse still, maturity is an abstract term. It is not like an education where we can measure it by the knowledge gained. And one's view of maturity itself depending on what one uses as a measure, what ideal one has in mind. Judging by our traditions, using others or ourselves as the measure, we are bound to develop a false sense of maturity. I went through a lot of phases, judging maturity by this or that. By that on-fire connection with God, spirituality, wisdom, the willingness to do God's will regardless of the cost and so on. Each time I would spend time feeling mature, and then God would hit me with something else, something that would make me feel like a babe again. In the end, I eventually have to consider myself perpetually immature. I could only come to the conclusion that we are never truly purified, never truly mature if we use Christ as the true measure of perfection.

Moral sanctification is the purification the Spirit works in us so that we may more fully live according to God's moral will, the Law. Moral sanctification is a gift that God gives us for our sake. The Sabbath was made for man, not man for the Sabbath, so how much more is it for those who are dead to the Law? Moral sanctification, like sanctification, is worked on us by the Spirit so that we can be free as possible from the ill effects which sin brings. To keep us out of those hardships we bring upon ourselves because of our lack of discipline. (Matt 26, Mark 14, Luke 22)

But the sanctification which comes to us with Faith is more than simply reasonable morality, one which can be derived from reason. The Law was never enough, for the morality only points out what is wrong. It gives us an image only of what can go wrong with violation of the Law (Romans 7). Sanctification is visionary in its nature, an imperfect vision of perfect Honor. Not simply a code of conduct, Honor is the ethical ideal. The Spirit works on us not only a purification of our morality, so we can avoid what is wrong, but purifies us towards the ideal of perfection, namely Christ, so that we can actively do what is right. While moral sanctification is worked primarily for our own benefit (Roman 8), virtue sanctification is worked on us by the Spirit so that we may serve each other better. So that we may better fulfill God's will for our lives. (1 Corinthians 10)

Knowing God's moral will is easy enough. It is clearly explained in Scripture, though there are many today that twist meanings to suit their decadence. But in their twisting, they teach us how easy it is to ignore what is plain because we do not like what we see. How much easier it is then to twist the vision? To ignore Christ as He appears in our hearts when we would prefer to see Him another way. The process of sanctification, as I have noted, is the purification of our ability to do God's will but it is also the process in which we gain a better insight into His will. Though we mystics like to use metaphors and hyperboles, in simplest terms we find it easier to know God's will simply because we are more willing to do His will, even if it is not always pleasant.

The choices we make which do not fall into the realm of morality are not as clear because they are abstract, as abstract as love. This would be easy to write if I could write about doors God opens, of seizing opportunities. But not all doorways should be entered, and the enemy can present opportunities as well, if we but bend our character. It would be easy for me to write that one just knows, but I remember a time when it was not so easy for me. Being a mystic, I was used to God communicating His will precisely and did not understand those for who God did not do this. But as I worked in ministry, I encountered many who did God's will without such clear communications. Without those mystical experiences I thought so important at the time. And so in my search for understanding, through much prayer, and a rather unpleasant time in my life, I learned that God does indeed tells us all His will for our lives, just not in the way I had been used to.

Knowing to go right or left, up or down, to go to this or that school, take this or that job, knowing if we should give our time to someone or if it is better spent on someone else, throwing it all away for a life of ministry is as easy as…Loving God. (John 8) There are those who will try to teach you some new form of prayer, try to sell you on the idea that what you need is this or that Bible course, classes by this or that teacher, or a mystical experience. That if you just do this or that (usually for a fee), your spirit will be refreshed and you will know God's will. It all sounds so easy, so spiritual, and is so completely nonsense. All who belong to Christ knows His voice, and all who love God knows His will. It is just, sometimes, we do not love it. (Jonah 4)

The problem is never about hearing God's will, for it is in our hearts already. His Spirit guides us in our daily lives. With Scripture and the work the Spirit we have all we need to know God's will. The problem is found in that what we desire His will to be is different then what His will is. And I say it is a matter of loving God because to love God is to love His will. I know you love God, that I am not questioning. So, I should say that it is a matter of loving all of God. His will is as much of God's Nature as His forgiveness and His righteousness. It is the same will in which God chastise us as it is when He blesses. The same will which we chafe against is the same will which forgives, saves, justifies and sanctifies. The same will, regardless of how it may seem to us, is purifying and edifying us.

We judge those things which we do not like as evil because we lack understanding. We do not see how God is using it to shape us, to tear and burn away those things we should be without. We are dead, still trying to hold on to that corpse we no longer need. Worse still, we look to God no differently than the pagan superstitious masses. We would turn God into a pagan god instead of the Most High. Thinking that we can manipulate Him into giving us our will. Find the right way to appease God and you can have wealth, health and all your dreams. Make a sacrifice, burn the incense, fast, say the right prayer, and God will bless you.

I am not writing here about prayers of supplication. Even if I had such authority, I would not forbid such. Pray for needs, pray for contentment, pray to ease the turmoil of your heart and the heart of others. Pray every request you can think of, but make it a request, not a demand. Coming to God with an attitude of manipulation is sure to get you treated like the ingrate you are. Treating God like some dysfunctional parent where you can get that toy if only you begged enough, or throw a fit, is bound to get you into trouble. And is obviously dealt with in Scripture (Mathew 6).

The extraneous points aside, and as I am sure you have figured out, virtue sanctification is what I am calling, at least in part, a purification so we can fulfill the law, not simply in avoiding wrong but in doing right. To fulfill the commandments all of the law rests, the love for God and the love for others. And our love of God needs to go beyond just His will. We give labels to aspects of God. His will, His forgiveness, His wraith and love. But God is beyond such distinctions, they are simply all God. For some, such as myself, His will was not much of a problem, except when it was His will that I should know His Love. Give me a mountain to climb and I am on it. Give me a dragon to fight and I will gladly sacrifice my life. Show me affection and I ran scared. To show affection, and to be shown affection was, and still is the hardest part of Life. Faith I had and liked, but Charity was not something of which I was all that fond.

Obviously, we cannot say that we love God if we do not love others (1 John 2). We may love God's will, and maybe His love for us, but not His will to love others as He loves us. We can get wrapped up in doing His will for works to forget that it is mercy not sacrifice that He wants. Is the Word we preach more important than the people who hear it? Is the bread we hand out more important to the hungry person in front of us? Are the words I write more important than you?

We can judge maturity in many ways, and in many ways be

wrong. There are obviously many areas in which we could seek perfection, but the clearest signs I have seen of one who is active in their own process, that is working with instead of hindering the work of the Spirit in them is an increase in a humility and reverence for God, and a love for others. Everything else is secondary, simply flowing from these two.

Saved for a Purpose

There seems to be some disagreements on whether God has an individual will for us, or only His general will. The argument seems to be centered around a point of view, from what traditional hill we sit on, rather than any true disagreement. An argument by those who have not the wit to realize that they are arguing two sides of a paradox. With prideful minds, unable to understand that God can, and did create a universe in which His plan will be fulfilled in every detail yet at the same time allowing us free agency. The same pride which turns predestination into fate or the concept of free-will into the idea that by our beliefs we can force God to save us. It is an argument about a Mystery, so words are just not enough. One must live it.

If one means that the distinction we make between the two, between morality and virtue is artificial I can only agree. As with most of the Mysteries, we put it in human words so humans can understand. Then we fail to understand that we only understand the words because and to the degree in which we already understand the Mystery. Or if by bringing up the artificial nature of our labeling one means that God is unconcerned, unwilling to directly guide the individual in their life then I am at a strong disagreement.

I obviously believe in the God's will for the individual, that He has a purpose for every person to who He gives the Grace of Salvation. We are saved for a purpose, though we do not always know or understand that purpose. But we can strip the heat from the argument if we change the words we use, while keeping the same meaning. God's moral will, the one which is clearly portrayed in Scripture is the Law, the very Law in which all the world will be judged (Romans 3). It is the general will that applies to everyone, the judgment that all are under. But being saved, justified and sanctified, we have died to that law of death by joining Christ on the Cross, and have been reborn into the law of the Spirit, the Law of Life. So, what we call God's individual will for us is that law in which we are under now, as Christians. It is the Law which the Spirit of God writes on our hearts. And this goes beyond just morality, as that is evident to the carnal mind even if they deny it, but also the passions and drive for those things of God. In simpler terms, God's moral will is what has always been expected us, while God's will for the individual is found in the virtues which God expects of us as individual Christian.

The distinction between God's moral and individual will and between moral and virtue sanctification is an artificial one. I use it simply for the ease of writing and understanding. Moral sanctification is also part of God's individual will for us. Those who do not strive for moral perfection cannot be doing God's will for them as individuals. For no one who is saved is ever so perfect or so important that they are allowed to keep on sinning (1 peter 4, Romans 6). Not only that, but as one desires to do God's will, follow their calling, they will have a greater motivation not to have that work ruined by their own behavior (Romans 14, 1 Corinthians 8).

Instruction in Scripture, being the source of dogma and doctrine, is important as it gives us the foundation to make moral decisions and theological statements. As Scripture holds God's moral (general) will, it is sufficient for the moral aspect of any choice we have to make. This is why many in the Church often mistakenly turn everything into moral choice, inviting an active legalism. Then, so not to risk the comfortable life of a mediocre Faith, refuses to suffer in the ways necessary for virtue. But the choices in life are most often only partially moral. Indeed, very often the most important choices are not an issue of morality at all. Is the calling into full-time ministry part of God's moral will or a matter of God's individual will? Is one morally obligated to become a preacher if they can speak well, or could God have other work for them to do? It is such choices, which may contain a moral element, that virtue sanctification becomes important.

The problem I have with most teachings on God's individual or specific will, or I should say how those teachings are typically applied is that it forms another form of legalism. More often than not, it is focused on what you are, on a label, instead of who you are, as a person. And more often or not it becomes a list of Gifts, talents and education, rather than truly about God's will. God's individual will for us is not base on our abilities, but on our love. It is not a question of how well we do, but how well we love. It is the love which creates the work that is pleasing to God (1 Corinthians 13).

We like to think of God's will in terms of some grand feat, a task list in which we need to accomplish. It creates the tendency, especially with the mystic, to think of God revealing His will to us only through those raptures, visions and burning bushes. We come to think of the guidance of the Spirit is only for special times, or maybe only for special people. So much so, we come to think that one must be like the Old Testament prophet to be guided by God. Indeed, is it not this belief that we elevate those preachers, some who are obviously charlatans, to the status of a god, an idol. They come with a flash and titillating words which are crafted to hide God's will from us.

Such preachers, false ministers are easy to spot. They always deny that God's will may differ from one person to the next. That all must be rich, or all must be poor. All should be in the streets witnessing or feeding the hungry. All must be like this, or be like that. And that is why they are worshiped as they are, for they allow their followers to deny God's will for their life, as individuals. It allows them to avoid the struggle, sacrifices and pain a life of serving God costs us, though the rewards are more than worth it, even in this life. It allows them to avoid the turmoil which caused by not pre-knowing God's will for our lives.

There comes a time during moral sanctification in which even the thought of our sins leaves a bad taste in our mouth. Righteous indignation, as it is called. For some, unwilling to deal with their own sin, repress it and become sin-hunters. Their hatred of the sin is so intense they are unwilling to see it in themselves, and so go to great lengths to attack those who show them a mirror, reflect the very sin in which they are struggling with. Unfortunately, even good preachers fall into this, and the clearest sign is when you have an obsessive focus on a very narrow subject. When your thoughts continually return to those same sinners over and over. In the same way, there is a time, or maybe times during our virtue sanctification in which we obsess on God's will for our lives. We put ourselves through great turmoil wanting to know what is God's will before we take a step. In which we come, in a way, to worship an ideal of the concept of knowing God's will. There is a danger in this, just as in coming to worship mystical experiences.

Grace is given to us, given freely by God by His will, according to His will, for the fulfillment of His will (Ephesians 3). As salvation is a gift, a Grace, it is given to us so we may be a partaker in that plan. But so too is the knowledge of His plan. That

God gives a knowledge of His will, either before or after the fact, according to His plans for us. And in my experience, when He does it has little to do with the task, but a means in which to motivate us to develop those virtues in which we need to live a sanctified life. In my case it has been most often about trusting that God knows what He is doing.

Sanctification is being put aside for God's use, saved for a purpose and we go to great pains to know that purpose. As we know if one cannot be saved, cannot enter the kingdom of heaven unless we are doing God's will (Mathew 7). But knowing God's will is a Grace, so a paradox is created. A Mystery which is the source of much contention and arrogance. For if being saved we must do God's Will, but if God's will is not always known to us then how can we do it? There is no divination, no special prayers or retreats in which will give you the details of what God would have you do. And while a spiritual director may help they will not, at least those worthy of such a label, tell you but help you learn how to discern it for yourself. So, how can we do that which we have no knowledge of needed to be done? While Scripture is silent on whether or not you should get your degree or drop out of college to become a missionary in some far-off land, it is clear on the manner in which we can be sure that we are living according to God's will.

As I stress, there is no quick and easy way of virtue sanctification, for it requires one to carry their cross, live their calling, to give up ownership of their own lives. To have our Life found only in Christ (Mathew 10). And though the details may vary from person to person, following Him is not the haphazard, what-ever goes path which is commonly taught today (Mathew 7). Knowing God's will for our life is obviously the work of the Spirit of the Lord, as only God knows the mind and heart of God (1 Corinthians 2). As I wrote above, we often think of the Spirit working only with flash and bang but it is far more common, even for the mystic, for this to be the subtle transforming of our minds and hearts (Romans 12) towards perfection (Galatians 3). We have the Spirit of Truth, who is unknown to the unsaved, who guides us in our understanding of Scripture and its application to our lives. To become more like our name sake, Christ-like.

Surrendering Love

It is the height of mediocrity to expect praise for living a moral life, for simply doing our duty (Luke 17). Even if we lived the most perfect of moral lives, we still would not be worthy of praise as it is expected, commanded of us. Our rewards are not based on simply being moral, keeping safe what we have been given (Mathew 25). It is not enough that we keep our bodies from sin, we must also strive to have our heart changed to be rid of the desire to sin (Mathew 5). The continual sanctification is not simply so we can share Christ's moral behavior but so we also share His moral character (Romans 8). Everyone who longs to see Him face to face seeks to be perfect as He is perfect (1 john 3).

Nor do I expect praise for the works of my hands, though these may be what our reward is based on. I spend time writing, giving my time and energies for the betterment of others, but I can hardly consider that a credit to me. My wisdom and understanding, my Honor and all the traits in which are praiseworthy are only because of the Cross, because I have been given Christ's character, been given Life. My growth in Faith, as a person and as a Christian, has been a Grace. The Spirit of Christ overflowing my Life. In simplest terms, like any traditional mystic I do not count my works in my favor for they are simply a product of the changes which have been worked on my heart.

At my conversion I was stripped of all my duplicity. I had this skill of being able to put on any personae I needed for a task. In essence, my wall and way of coping with challenges was to create a personality which was unaffected by the hardship. So much so, I could not tell you, even now, which one of those 'personalities' was me. But in a moment, they were gone, and it took me years to learn to be comfortable in public, when I could not be a jerk or friendly in order to achieve what I want. So, why did not God do the same with my pride, with my lust, or with my depression? Why did he not remove the 'wound that will not heal'. Though not as it once was, why do I have to continue in my struggle with such imperfections? Is it only so I can call the struggle my own, even though the overcoming of the sin and the vice has been a Grace? Or maybe, as is my view, so that we can learn that post-salvation sanctification is very much about surrendering our lives to God (Romans 6).

Regardless of the words used, that surrendering is the main thrust of biblical Christian mysticism. Death of our self, being nothing and all that is our constant, sometimes obsessive drive for a purification in which removes us from our carnal desires and worldly worries. So much so we often neglect in our teachings to put in the qualification that one must first be saved before any of this applies. All in all, not that much of a problem except that it gives the impression to the unsaved that one can reach God by becoming nothing, instead of us becoming nothing because God has touched us. None-the-less, and hyperboles aside, the focus of my Faith has been the subduing of my carnal mind so nothing can prevent me from living according to the Life I have.

Easier said than done, but the problem is that we are taught this idea that Faith is all roses and no thorns. Beyond the neo-mystics with their slogan-based theology, Church culture across the board is more complicity than cross-carrying. Even among the traditional mystics there is the tendency to see detachment from the world not as a means to better serve but a way to avoid the pain. Settling for the comfort of a mediocre Faith instead struggling for a total conformity to Christ's Life. And then we wonder why we find no real pleasure in our Faith, why we do not grow. But we cannot enjoy the love, joy, peace, longsuffering, gentleness, goodness, faith, meekness and temperance unless we add to our Faith virtue; and to virtue knowledge; and to knowledge temperance; and to temperance patience; and to patience godliness; and to godliness brotherly kindness; and to brotherly kindness Charity (Galatians 5, 2 peter 1).

Mediocre Christians, pew-sitters, lukewarm…do not let others judge you in this, but judge yourself honestly. Or more to the point, let God show you. If you are content with the perfection which you already have in Jesus Christ, then be content. I have never had any teachings for those who have been content simply being saved. I even question the salvation, or at least their desire for salvation, of those who do not see Faith as a continual life of growth, of purification (1 John 3). But God has made it clear, more than once, that it is not my place to judge such things, only to help those who desire to strengthens their Honor. More than likely, such judgment is not needed anyway. There is something, some area of your life in which you are driven to be that which Christ would have you be.

Unless you are thinking that you have already become perfect, as God is perfect, there is always something in which we can to improve, always something for us to be working on.

There are times in which it nags on us, our weakness. There are times which God hits us with a baseball bat. There are times in which the changes are pleasant, and times when it would be easier to rip out our own heart. Through it all, if we reduce it to a single issue the struggle is to keep our focus on what is holy, to keep our inner-life focused on God. Whether in pain or in pleasure to never be separated from our love for God. Easier said than done, to be sure, but that is all there is to it. In fact, one could say that both our pains and pleasures are gifts from God in which to strengthen our holiness.

Moral sanctification is the struggle to live according to Christ's moral character, to be righteous, blameless according to the Law (Phil. 2). Virtue sanctification is the struggle to live according to Christ's holy character, separated onto God, to live perfectly blameless according to God (Col. 1). And regardless of the teachings of others, this does not happen by donation, special prayers, the touch of some preacher or anointed oil. It happens only by the struggles in Life, in our everyday life.

We are a mirror who reflect a small, a very small part of God's light, and it is our task to polish that mirror so that more of that light is reflected. But the polishing is not in the work that we do, but in the struggle of doing. As you most likely heard before, building moral character is by habit. Resist a sin and it becomes easier to resist, succumb to a sin and it is harder to resist next time. The same is true with the struggles in holiness. Keep our focus on God and His will during hardship and it becomes easier to keep that focus next time. Get distracted by a pleasure or a pain and the easier it is to lose your focus the next time.

I am fond of saying that my experiences does not doctrine make. It is slightly dishonest though as the one doctrine in which my experiences have created is; my experiences does not doctrine make. I can say that for me Grace was given before the vision. That visions, the raptures, all of my mystical experience has been a product of Grace, not the origin of it. Both in my experiences and observance have indicated that the Grace of the Spirit moving our lives happens prior to the vision. That God is active in His will to bring us to revelation, or what is technically called illumination. And it appears, especially when we are young in our Faith, that God leads us to desire the revelation, to want the understanding.

It appears, only appears such but the desire for understanding is a byproduct, a result of our love for Him. For when Faith was born in us, we knew God in a way we did not before. By being in the Son we are united with the Father, by knowing Christ we are united with all of God as fully as we can be in this age. And in that unity we know that we do not know God clearly, and we long to know God in all ways, and all His ways as we would any true lover. We long to know God as we will in the next age. But when we desire revelation, when we long only for the understanding we are acting like a poor lover, like a spouse who never stops to think that maybe it is the fact that their obsessive focus on sex is why they are unsatisfied with their partner. (Philippians 3)

There are those who teach that the mystical tradition is a means in which to force God to give a revelation, to give us illumination. I call them neo-mystics because they have the language of a mystic of the Cross, but lack knowledge of God which only comes in Christ. I say they lack this knowledge for they will teach you that what is wrong is that you are not praying correctly. That if you pray this way or that way, if you fast, if you just tithe more, if you do these works, then you will have that revelation and Life you long for. They prey on that temptation which comes when we are not feeling our union with God through Faith in Christ.

They irritate me, sometimes more than they should, for in those times when the Spirit is trying to show you that your Faith is enough, they teach that you can reach to God without Faith. At the very moments in which God is trying to tell you that His Grace should be all you need, they come and say that you need more than the Cross. Which to, I have to ask; what if it is not God's will that we should have a revelation, vision or mystical experience at that time? Is it not an overgrown sense of pride, and a lack of Faith to think that we can force God to act other than according to His will?

Yet such teachers could not be so common in the Church if this was not already believed. If it was not already common teaching that we can force God to give us revelation. That is, if the teaching that conversion is a work of our own hearts, we would know that all which God gives, His Grace is done according to His works and not ours. That we go out with the arrogance that we can convert, that we are the one who calls people out of the world. Because we are the light of the world, we forget that the Light is Jesus the Christ. We think that we bring people to Jesus, when it instead it is the will of the Father calls people and gives them into Christ (John 6, John 10).

With convincing arguments, we may convince, with social pressure or a pleasing promises we may get one to change their beliefs but it is only God who can convert. It is easy for us to overlook that it is the Father who decides who to bring into Christ. Easy to forget that it is Him who decides who to convict, give them a longing for the Life we have in Christ. That is, it is an easy misunderstanding when we base our doctrine on our own experiences. Indeed, God gives such Grace corresponding with our preaching so there will not be misunderstanding on who the Light is. We preach repentance so that one who is convicted knows that it is sin in which is what is wrong. We preach the Cross so they know that the Grace forgiveness and freedom of that has come from the work of Christ on the Cross. We preach the resurrection so that they know that the Hope they have in their conversion is on the promise of even greater sanctification.

If this was simply a matter of a theological position, I would leave it to the theologians to argue over such. If it was only a matter of conversion, I would leave it to those whose calling it is to be focused on harvesting those in the world who God is calling. I would not bring it up if it was only an issue of this obsession over numbers, the condoning of counting cultural Christians as being in Christ which is obviously derived from the Armenian view. But our doctrine on conversion, our view on justification greatly affects how we see sanctification. When we think that our salvation comes from someone other than Christ, we look too much to others for the growth which the Spirit is performing in us. Just as those who see Scripture as their justification will see the Word of God as instruction of gaining Grace rather than the story of how we gained it, and instructions from God on what to do with it.

Though we should not imbalance the paradox in the other direction by basing doctrine on my experience and say that because it is God who draws us to Him there is no reason to preach. It is certainly wrong to say that it is unimportant what we do, and what we preach just because I was too arrogant to listen to your words .

But then why? Why do we preach the Gospel, why are we to be a light for the world to see? (Mathew 5) Some say that we do it simply because we are commanded. To be sure, I preach because that command is so complete I can do nothing else. But we preach to gather those whom God has graced to no longer love the darkness. We preach so that we may let those who God has given a longing for the Light it is Jesus the Christ they are looking for (John 3). We preach because though God gives Grace only according to His will, He has ordained that He gives it through our works.

We preach repentance so that they know that it is God who is convicting them of the sin for which they are condemned. (Romans 2) We preach the Cross so they know that God that the forgiveness and freedom, the Life they now have comes from the work of Christ on the Cross.(Romans 5) We preach the resurrection so that they know the promise in which they have Hope, the perfect sanctification which will come in the next age, comes from the same Spirit which we are dependent in the sanctification in this age. (Romans 6, Philippians 3).

Judgment

EMPTY . . .
The nature of our faith
No cost to high
As long as someone else can pay

WITNESS . . .
The darkness of our hearts
We will forsake even Him
To fill our seats with the dead

LOVE . . .
All that glitters
If you have the gold
We will call you brother

ASK . . .
For all but what we need
His will does not matter
As long as we have our miracles

GIVE . . .
To feed our ego
Go with His blessings
Forget your empty stomach

BLOOD . . .
To wash away our sins
No need for His
When yours will do

FREEDOM . . .
From the law of death
But if you are true
You will wear our chains

BELIEVE . . .
All that we tell you
Don't listen for yourself
You do not have our ears to hear

REPENT . . .
Kneel with tears in our eyes
Poor out our heart on the alter
What does it matter?
Tomorrow we can return to our ways

The Circle of Harmony

My heart now wonders through time, not of what could have been but what can be, through Tym, so many threads, so many currents flowing into the future. So many pressures, so many forces working on how that future will take shape. I sit, I watch, I smile. We work so hard to forge our world into an image that would better suit our tastes. We struggle, we strive, we desire. We waste our vital energies, until our lives are spent, as if our will alone can bring the world in which we want. This too we call chasing the wind. We strike, we push, we grab. Strength eventually gives out, power corrodes the foundations on which it is built. The very force we use weakens the structure we are trying to save….in the end, none of it will stop the call of the Bear, the gathering of the Wolves and the return of the Buffaloes….

There is this idea that our nation is a holy nation, or was at one time at least. As much as I would like to I cannot agree with that. We are a nation built on stolen land, the backs of slaves and with the blood of the poor. Yet, let us not forget that every empire, every great nation has been built in the same way (great only in one way of judging such). Human empires are built by force, by fire and by sword. Every nation is built upon the ashes of what is destroyed in order to create it, and gathers insides itself the seeds of that destruction. And when those seeds mature and bear fruit, the nation itself is destroyed. The trees of one nation are cut down in order to build the structures of the next. Life and death, growth and decay, thus is the rise and fall of every empire, thus is the cycle of a nation's life.

Like a ship with a broken keel there comes a time when a nation is no longer redeemable. There is a point which is reached where the keel of a society, the very ideology on which it was built, becomes so corrupted and decayed that no amount of whitewash or bracing is enough to prevent it from snapping in a storm. But maybe no storm appears, and the rot continues until the keel cannot take even the stress of a wave. But a wise captain knows that before that time comes the ship must be returned to shore. So that even though the ship will not sail again it can be stripped of what is still useful on it. That everything on the ship which has not rotted and decayed may be salvaged and used in the building of a new ship. It is in this way which wisdom of the past is passed on in our hearts, the way we may learn, if we are willing, to slow the maturing of the seeds of destruction.

Let us not stall our progress by pointing out all which has gone wrong, or those things which has brought this time upon us. Let us not talk in terms of the darkness or destruction, but instead of what needs to be accomplished. There is not energy left for both lamenting for what could have been and for the wisdom needed for what must be. There is too much to be completed to distract ourselves with worry or crying out like Habakkuk. So let me stop wasting time with artful words and get onto the task at hand.

It is time for us to build a circle of stones, or more precisely to start with the work which will be the preparation for laying that circle of stone. It will be called the Circle of Harmony, a holy circle atop a holy hill. Maybe there are those out there, who have seen the circle as well, who understand. In the months since the vision I have exhausted all my resource materials and the only reference was of a Navajo concept in Deswood Tome's Living Dine Harmony. It leads me to speculation but let me share what I know.

The building of it is a simple matter in a physical sense. That is it is just a matter of placing a number of rocks in a circle. But if it was that simple I am sure it would have been accomplished a long time ago. Each of the stones must be placed in position by 'bears with the appearance of men' and while this is going on the hill itself will be surrounded, protected by 'wolves with the appearance of men'. To complicate matters further, the stones themselves, besides being blessed must also come from the community in which the each bear represents, chosen by that community with the understanding of the seriousness of it.

The circle will have many meanings. There are some who will see the building of the circle as a return to the ways of the distant past, some will see it as the symbol of a new ideology, but it is much more then that. It will be a covenant between God and the communities of the Circle. It will be a vow of the communities, and the individuals of those communities to live a life of harmony, with God, with nature, and with each other.

The hard and cold truth is that the People will not survive with our current mindset. The egocentric doctrines of our current culture have not only destroyed the community it has poisoned the hearts of the People. We must do more than simply reject the preconceptions of our 'modern' society, but we must actively promote Harmony. We must stop thinking in terms of how our actions will benefit us but how they may benefit the community as well. We must not think in the simple terms of retirement but with the goal of building real wealth for generations to come. As Jesus said, a kingdom divided against itself will not stand, and if the community is not united in Truth and in Charity, it will not survive. And without community, the People will not survive.

Sanctification

The Grace of salvation, the union with God in Christ is almost tangible to me. There is an awareness of God which has grown over the years, both of the indwelling of the Holy Spirit and God's hand in the threads of fate. Undoubtedly, some of the reason I am able to draw a sharp line, sometimes too sharp of a line between flesh and spirit is because I am a convert. For me there as a moment in which a sharp line was drawn between who I was unsaved, and who instantly, or at least very quickly, became being saved. Repentance drawn from the awareness of sin which I was unaware of just moments before. It is a theme I hit on time and time again, the holier we become, the more aware of God's presence in our life we become, the more aware we become that we are sinners falling far short of the glory of God.

Obviously when it comes to both justification and sanctification, I lean heavy to the Grace side. Regeneration, being born again and our continued sanctification is an active work of the Spirit of God and thus is dependent entirely on His will. All the Grace we receive is a gift from God, unearned by us, but that does not mean that regardless of what we do. Though my own experiences seemed to leave me no choice, I cannot accept that Grace is irresistible. Not that we have a choice in whether or not God gives us Grace, but in so much as it is up to us in how we accept and keep that Grace. (Luke 8)

While it is typical at this point to jump to the work which is the God has ordained as the vehicle of Grace, I would rather first focus on the means through which all the Grace we receive passes. Our prayers, fellowship, study of Scripture, our hardships and obedience only bring us Grace by and through our Faith. As I wrote earlier, I have not studied this enough to know whether it is true with justification, but our sanctification depends greatly on what we do with the Grace God gives us. Our sanctification, the purification of both our behavior and our character and the maturing of our Faith are so intertwined they often appear that they are the same, that it is only a technicality in which they are separate. (Colossians 1)

Indeed, as there cannot be one without the other, we often write and preach as if sanctification and maturing in the Faith is the same. We could go as far as to say maturing in Faith is part of the sanctification as Faith is an aspect of our character. It is without doubt a paradox that we can only overcome our sins by the Grace God has given us, the indwelling of the Spirit, but that we must also struggle and work to put aside our sins. An easy paradox to unbalance. To sit back and say as it is only by Grace then God if God did not want me to do this sin He would take away the desire for me to do it. Or to go in the opposite direction and think that we can overcome our sin simply by beating down our own flesh. Which is, of course where Faith comes in. (Romans 4)

The Faith through which we are saved is our belief in the work of God upon the Cross for the remission of our sin (Hebrew 10). While I have been called heretic for saying so, the Faith through which salvation comes is not simply believing the Gospel, it is believing it in a way which we put our trust in Christ. Again, I have not studied enough to enter the Lordships/Free Grace debate about justification, but our continued sanctification and the maturity of our Faith requires us to trust God as our king. Faith is not simply believing certain things about God, it is believing in God. Faith my start with believing that the Son of Man was lifted up to save us, but only whoever believes in Him will not be condemned. (John 3) Believing in someone implies trust. Our struggles to hold onto and mature in the Faith, in one way or another, revolves around that trust. Some people struggle with trusting God for their sanctification. They feel that their sins are so severe that God cannot forgive them. Some people struggle with trusting God with their sanctification. They feel that their sins are so addictive that the Cross cannot overcome them. Others struggle, as is been my main one, with trusting in God's Love, or His wisdom. While going into the struggles and sacrifices God asks of us it is hard to see how they can be for our own benefit. But then again one must also trust God that sanctification which He is working in us is well worth it (2 peter 1).

Sometimes He seems to move to fast, asking too much of us. Other times He seems to be moving too slowly, we want the sin gone now. Still other times we have no clue about what is going on, there is only pain. In those times, and the times when things are going so well, and in all we do there must be Faith. To place our trust and hope first in God, in the Grace He has given us, and only then in ourselves. It is my opinion that the reason we cannot separate sanctification and maturing in the Faith, and the source of many heresies, is because Faith itself is both a Grace and a work. We are given a measure of Grace which allows us to put our trust in God, and only by continuing to place our trust in God can Grace grow. Our continued sanctification, the growing in Grace comes through our work, but only if we work trusting in God to do the sanctification because the growth is His Work. (Hebrews 4)

Balanced Grace

For those unversed in technical terms, a vehicle of Grace are those things in which God has ordained as the means or ways in which we gain or grow in Grace. They are the things which we must do in order to mature in the Faith. Even though the Church seems to be locked in debate over oddities and obvious heresies, what are those vehicles and the mechanics of how they bring Grace is what most of the old-school arguments are about. In fact, the theological traditions are more or less defined by their views of the vehicles of Grace. Of course, the arguments typically surround justification, are we saved by Faith alone, or 'by the works done', or a combination of the two. While historically this was a Catholic/Protestant divide this can be seen clearly within Protestant circles with the argument over the 'sinner's prayer.'

I do not doubt that there have been many saved while saying the prayer, but the question is are they saved, did they receive the Grace of Salvation by saying the prayer or through their Faith? The position that by saying the prayer and meaning it guarantees Grace will come, is by definition 'by works' theology. I do not see any real difference between that prayer to salvation and baptism, except of course that baptism is actually commanded in Scripture. Those who use the 'sinner's prayer' in its various forms mean well. Most of the ones I have heard do a pretty good job of presenting the Gospel, until they get to that alter call, until they get to the prayer. I am not opposed to the prayer in and of itself, only in it being presented in that 'if you say this prayer and mean it you will be saved, which turns it into *ex opere operato*, 'by the work done'.

Are we saved by our prayer or by Christ? I bring this up, not to point a finger, but to point out how easy it is to unbalance the paradox of vehicles of Grace. They are things which we must do in order to grow in the Faith, but they themselves are not, in and of themselves, the cause of the growth. It is easy enough to unbalance it the other way as well, to say that what we do is unimportant. Though we are saved by Grace, we are saved through our Faith, through our belief and placed our trust in Christ and Him alone for our Salvation, for our justification and sanctification. (Romans 3). This is also true for our continued sanctification, that though it is through our works, it is only by His Grace. That we must place our trust while working in the will of Christ as our Lord. (Galatians 3)

Now, I wrote that the vehicles of Grace are those things that we must do in order to grow in our Faith, to grow in our ability to live according to the Grace we have through our Faith in Christ. I am in agreement with those who say that if we are saved our vows are to Christ as our King as well as our Savior. Because we have Grace we desire to be pleasing to God, we desire to serve Him. I would also go as far as to say that if you have Faith you will produce works (James 2), though if you may go way off course and not do those things which God would have you do. I cannot agree with those who make salvation a matter of having works which are pleasing to God. There are those who will try to do all kinds of works out of the desire to serve God which Grace produces, but will not do any which are of His will. (1 Corinthians 3.) With the point being that the vehicles of Grace are the works which are pleasing to God, and how we make sure that our works are pleasing to God.

Unarguably the vehicles of Grace are the 'blueprint' to gaining Grace, the four things which you must do in order to grow as a Christian, grow in the image of Christ. But from the start it should be understood that it is not simply doing them in which brings the Grace. They must be done from Faith to Faith, and by the guidance of the Spirit. Without Faith, without trusting in God, our prayers avail us little, if at all. (James 1, Hebrew 11). Instruction/study of Scripture benefits us beyond measure but cannot truly understand without the illumination the Spirit of God brings us. (1 Corinthians 3) We can surround ourselves with the most holy of saints, and their words will fall on deaf ears if we are avoiding the edification which God has intended for us in fellowship. (Ephesians 4) And we can impose on ourselves all kind of rules, fast long and frequent, do all kind of works in our drive to put away sin but as long as we are relying on ourselves instead of the Power of God it is useless, and not true obedience. (Colossians 2, Galatians 3)

I should also bring up at this point, that we could easily lump them all together and call them the vehicle of Grace. It is a mistake to think of them as separate things, in the sense that they work together in such harmony that they all meld together into each other. In my desire to live more according the Life we have been given I seek mortification, to subdue my flesh, and I do it primarily through prayer. Without the study of Scripture, I would not know if I was truly moving towards an image of the Glory of Christ or simply one crafted by my own imagination or by popular culture. And not being perfect I rely on my fellow believers to keep me pointed and pointing to God instead of my own ego. Which is really what it is all about, that we place our Faith, the belief and trust of our hearts in the Power of God to save, and not in what we believe or the works we do. (Romans 10)

Resist Temptation

Though I frequently fast, and frequently bring up fasting in my writing, I have never felt compelled to preach fasting. This has always struck me as odd, as fasting has been so important to my own growth, and important for my understanding between my desires and what God would have of me. At times God has commanded me to fast, but does He command you? I can easily say that He does, or if you really, really-really want to be righteous as God is righteous then you will fast. Doing so I would convict those who God is guiding to fast, and also those who want to having something else in which they can boast, to feel superior to all us struggling Christians. (Luke 18) The problem with such an approach is that it runs counter to what I have actually learned from fasting. I fasted, and continue to fast because I am incapable to do anything, or at least any work pleasing to God outside of Christ.

More importantly, fasting is assumed but it is neither emphasized in or commanded by Scripture. In my studies I have yet to find even a single verse which says that if you Love God you will fast, or if you really want to please God you will fst. Though there are several examples of a fast being called by leadership, there is no general command to fasting. No instructions on how often to fast, but more than a few on how to fast. Fasting is a private affair, something between you and God (Matthew 6). It is strongly linked with repentance, the tearing apart of our hearts and the desire to know God and His will (Joel 2, Acts 13). And more than enough evidence that a true fast is one which produces the works of Love, placing the welfare of others over our own desires. (Isaiah 58). So I think that whether or not one fasts has been unimportant to me because there are plenty hardships and sacrifices which God uses to sanctify us simply from the Love which comes from being in Christ.

Though we often think of mortification in the self-induced suffering such as fasting, it is found more commonly with that struggle to resist temptation, with those things which test and challenge our Faith. Hardships and struggles in which we place our trust in God builds in us a patience which allows us to resist temptation. (James 1) But I cannot leave it there because then we become trapped by the Law. After all, if God uses our suffering and hardships to sanctify us, then why not sit on a pole or whip the flesh off of your bones? In the modern terms is it seen in all those you shall not touch, you shall not eat, you shall not drink rules. Such outward religiosity, while maybe capable of modifying behavior, does not have any true ability to mortify us, put the Self to death. (Colossians 2)

Any teaching on works, even the work to put away sin, is bound to bring up the accusation of legalism. And it is true, as with all the vehicles of Grace there is a danger, even more because we can do it out of our hate for our sins rather than our love for God and others. It is bound to happen from time to time, to place our trust in our works instead of Christ. Though I struggle against sin, most notably pride and lust, I learned early on that Christ saved us, not only from the wraith and punishment which is due us for our sins, but also from our sins, that we may be free of them and free to Love. Though we suffer, strive against sin, Christ has showed us mercy, and our comfort, by being both the author and the finisher of our Faith. (Hebrews 12).

Virtue, though, is only part of what we seek. To our Faith, and through our Faith we also seek to add knowledge, self-control, perseverance, godliness, kindness, and most of all Love (2 Peter 1). Indeed, *miseria et misericordi*, Misery and mercy. What is the point of suffering if it does not teach us to be merciful? Is that not what Christ did for us, suffered even onto death so that we may have and know God's mercy? Not only to give us an example of sacrificial love, having been shown mercy knowing what mercy means, but also given us the ability to show mercy ourselves according to the Grace of being in him. And is not mercy, the ability to put aside our own desires to show mercy something worth suffering for? (Ephesians 2)

Beyond Religion

Mystics, rightfully so, have always been considered a rebellious lot. We are never happy with simple religious practice, we want to know, to experience the truths in which they represent. The Cross, which is the symbol of our Faith is more than a trinket to be worn as jewelry or a symbol of our group but an expression of our Union with God, of being in Christ. We ask those questions from our honest doubts, and from the curiosity often seen as lacking Faith. So, mystics, rightfully so, has always been a thorn in the side of the legalist, who see Faith as only in its social context. We are a remainder to them that Faith is in a person, namely Jesus Christ, and not in our religious practices.

Mystics are the philosophers of the Faith, wanting and pointing to the deeper aspect of our Life. Our religion is not enough for us, we want the spirituality on which it is based. But this is also why mystics have, especially over the last hundred years or so, been so prone to error, of becoming heretics instead of staying true to the Faith. That in the pride of an immature Faith, we mistake our place as being a rebellion against the religion, the dogmas and doctrines, instead of the legalism which believes without Faith. One saying they are spiritual but not religious are akin to the one saying that they are into politics but not government. Spiritual anarchists, like the political ones more often than not are simply exposing their own rebellious nature rather than the faults of the establishment.

Most people I meet who say they have gone beyond religion but really mean that they have rejected religion. More often than not, when a Christian claim this, mystic or not, they mean that they have ejected their desire for truth. I can honestly say that my goal has always been to go beyond religion, beyond the doctrines and dogmas of our Faith. Words are nothing, only symbols we use to represent something else. To truly go beyond one must go through the words and symbols we use. And with the core doctrines of our Faith, to go beyond is to see the truth they represent, and thus confirm them as dogma and doctrines.

I can also honestly say that I am beyond the mystical tradition. I do not rely on my experiences for authority, or do any of those things which are expected of mystics. Obviously I find no need to obscure what I am saying, and in fact, find it often counter-productive to do so. If I was still a pagan, I am sure I would, as the paradoxical language is an important tool in getting someone to think deeply, to think on the spiritual level. But as a Christian talking or writing to another Christian it is not needed. I rely on the Spirit of Christ to provide such depth to my words, and your understanding. There is no need because we already have that spiritual life living in and flowing out of us. (John 7)

That being the case, as there is no need to get you to be spiritual, my task has generally focus people on the mystery they need to be pondering. Even in this I cannot really say mine, as this is a product of the Spirit as well. Sometimes it is overt, such as saying something or writings such as this, but most of the time it simply is how I live my life. Thus is the nature of fellowship, as we mature we become living apostles to one another. I have been convicted by the Spirit more than a few times by something someone said or wrote, or how they lived their life. But for the mysteries, the paradoxes of our Faith there is but one source, Holy Scripture. (2 timothy 3)

Now, I differ greatly in my view than many others regarding Scripture alone. I can honestly say that only God has any authority to me. That it is Christ and not Scripture whom is my King. For me Scripture is not simply some framework in which to apply my logic and reasoning. Some text book in which to learn from. I am a mystic of the Cross, a poor knight of Christ, I serve only Him. Scripture's authority over me is that it has been proclaimed by God, it is His message, and His decree. I submit, and teach submission to Scripture only because I serve God.

Today, too many theologians, pastors and people in general seem more like wizards then students of God's words. They treat verses like ingredients in which if they can just find the right combination, they can produce an elixir for enlightenment. They treat Scripture as if they were magic, reciting them like are some sort of incantation to ward off their adversaries. The legalists on one side and the Gnostic neo-mystics at the other extreme fail to realize that the power of Scripture comes from God. Scripture does not have authority for its own sake, it has authority because God has made it so. Scripture has no power, cannot be truly understood unless one has the Spirit moving them. Unless they have Faith in

Christ which has removed their blindness, and with Faith a sight that makes Scripture not only understandable but something for which to give praise to God. wonderful. (2 Corinthians 3)

It is, however, far more fashionable today to reject Scripture and the importance of proper doctrine it seems somewhat silly to worry about those who worship the Bible. It is far too common that in order to be considered right one now has to be unorthodox. It seems in order to be counted as a 'good pastor' today one has to be not only a heretic but a bold one at that. This is, without a doubt, a product of pride. Something I do have some experience in. It is most popular to be a mystic, to be in rebellion against the legalist, but this is a childish rebellion. I can easily put it in terms that the rebellion against Scripture is a mirror to our rejection of God, but as a mystic I have to say that it is cutting our nose off to spite our face. God gave us Scripture to edify us. It is a tool just as important as prayer. (Romans 15)

When I say I have been trained by God it is usually in reference to the fact I have had no formal education. That I am self-taught, relying on the Spirit of God and my own reason for growing in knowledge and Faith. I cannot agree with those who say that our growth is because our theology is correct. One can be completely correct in all their doctrines and not have Faith. This is the origin of being legalistic, a moralistic faith. This is just an informal form of spellcraft, in which if we just do the right things God has no choice but to bless us. Without the Spirit revealing the truth in Scripture we study in vain. But I cannot agree with those who say because we have the Spirit our doctrine is unimportant. God has trained me directly. Through the Spirit's work to-be-sure, but also through Scripture. Though we do not grow because our theology is correct, we are surely hindered in our growth when it is not.

In this rebellious time, we too often see Scriptures and the dogmas and doctrines from it as something given to restrict us, too control us. Indeed, that is true for one who does not have Faith. As a slave of sin, the Law shows that they are condemned. But to carry this rebellion into our Faith, after we are justified, greatly hinders our sanctification. Our growth in Faith comes from the study of Scripture and from the moving of the Spirit of God. We need Scripture, and proper dogmas and doctrines derived from it, simply because we are not yet glorified, completely sanctified. While in this age we will always need Scripture because our sinful nature which will, even if we deny it, hinder the Spirit in His work. To say otherwise is simply saying that you have already become perfect, as God is perfect.

Tradition of Scripture
1 Corinthians 15

As it often happens, while writing I get distracted by Scripture. It is one of those behaviors I consider a benefit rather than a hindrance and is, in fact, why I only give book and chapter instead of a verse. Besides the point that the greatest hindrance to proper theology is taking something out of context, I like the idea that you may get distracted by Scripture as well. I am not a teacher in your tradition so it is not my role to tell what the bible is saying, but rather how Scripture brings relevance to our inner-life, in our modern-life. And though I am arrogant about my abilities, I find that Scriptures speaks far plainer on that than I do.

My mussing this week has been focusing on the role Tradition plays in our life, and especially in context of how it guides our understanding of Scripture. There are those, of course, who claim they have no Tradition, but what they are really claiming is that they have no Tradition except for sola Scriptura. The doctrine of Scripture Alone itself requires an appeal to the Reform Tradition. Its defense requires reasons not found in Scripture. Most notably that which writings to be considered Scripture was and remains clearly a declaration based on Church authority, but less noticed is that it is simply the safest course. That is, Scripture being the words of God, are the only source of God's words in which we can rest assured in their correctness.

Though I am inspired by God, this inspiration is not equal to that which gave us the Bible. Scripture is simply infallible in the way that you and I are not, cannot be. In essences, the Reformation was not about throwing out Church authority in its entirety, but ultimately an argument and bloody conflict to limit that authority to be submissive to Scripture. It was a return to the understanding that the Church has the authority to confirm that those books we call the Bible came from God, and a rejection that they are only the Word of God because the Church confirms it.

Though I am a mystic who has a fondness for Catholicism and influenced by mystic philosophy, both east and west, I am very much of the Reform Tradition. I am not a Protestant in the traditional since simply because I can see little point in protesting the Catholic church when the majority of Protestant churches are far more heretical at this point in time. In fact, I would probably would have become a Catholic Priest if God had not told me no. And now I see it would have been dishonest as I would have converted and then became a rebel against those dogmas which I cannot accept. As I see it though, Reform Theology has been hindered by its anti-mystic bias in its Tradition, though mystic teachings, such as Faith alone, was a large part of the Reformation. The Reform Tradition split most often because the theologian's argument over whose Kungfu is the best, whose view gave us the best understanding of Scripture. I could easily join the argument as in my way this work is a mystic of the Cross view of Scripture, but that is not is not important to me, in so much as I have another purpose in mind.

Mystics who truly had Faith have had little choice but to find a home in Catholicism, in one of the charismatic cults or go it alone. While I am unashamed of my fondness for Catholicism, my theology is purely and uncompromising Faith alone. Which means that I have had to go it alone. Ironically, I would rather have had the Church stay anti-mystic then to see the mysticism we have today, which can be seen as an extreme reaction to the legalism of the past. Far too many see mysticism and anti-intellectualism as the same thing. Indeed, the fruits of this today is not only the alienation of individuals such as myself but even those who feel the Spirit active in their Life.

The Protestant branch of the Church is crumbling because more and more in order to remain in a church one must choose between those who believe that God is not active anymore and those who see every whim as a movement of God. More and more we are being forced to make the choice between a Theology without God, or God without Theology. Being asked to make a choice between the God of Scripture, and the God we know. More and more we are having to reject this as a false choice.

In fact, my first revelation after the Gospel was the core of sola Scriptura. I was politically a liberal, and remain so for the most part, so obviously there are aspects of Scriptures in which I did not agree with. Some I thought were just plain wrong, and others which I thought I had a better understanding than those who wrote Scriptures. At the time I even kept other writings, such as the Toa Te Chang on the same shelf and on equal footing in my heart. Yet, time and time again God showed me the meaning of the Scripture, and in that I was the one in error. I continued for a better part of a year until I had that revelation, that knowing that any time in which I disagree with those books we call the Bible, as they are words of God, I am the one who is wrong, immature or blind.

Most of the problem of the Reform Theologians is the assumption that the revelation of the Gospel automatically means that one knows the authority of Scriptures. They expect that people to have faith in the Tradition of Scripture alone. Indeed, to a Reform Theologian it does not even make sense that one would doubt this Tradition. Being educated, the theologians see how Scripture is the real record of the revelation of the Gospel. So, they understand that to reject it is to in fact to reject the Gospel. They forget that for those who have not studied as much, who has not pieced it all together, who have not had the revelation of the inspired nature of Scripture, who have not yet matured in their Faith, have only the Tradition and do not see how that by denying the authority of Scripture is denying the Gospel itself.

Which is what many of the neo-mystics are doing today, is it not? Denying the Gospel. They claim to be Christians but then claim that our union with God can be found outside of Christ. In that same arrogance which I had that first year or so they place their own understanding above that which God has revealed in Scripture. They place their own understanding and reasoning above what God has clearly revealed in Scripture. Some of them love mystical experiences to the point of seeking them, which is a quick way to go astray. They elevate the ways of the mystics to be equal to the Way, namely Christ. They say that our experiences and revelation are proof and means in which we know God, but we know God because we are in Christ and we are in Christ because of the Cross.

Though we strive for a greater sanctification, our union is given and perfected by the passion of Christ. Our regeneration, our repentance, the forgiveness of sin and our striving to overcome them is based on the Gospel. Even the work we do on our own purification and sanctification is possible only because of the work which Christ did on the Cross. Because of this, to elevate our revelations to be greater or equal to Scripture is arrogance, plain and simple. It is in fact, to say that the revelation in which God gives you is more important to the Gospel itself. To say that anything God has to tell us is equal to Scripture, the revelation of the Gospel denies the Gospel presented in Scripture, and then you really do have to choose between the God of Scriptures and the one you know.

Without a doubt being a mystic influences the way we read Scripture. Having those revelations, it is natural for us to see God's word, not only as Scripture but to be living and active. Having experienced the Spirit as that two-edged sword which cuts a deep divide between our old and new selves, it is natural to God's word as His movement of our inner-life (Hebrew 4). However, I cannot express enough that Scripture, and its study simply cannot be replaced, at least for a mystic. As our desire is for increased sanctification, there is no substitute for Scripture in this manner. You will learn in time that though we have revelations, it is Scriptures in which gives them meaning. That Scripture is God's word which cannot be rewritten to our desires, warped by our desires.

While one may ask where the wisdom is today. We may, in fact, be arrogant to believe that no one knows the Way of God as we do, but are we really so arrogant to believe that we are the wisest who have ever lived? That the wisdom that I have, that you have, that our current culture has is greater than all the minds and hearts of our Faith before us? All those saints before us, the ones who gave us what some refer to as historical orthodox Christian doctrine, may not be easy to understand because they wrote about the deep truths of our Faith in a world much different than our own. They lived in worlds radically different than each other. But they and us, come to understanding of those truths by meditating and living what is found in Scripture.

I cannot stress enough that if one is truly seeking sanctification, Scripture is as important as prayer. The fact that the neo-mystics ask us to choose between knowing God and biblical theology far more often than theologians do should speak volume to the importance of Scriptures. By Scripture we are asked if we are in fact preaching the Gospel or only what we want to be the Gospel (2 timothy 4). By Scripture we will continually be challenged in our seeking sanctification, and that this is not done by external exercises (Mathew 5). We find in it the reward of the simplicity of being able to trust in God in spite of what is happening in our lives (Mathew 7, Mathew 10). Without exception, in Scripture, in sola Scriptura, you will find understanding of every lesson of your inner-Life.

Frustration of the Flesh

I read, or tried to read Plato's Republic for the first time when I was fifteen. I did not understand any of it, not really. In my early twenties, I read it at least six times and understood it. By the time I was twenty-five it was simplistic and frankly a bit childish. I read, digested and reread all the books of philosophers both east and west I could get my hands on. I approached them all as a mystic, looking for the truth behind the words. Some had more depth than others, some spent volumes saying the same thing over and over. All of them came to the point in which they had no more to teach me. And I had reached the same point with the Bible. Then came my conversion and Scripture became so much deeper than I could ever have believed. In the years since then, there is still so much in the bible to explore, to understand, to live.

We each going to approach Scripture according to our calling. A theologian, a preacher-teacher, is going to approach it for its dogmas and doctrines. This is fitting for their calling, as they are responsible for teaching those dogmas and doctrines, or in some cases defending them. As my calling is helping people with their sanctification, I approach Scripture from the view of applied theology. Obviously, it is important to me that your dogma and doctrine is correct, but this is because I focus more on what they mean to us. That is, in my calling I study more towards how Scripture applies to our lives rather than towards what they are saying, in that dogmatic sense.

Though I am not in ministry, I still study for my own benefit and not just for the sake of making sure what I am witting is correct. This is simply because, again, I am not yet perfect, as we will be perfect. In writing I can spend a day of prayer and study to write a single page. In life I often have to have the wisdom to know what to say and do in the moment. So until the next age I spend time in prayer and study to increase the wisdom in order to help others. And the edification we find in Scripture I call the paradox of the compass.

While those who do not spend much time in the wilderness might be unaware, you cannot get anywhere looking at your compass. No matter how clear your sight of the compass, if you cannot see where it is pointing it is of no use to you. One uses a compass to set a landmark, and then you head towards that landmark. Pulling out your compass again when you get there. Scripture is the same way. Studying Scripture only for the sake of theology is like only looking at compass. Theology is not our goal, but it gives us the landmarks we are trying to reach. And, I might differ from you because I say that heaven is not our goal but our destination. Rather our goal is to be Christian, to become Christ-like as much as possible in this life is our goal. We strive and struggle in that impossible task to live now our Faith, our Life in Christ as it will be after the resurrection. So, in order to do this, we need to set our landmark on Christ. We need a clear image of Christ. We must be able to see what it is we are to be like. We need a proper view of Christ. (2 Corinthians 11)

This is why is say that Scripture is unlimited value to us. I could write a whole book on the wonders of Scripture. I have spent more than a few prayers giving praise to God for giving it to us. For in the next age, we will be face to face, with a unimpeded constant view of Christ, but in this age we have but an imperfect vision. There are times, to-be-sure, that we have reached some mountain peak in which we gain a line of sight to Christ, but many times we live in a fog in which we cannot even see the next peak. And that is the purpose of Scripture, to be our compass when we need to know which direction to go. This is true for every one with Faith, but even more so for a mystic of the Cross. (John 15)

For if we turn to the popular view of God is love we see this clearly. There comes a time when the commandment to love strikes home to us. Where we know in that deep way that we must work on our Charity, to love the way which Christ loves us. Far too many turn to themselves, using their own imagination in creating an ideal of what God's love is like. That can only end in a warm-fuzzy feeling kind of love, a love without pain, a love without the sorrow for sin. But if we turn to Scripture to define how to love as Christ loves, we see the end of that love is found in Cross. That God was so sorrowed by sin that He was willing to die so that those who turn to Him in Faith can be free of it. It is a love which does not ignore sin, but does something about them. It is a love which says I have no rights, you may sin against me, even onto my death. I will not return evil but instead absorb it by turning the other cheek. (Mathew 5)

This is why Scripture always stays relevant. It is easy to say that you follow Christ, and it can even be true, but to be perfect as God is perfect is a process which takes some time, and many trials. While it is our desire to be perfect as God is perfect motivates us, we have a tendency to become frustrated because we are not perfect now. Scripture helps us with that as well. For Holy Scripture points not only to God but to the next landmark the Spirit is bringing us to. That when we reach that landmark, in which we have grown more Christ-like, it shows us how even more perfect God is. We know where we are going, but the twists and turns of life get us turned around sometimes. So, we use Scripture to point to that next landmark, to create the ideal in which we are striving for next. An ideal we can then strive to accomplish (James 1). It shows us yet another way in which we can strive to be more like Christ.

Idols of Prayer

I have practiced contemplative prayer since my conversion, or at least what I thought was contemplative prayer. It was and is how I start my daily prayers and the majority of the spontaneous ones thought out the day. So, for a long time I simply dismissed the heretic-hunters when they wrote about how evil it was. That was until I did an internet search and found what the neo-mystics teach under the label of contemplative prayers is not what I came to understand by the term. One of them, called centering prayer, is clearly a form of trans-dimensional medication using Christian words. Most of them being called prayer were simply zazen, of which I have more than a few hours of practice. Regardless, none of them wrote about contemplative prayer as I understand it. Which can be summed up as: Our Father who is in heaven, hollowed be your name. (Mathew 6)

My problem with the neo-mystics teaching of focusing on some word or sentence, or the no-mind goes beyond the formalizing or ritualizing prayer. It is that these teachings are sure to rob the wonder and greatness of our prayers. In this case, they deviate from contemplative prayer really is, the expressing of our Love for God in an intimate and total way. It is a praise and worship of God with all of who we are, mind, body and soul. Anyone who has been in love knows this, for we may say 'I love you' but the words do not fully express our hearts. Yet God knows us in a way and to a depth, with an intimacy which no human can match. God knows our hearts and our minds, so saying 'I love you' requires it to be true. Sometimes we want to express our love just because we are in love. Other times we go Him in prayer through Christ out of the love for the one who knows our pain. That alone is worth at least a few years of worship. (Hebrew 4)

In a real way, I could say that our life should be contemplative prayer. That our lives, not only our prayers but our deeds as well should be an expression of our love for Him. Sometimes God will bring us up, show us and allow us to feel His love for us, most of the time we simply have to accept that He does. Bluntly, all these teachings called contemplative prayers which are trying to create a communion with God seems to be very much like someone always asking for their spouse to prove that they love them. A spiritual lust, an unlawful desire for the feeling of God's love, rather than His love itself. He justified us and gave us His Spirit. Do we really need more proof than that? (John 3)

I see in these teachings a desire for God, but a desire for God on our terms, not His. In essence, they deny that God is Holy, and by our inner-works we can manipulate God. It is in that I can only see these teachings as most dangerous for a mystic of the Cross. While those who tend towards the legalist side have to come to understand that our outer-works do not sanctify us, those of us who tend towards the mystical side must understand it is not therefore our inner-works which do. Not by works but by Grace through Faith. Our works, both inner and outer flows from our sanctification, which is the work of the Spirit of God. Indeed, these teachings are sold as a means for you to hear God, for you to experience God, for you to know God's will. They are not contemplative prayers, as they focus on you what you want and not on God, and His will. It is proper for us to pray for things which trouble us, but we should ask according to God's will. (James 4)

Obviously, I link these two. To love God is to love His will, and to desire to live according to His will. To have His will done on earth as it is in heaven. I say that these centering and zazen style prayers are a form of spiritual lust because we are not asking for God's will, or having Faith in Him to give us what we need. They are about you, about asking God to give us a feeling, a sign that He is with us, or simply creating a feeling. While there is nothing wrong to cry out to God in our turmoil, we should start by asking for the will to live God's will. I have prayed for my daily bread, and have learn to be content when it was God's will that I go hungry that day. I have prayed in repentance and for the strength to forgive others and to overcome my vices. There have been many times in which God saw fit to bring me to that point in my prayers where everything faded and it was only me and Him. But most of the time it has simply be me praying in the Spirit. (John 4)

The problem you will run across in their practice is primarily the same we always see in the formalization of prayer. While there are occult aspects to centering prayer, the primary danger to one with Faith is it becomes something to do instead of being a spontaneous expression and outpouring of our Love for God. I write as someone who fell, several times, into that trap in avoiding God by seeking Him. I know that danger now. Do more, pray more, study more, read, fast more, write more…frustration of the emptiness. Of course, I write this from the maturity of Faith I have now. I know now that such attempts are futile because we are looking for God in the words or in our prayers instead of having Faith, having trust in God which comes from being in Christ.

In His Name

Those without Faith, even if they say otherwise, simply do not want God. That is to say, they want God if…if He is how they want Him to be. If they do not have to change their lifestyles. If God would give some proof, If God would just make sense to them. It is that which I define as the fallen state of humanity, the flesh, the carnal mind or ego-self. That our carnal minds do not, cannot truly want God, but instead wants a god of our own making. This changes when we receive the Grace of being in Christ, when we are regenerated, born again, made into a new creation. We truly want God, but be must still struggle against a flesh so what we do is want God and… And Him to be how we want. And we get to hold on to our sins. And He gives proof that He is with us.

Being a Christian means seeing the sanctification in this life as being getting rid of the 'and'. It is very much about have Christ as Lord in every aspect of our lives, both inner and outer. It is about belonging to God completely body, mind and soul. Being a mystic of the Cross means seeing the importance of prayer in living this out, to make it real in our being as it is theologically. And that requires meditative prayer. Meditative prayer is not prayer in a meditative state but instead prayerfully pondering aspects of our Faith. Not time spent in meditation but time spent meditating on Godly things. (Philippians 4)

Christ is my Lord, I am his poor knight, but I still sin. I do what I should not, and do not what I should, because though I am a knight, a servant to the King, I am not the King and so I am not a perfect knight. But I want to be and so I pray. But what do I pray? What should it be that we pray for in desiring to serve our Lord perfectly? The answer is nothing…nothing except for God's will to be done. We need to approach God in our prayers with a Faith in God. No matter what we ask for, we should desire God's will knowing that God's will is more in our favor than even our own. God being perfect in a way in which we cannot fathom, perfectly knows what we need even if we do not. (Luke 11)

Do not mistake me. I am not saying that prayers of supplication are wrong, only that there must be Faith, a trust in God, and His will in all our prayers. Their needs to be an understanding that we may not get what we pray for, but we will get what we need. We may not get what we want because we are not asking for what He would give us, or for reasons He does not approve of. Indeed, we may not get what we pray for because God has already given it to us. With contemplative prayer we praise and worship God from our love. In meditative prayer we pray from that Love which desires His will. Without Love for God contemplative is unproductive, likewise without a trust in His will meditative prayer is pointless. (1 Corinthians 14)

There are those who see sanctification, the progression of holiness as some kind of disease, or an extension of the Law of death. They see it as another kind of 'do it or else' list of rules. Maybe they are cold in their Faith, or lack Faith all together. Maybe they are simply caught in one of those times when the work the Spirit is doing for our sanctification seems painful and cruel. I enjoyed those early years when I first was taught about Charity, but I did not like any of those things which came after when God was teaching me humility. There are some fruits will come easy to you, others will let you understand why we mystics of the Cross speak about crucifying our flesh with its passions and desire. (Galatians 5)

That is why I say that when we pray, we must have Faith, a trust in God and His will. That is also why I say that our work, our only work in sanctification is to hold on to our Faith, our trust not only in His existence but also in His will. Because there are times when that Faith is tested, there are times in which we do not like the will of God. It is also why I often write and mean by being nothing. It is being a wisp of smoke in the Wind. Some desire experiences which bring them into heaven, but as a mystic of the Cross I desire to let go of those things which prevent me from moving to even the slightest blowing of the Spirit. To be rid of anything which prevents me from doing His will from my heart. (Ephesians 6)

Meditative prayer is seen too often as a means of gaining insight into the will of God. It does happen sometimes, but as I have already noted that is a movement of God and thus is according to His will. In fact, I have learned to take the opposite approach. I no longer seek to know God's will, as I seek to live more fully according to His will that I already know. That it is a time in which I pray for God to change my heart to be more according to the virtue which I have come to understand with my intellect. In context as we want to have God's will be our will, it requires is to completely give ourselves, to fully put our trust in His will. (1 Timothy 4)

Truth and Spirit

Before my conversion, though I was a Christian by popular definition, prayer seem just plain silly to me. Before I had the Grace of being in Christ, when I believed in God up there/out there, talking to God seemed stranger than having a conversation with one of my fictional characters. Since then, however, prayers have been a gift almost as wonderful as justification, almost as awesome as being united with God in Christ. In Faith not only do we have a belief and trust in the existence of God, but in God Himself. We have trust that we may go to the Father in prayer without having to perform rituals and rites. (Hebrew 7)

In our daily lives, we more often do or do not do the will of God according to our hearts rather than our intellect. We may like to think otherwise but the majority of our behavior is governed not by rational thought but by our impulses, our desires. If we were completely rational, being aware of our own sinfulness we would have never have a problem trusting in God. We know and even desire to do what is right, but still we sin. We know that God will sanctify us but yet we try to do it ourselves. We know that God works His will in our favor but still we doubt and worry and want to have things our way. These things we know with our mind, but doubt with our hearts. (Romans 8)

Those on the legalistic side have a tendency to focus on the mind and neglect the heart. While we on the mystical side have a tendency to focus on the heart, on purifying our desires and neglect our minds. We will even argue one against the other, like children arguing on the best way to make a cat fly. The legalist will say that it is all about the study of Scriptures, have proper theology and the rest will follow. The mystic will argue that it is all about prayers, If your relationship is good then the rest will follow. And we argue such things when we are immature, but when we grow wiser, we argue that the two go hand in hand, are two sides of the same coin.

I can easily say hold on to your Faith and the rest will follow. Draw closer to God and everything will fall into place. But we should seek to be as Christ in mind as well as in heart. Prayer and Scripture goes hand in hand to do just that, to sanctify mind and heart, both our desires and methods. One without the other is futile.

I reject the notion that study alone is a means of Grace. I reject it because that would mean that my sanctification of my mind has come from my genius rather than illumination by the Spirit. I reject it mostly because it makes the understanding of the Mysteries more important than the understanding of morality. (1 Corinthians 13)

Obviously as a mystic of the Cross I am all about sanctifying, purifying the heart. I desire to desire nothing except for God desires for me. And as I pointed out the poor knight paradox, the paradox we live is that of desire unfulfilled. We desire righteousness, we desire sin, and it is precisely the part of our intellect, our will which chooses which desires to fulfill in which needs to be sanctified. Scripture teaches us which path to take, which moral road is the proper one when our heart is being stubborn. We study Scripture so that we know which desire is from our ego-self, our flesh and which one is from the Spirit. Or in the language of the mystics, we learn the image of Christ portrayed in Scripture so that we may still live according to His example during those time which we do not see Him clearly with our hearts. (Hebrew 3)

Certainly, the paradox cuts both ways. Not the paradox it creates for our intellect, but the paradox of our very Life in Christ. It is not the paradox of being both a saint and a sinner, but the awareness of being both justified but still sinful. Indeed, the more sanctified, the closer to God, more Christian, more Christ-like one becomes the more they become aware of how far they are away from that ideal, from Him. There are times in which the awareness of our own sinfulness weights on us. When we face not some sin specific but that we are sinners general. Conviction of a sin brings contrition and repentance and are easy, pleasing compared to such times that we find that simply being a sinner, still being in this flesh is difficult. When we feel repulsed not by the sins we do but the sins we are capable of doing. (Romans 7)

That is, if we study Scripture without prayer, without allowing God to purify our hearts as well as our minds, we will soon be overwhelmed by the fact that we are a sinner. If we view Scripture only as the Law, only as a text book in which to formulate our doctrine and dogmas then we are bound to become hopeless without the council of the Spirit of Christ for we would be unable to live it. Likewise, if we neglect the council of Scripture we are bound to become hopeless by having no direction, no doctrine and dogma in which to point towards maturity. One who rejects the importance of prayer is like one who throws away their riffle before entering combat. One who rejects the importance of Scriptures, and proper instructions derived from them, is like one who cuts off a leg before a race. (1 Timothy 4) God has given us both prayer and Scripture as a means to grow in Grace, and for those times when we are being stubborn, when we are refusing to listen to either the Spirit or Scripture, God has also given fellowship.

Illumination

Very often it is words, our understanding of words which hinders our communication. Very often words that have technical meaning in one group only has a general meaning in another. I pointed this out earlier when I wrote what we often call revelation is in the technical language of theology an illumination. For some this distinction is unimportant, for others, those of us who sometimes gain understanding through extraordinary means, it is a necessary one. Not in that it matters whether we us the common name of revelation, or the more accurate illumination, but that we do not allow our pride to puff up the importance of the information. Whether by vision or those times Scripture pops and sizzles for us illuminations, the gaining of understanding is simply the next revelation in that process of maturing. That regardless of how grand they seem, we are still sinners and in need of the Cross. (2 Corinthians 12)

Likewise, and I believe far more dangerous is the misuse of the duel meaning of inspiration. I am inspired by God to write this. But in the language of theology, I cannot claim that for inspiration is inherently tied to Scripture. I can only say that God has inspired me to write this in the sense that God has placed the Charity, the love for those who struggle with those things which I have struggled with. It is inspired by the desire to help those struggles I have seen others go through. And I can say that it is inspired by God because writing is my art, my calling. As some preachers must speak, I must write. That is, the inspiration which moves my writing or a preachers speech is no different in how God may inspire you to choose your major, or throw it all away and work in a soup kitchen.

My writings, especially those in regard to Faith, is the product of long hours of prayer, thought and study. It is inspired by God in the artistic sense. It is not inspired, in the theological sense, which goes far beyond the way in which a mountain view or a muse inspires poems. That is such inspiration goes beyond the Spirit of God moving someone in the motivation to write, or the understanding on what to write, or even the words. True inspiration is God putting Himself in the very essence of what is written. And that belongs to Scripture alone. What I write comes from the heart.

It is simply me sharing what I have learned about God and from God, but Scripture is God sharing Himself. Though I would argue that the Word of God is properly Christ Himself, we call Scripture the Word because it is God saying 'this is me.' It is God giving us the ability to know Him in written form, as He has given us the ability to go to Him in prayer.

There is a subtle pride which can grow in our callings, even for those who are not given extraordinary experiences. Being inspired in the common use of the words, we can slowly start moving towards a view of it being the theological inspiration. Maybe it was just me, but I have seen it not only in those who are gifted in words but those who read us. Though there are those who see their own words as being on par, if not greater than Scripture, but such people are obviously heretics. I am writing of that pride which sees our words theologically inspired, but just not as inspired as Scripture. The pride can grow were we see the words as being just slightly under the Word, just shy of being Scripture. A pride which reveals itself in the fact that we compare our words with Scripture, instead of considering it what it is, fellowship. (1 Corinthians 13)

It is tempting, always a temptation to declare ourselves to be the authority, our own little medieval Pope. What I write is inspired by God so therefore if you reject it then you are rejecting Him…if you reject what I have to say then you are rejecting Christ…to declare myself a prophet of God and therefore you must accept whatever I write, without question, without debate…unfortunately this is a common arrogance found in the Church today (probably always has been). The authority of the leader to speak for God cannot be challenged. And many of us know the price to be paid for challenging that authority, but that is a topic for another time. We use different words for the guidance which Spirit of God gives us, inspired, led by God, called and so on. There is no danger in the use of the common language, as long as we do not allow that pride set in where we start to think that the purpose of that guidance is authoritative rather than Love. (1 Corinthians 14)

There are those who would argue that we are not inspired at all. Some of them are deist, and do away with all which is supernatural, do away with all guidance of the Spirit of God. Others, who are guided by the Spirit themselves, protests those who believe that their inspiration competes or even replaces Scripture. Though I often disagree with their method, dislike the manner of their protests, I have to agree with them because inspiration in which we write, or preach or teach is not in doctrine and dogma but in fellowship. Even the theologians, those who teach doctrine and dogma, claim inspiration that in teaching they may aid others towards maturity. (Philippians 3)

At times I cannot help the play on words, for indeed I and my words are inspired. I am inspired to be the knight God would have me be, and I am inspired to write in such a way that shows you that it is indeed possible for you to be the knight God wants you to be. We are inspired by God so that we may be an inspiration to one another. Through words and deeds we are guided by the Spirit of Christ not only so that we may mature but that we may be an aid to one another's maturity. But the words aside, it is a sure sign of pride in which we focus more on the inspiration then on the Love. It is a pride, a pride without Charity, when we deny responsibility for our own words or deed by claiming inspiration. Undoubtedly there are times in which we must convict, times when our words are harsh, but if they are not motivated by Love then they are not truly inspired by God.

Inspiration

There are those who reject God talking to and moving us today because Scripture is sufficient as a guide to our spiritual growth. There are others who claim to be inspired and so claim that they do not need submit to Scripture. Both of them use the faulty assumption that inspiration would mean that Scripture is insufficient as the authority of our Faith. While the first group I can hardly agree with, unless I am delusional but then it would hardly matter to me, the second group I have honestly doubt that they know the Spirit of God at all. But I have to be careful in that because they creep me out a bit, too much like the stereotype of a used-car salesman. (1 timothy 4)

For obvious reason, I have given this much thought and study in regard to our sanctification. Which is why I am splitting hairs with the word inspiration. Because the inspiration we count on is God focusing us in the direction He wants us to go. Not in the left or right, up or down kind, but in the direction of character, the sanctification of our desire. Inspiration is not so much about to do or not to do, to know or not to know, but the changes God makes in our character.

We may repent in a mild way when confronted with something we did wrong, like with my spelling errors. But we are inspired to repent when God shows us our sins. We are inspired to believe through our Faith. We have knowledge of the truth of the Gospel because of the Grace we have been given through our Faith. And we are inspired to do, or not to do according to our Love. I am inspired to know God so I pray. I am inspired to know about God so I study Scripture. I am inspired to fellowship, to write and share, driven to be better, to do better because of Love. Not a human kind of love, not from the understanding of love, but the kind of Love which can only come from God. (1 Corinthians 13)

Most of those I have read which has problems with the mystical tradition is that this kind of inspiration is subjective. Love by its nature is subjective and so can never be completely relied on for determining our actions. To the neo-mystic I will never be a real mystic because I agree with this full heartily. There are times, to be sure, in which God will hit us upside the head to get us going the direction He wants. But it is either pride or laziness in which we think that this should be the normal rather than extraordinary aspects of our Life. Pride in thinking that our life is so important that everything we do is important to God fulfilling His Plans. Laziness in the desire to have God make our decisions instead of using our own reasoning and wisdom.

God inspires me to write this, I can even say commands me because of the strength of the impulse, but the writing is mine, my work. Or if you would, my words are not inspired, they are work. I must struggle with my pride in order not to think more of this than it is, and accept that there are going to be mistakes in it. And I must work to make sure that it is the best I can do, that my words are as correct as they can be out of a Love which wants to give aid rather than my pride which simply wants to always be right. So, if you condemn me for writing, I can honestly say that you need to take it up with God. However, if you condemn me for something I write, or how I write it, then I should thank you if you prove to be correct. Far better to be judged by you and corrected then to face the judgment of God for improper teachings. (James 3)

I do not expect to get much criticism because I do not expect that many will read this, at least not in my lifetime, but that is hardly germane. Like I wrote before, when we are young in the Faith we are inspired primarily in our own sanctification. When we are a child life is about us, but when we come of age life shifts to become about others, our family. When we are young in Faith, fellowship is about us, about our own sanctification, but when we mature our inspiration starts becoming about others, helping them in their sanctification. The more we trust in Christ for our sanctification, the more we are motivated by our Love for one another. Fellowship becomes less about our needs and more about the needs of others (1 John 2). Love is the true inspiration from God.

Spirit and Truth

As mysticism is about sanctification, about achieving as much righteousness and holiness which God will give us in this flesh. So, it seems odd, does it not, that some would reject the authority of Scripture. I have, and will continue to point out that this is simple pride. Understandable to be sure, but still pride. Prayer is the vehicle, or the most common means in which God gives us the Grace which sanctifies our heart, our desires. We pray with devotion and praise from the love of our heart. We pray for intercessions from our desires. And we pray for the strength to resist temptations when we desires is not what God desires. Knowing that there is no temptation which we cannot endure with God's help. (1 Corinthians 10)

To deny the importance of the instruction of Scripture is basically to say that you are not a Christian mystic. You may be a mystic, but you lack the Guidance of the spirit of God. I know that is a rather bold statement, but to claim that we do not need Scripture is to say that our hearts are already perfect, that our desires are perfect as God is perfect. Just as prayer is the common means that God uses to sanctify our hearts, so too is Scripture the common vehicle which God uses to sanctify our minds. While prayer is Grace which allows us to rely on God for our strength, Scripture is the Grace God has given us for the wisdom on how to apply it. (2 Timothy 3)

There are some, it is true, who would make our Faith a matter entirely of the mind. Make it all about the rules. The legalists as we call them, who would make Christianity a 'religion of the Book' rather than a Faith in Christ. Those who study Scripture day and night, not to allow the Spirit to transform their minds but because they think salvation is found in Scripture. As they believe that the heart is unimportant, they are obviously such people are the polar opposite of the neo-mystic, who believe that the mind is of little importance. But never having being such myself, there is not much insight I have for them, except to say that sanctification is the transforming of both heart and mind. That those on both sides of the argument, those who would pit Scripture against prayer, who would create a false paradox between the guidance of the Spirit and Scripture obviously lack the wisdom to teach. (Proverbs 16)

There will be no need for Scripture after the resurrection. When we are raised in that final sanctification, we will do what God wills of us without hesitation or struggle. And undoubtedly prayer will be an entirely different experience as well for we will be truly face to face. At this point, for this writing I am less concerned about dogmatic statements of how we need both as I am expressing the sheer stupidity for a mystic of the Cross to disregard either one. As we are not content with simply getting by, we desire for as much sanctification in this life God will give us…but to what end? Neither Charity nor knowledge is sufficient without the other, both of which points us to fellowship as both a means and purpose of the Grace.

There is a considerable amount which needs to be written about fellowship, but I will not go into detail here as my focus is on sanctification. I likened the inspiration to write this to the inspiration God gives us in fellowship because it is a labor of Love, comes from the desire to share what I have learned. I have written before, when we are young in our Faith sanctification is about us but as we mature, as our Faith grows so does our Charity. We use different words, our calling, ministry, and sometimes we make a big show of what our position or work. But regardless of what God calls us to do, it is simply what we are compelled to do from how Charity manifests in us. We are not given Grace, sanctified in this life solely for our own benefit, but also for the benefit of others. And in being an aid to others, we are also aiding our own sanctification. (1 Peter 4)

While the sanctification in morality (outward acts) and virtue (our character) are two different things in our language and views they are so closely related that any distinction is purely an artificial one. Without a doubt it starts with virtue, as it starts with our regeneration, our rebirth, when we receive the Grace of being in Christ through Faith. But the regeneration of our character produces outward works, which in turn is used by the Spirit to further purify our character. Sanctification which the Spirit works on us is in our totality, both our inner and outer life, both morality and virtue. Though, at times the Spirit will have us focusing on a specific virtue such as chastity or humility, or dealing with some behavior, these are not separated from the whole. So too, prayers and instruction in Scriptures work together in such a way as they cannot be separated from the other.

Fundamentalist, teacher-preachers have a tendency to focus on Scripture, the concrete and objective aspects of the Faith. On the facts and details of doctrine and morality. They often run into the problem of applying the rules of the concrete to the abstract. It matters less to them that there is pride in their hearts as long as they do not act prideful. They can become heretical by over defining the Mysteries and paradoxical aspects of the Faith. As mystics we have the tendency to focus on prayer, the mystical side of our Faith. We focus on the abstract and subjective aspects of the Faith, such as having Hope or Charity in our hearts. The problem we often run into is trying to apply rules of the abstract to the concrete. We treat our minds like it is our heart. We are less concerned with our doctrine as we are with virtue in our hearts. And thus become heretical when we start defining doctrine and dogma by the virtue we have, rather than by Scripture. By denying that there is no way to define the Mysteries and paradoxical aspects of the Faith.

I went through the phases, through those things we go through maturing in the Faith. That pride which says that everyone should experience God just like we do. Then I met a fundamentalist who was moved by the Spirit. No visions, no raptures but strong Faith none-the-less. In fact, I would come to say a stronger Faith, for he held onto to his trust in God without need for all the proofs my life had given me. Which for me is one of the primary reasons, and one of the major deficits of fellowship today. I, of course, had an advantage that I am rather analytical by nature. That is, if God had not trained me through the mystical tradition I would obviously tend towards the theological side. Regardless though I am not stranger to pride, and it only pride which we think that one's position is more honorable than another (2 Corinthians 12, Ephesians 4).

Of course, there is also that pride because I have had such events that somehow, I am special. That God was training me to walk on water and throw mountains around. Now I am crazy enough to believe, to truly believe that with God such things, all things are possible, it is just that there a lot of people on the lakeshore who you will miss ministering to by not going around. But more germane, God trains each of us according to the purpose He has for us in the ministry of the Church. Fellowship, as the third means through which God has ordained for the growing of our Grace, requires not only the humility which allows other to minister to us but the Charity which gives us the desire to minister to them. (1 John 5)

Think on this. We mystics of the Cross often lament over those who are legalistic. Who do not listen to our warnings that Faith is more than simply believing some facts, that one must be regenerated, born-again, to enter the Kingdom of God (John 3), or that one must follow Christ with their hearts and minds, be transformed into the image of the Glory of Christ (2 Corinthians 3), must seek sanctification to be secure in their election and calling (2 Peter 1, Mathew 7), or if they are not loving each other then they know not God (1 john 4). So then, if we are not hypocrites should we not also listen to the theologians and teacher-preachers that we are in the same danger if we do not hold onto sound doctrine (1 Timothy 3, 2 Thessalonians 2). Or that it takes sound doctrine in order to become wise enough to exhort, edify and convict (Titus 1, 2 Timothy 3). And just as we may say that one must prayerfully search their hearts to make sure they are truly in Christ, so too should we listen when they say that we should study Scripture in a way which make sure we are not twisting it to suit our own desires (2 peter 3).

This is, of course, why we need fellowship with each other in Spirit, in Truth and in Charity. No matter how smart, how well educated, how spiritual we are, regardless of how we experience God we still need each other, and each other's views. Each of us have our roles to play, our place in the ministry of the Church (Ephesians 4).

Mortification

Obedience is not universally accepted as a vehicle of Grace. I am simply going skip over the objections which are rooted in a lack of Faith and selfish desires which sees the Word of God as a means to wealth or power (2 Peter 2). But for some, their opposition to obedience as a vehicle is simply because their theology does not go beyond regeneration. For them 'being saved' is all there is too our Faith, so to them any talk of obedience equates to salvation by works. Obviously, in that regard I agree with them in so much as it is not a requirement to becoming saved, as a union with God in Christ, is a Grace, given by God through Faith in Him alone. Grace given according to His Will and not our works.

And personally, I like to go a step farther and always make it clear that one cannot truly obey, put their self to death, to subdue our bodies, or do any good works unless one already has that Grace through Faith. Just as prayer or Scripture only brings Grace through our Faith, so too is our struggle to live as we should only bring Grace, is only a vehicle of Grace when it is done while placing our trust in God for the strength to overcome. The entire purpose of our struggles is not to grow stronger, though we do, but to learn to live by the Grace we have in Christ. (2 Corinthians 12)

Others who object, see obedience, most specifically mortification, as the goal of the Christian life rather that a vehicle of Grace which allows us to live it. I certainly sympathize with that position, after all if you love God, you will desire to live a life pleasing to Him, to live according to His ways. (1 John 2). Indeed, we must 'endure hardship as a good soldier of Jesus Christ' for one is not 'crowned unless he competes according the rules'. (2 timothy 2) But is our goal and purpose of our Life in Christ simply to be moral, to better follow the Law? Where is glory given to God in that? Does that not make Christianity just another twelve-step program? It is a hair I am splitting, but an important one. We obey not so we may be righteous but that we may be the righteousness of God (2 Corinthians 5). Jesus Christ fulfilled the Law, and died for our sins so we could walk in His righteousness, and in His Love. (Ephesians 5).

Obviously, my point is not that we are permitted to sin

freely. Just the opposite, as I am making the point that because we walk in His Love we strive to walk in His righteousness. To state it plainly, you cannot expect to grow in the Faith unless you are striving to be obedient to God. How can it be written that Faith without works cannot save when it is also written that we are saved apart from our works? Would this not be a contradiction if it was not also written that if we have Faith, if we know Christ then we will Love each other? It is rightly said that if we have Faith, a faith that saves, then works will follow. They will follow because the works are based on Love. Indeed, Grace comes only from those works which are born from walking in God's Love (1 Corinthians 13).

Considering how difficult it is at times to live according to the righteousness we have in Christ, especially when we are young in the Faith, mortification is often a major concern. Mortification of our body does not sanctify us any more than prayer or Scripture does. That work belongs to the Spirit of God alone. Sanctification is the work God does, it is the Grace we have to be better able to live that holiness and righteousness in which have by virtue of being in Christ. Obedience, both putting aside our sins and works of Charity are the works we do when we are facing the hardships and struggles of life, are simply what we do to not be distracted by our desires and keep our focus and trust in God. (1 John 5)

Still some object because of the extreme measures some have taken to discipline the body and 'bring it into subjection' (1 Corinthians 9). Such abuses only come from the belief that sanctification and mortification is the same thing. We mistake sanctification with mortification when we define holiness only as righteousness. If I am able to fast for a whole week, as I do from time to time, that must mean that I am holy, does it not? If fasting once a week means that I am dedicated to my maturity, then three times a week must make me a Saint. We often make this mistake because mortification is more noticeable, less abstract than changes to our morality and virtue. We do this because mortification is the most obvious product of sanctification, our growth in Faith. It is far easier for me to notice those sins which no longer tempt me, to judge by the hardships that I no longer struggle with then it is to define if I am living more according to God's Love. It is easy to mark the progress in my humility by the decrees in the temptation of my pride towards outburst of anger, then it is to measure how much Love I am able to show.

Many object simply because of the works focuses us on our selves, sins and hardships instead of Christ. That mortification with places the focus on the Self, by trying to put it to death. That works focus us on what we are doing. To this I agree…to a point. Certainly those in Christ are dead to sin, no longer a slave to sin and so by Grace we are able to overcome sin. It is only by Grace, by virtue of being in Christ, by virtue of His Life and death that we are able to live according to His righteousness. So too is it only through Faith our works produce this. Which is why I have always preferred the word mortification, not because we are dying but because we are already dead in Christ. As I have brought up, the poor knight paradox is that we are dead to our sins, but sin still lives in us. We have become a slave of righteousness, but there is a struggle to be a good slave. (Romans 6) That there I a appropriate level of attention we must give ourselves, if we are to be an aid to others we got to get rid of that plank (Mathew 7).

More often than not however, a focus on the self will cause one to view obedience as a form of punishment instead of a blessing. As a work instead of a Grace, a sacrifice, rather than a mercy. We desire to obey the Law from our Love for God, and for others. It is from the Love which Grace brings we desire to be righteous, and to obey. But our ability to obey, just as our ability to pray and to understand Scripture comes from being regenerated. Comes from the work the Spirit has performed on us, and is performing on us. It is easy to be enlightened, to feel love while sitting in my cave, but if I truly want to Love, to have Charity I need to be where God wants me to be, working to show the Charity God wants me to show. If I really want to be chaste, then it requires me to beat down my body. These things are not always pleasant, sometimes they are very much work, but if we keep at it, God will give us of the Grace to mature.

Though I often use the death-of-self terminology, obedience are really about living as one who is dead to sin. It is about Faith, and humility. It is about understanding that there is no Life, no Life at all outside of Christ. I consider obedience a vehicle of Grace because the more you strive to live as one dead to sin, the more we struggle to overcome sins and subdue our bodies, the more you realize how futile it is without the Cross. I have the Grace to know this through the study of Scripture, but I received the Grace to be able to do it only by struggling to face my hardships and struggles, not with faith in my ability to survive, but in Faith that Christ will see me through. Or, I consider obedience a vehicle of Grace because one grows in Faith by Trusting God and His Word and not simply by hearing it. (James 1)

Trust in Christ

My Faith, from the beginnings, has been fraught with doubt. I have never doubted the existence of God, or the truth of the Gospel. Rather, it has been a life of constantly doubting myself. I cannot say that such doubt is a sin, or even wrong, except of course the part which is derived from pride. I can say, without a doubt, that doubt is an important aspect of sanctification.

Sometimes what we consider doubt comes from the workings of the Spirit. It is a question of what we do with the doubt. Do we let our pride seek for answer which we want? Or do we take them an invitation to gain a deeper understanding of our Faith? Sometime during the first or second year of my Faith I came to doubt the humanity of Christ. His divinity hit me so hard it left little room for His sacred humanity. If you would have caught me for those couple of weeks, I would have had to admit that I doubted that Christ was fully human as well as fully divine. I was curious, which is how doubt works when we are honest about it. It is acknowledging that you do not know something, and so motivated to finding out. It would be Christ's tears and blood in Gethsemane which would strike his humanity deep into my awareness.

It is a shame, but true that sometimes our questions are taken as prideful doubt instead. The kind of doubt which people have in which they just do not like the answer. Fear is the mind killer, but pride kills the heart. I have never been good at addressing those with hard hearts because my pride has rarely manifested, at least with Faith, in a way in which robbed me of my curiosity about God. And it is the doubts which most concerns me here is the one which affects our Faith. The doubt of salvation which rise from Pride.

Maybe because of the nature of my conversion, or maybe it is an aspect of my personality but salvation as it is typically understood did not come into my understanding until later. I have yet to do a study on our resurrecting to glory. I have never doubted it, have never been concerned about it, and simply took it for granted. I vowed to serve Him, to be His knight as He is my King, and as such whatever God does with me after this life I leave up to Him. I started with Hope, an unshakable Faith in His promise as found in Scripture to save me, save us from His wraith. I have had people envy me for that, as they struggle with that Hope. They often doubt and fear that they will not 'make it'. But I once envied them because though my Faith was secure in that I will be saved, my pride manifested in doubting if I am saved, no longer a slave to sin

It is almost ironic, and more then silly considering there was such a sharp line between who I was before and after my conversion. but though God saved me from so much at that moment I was, and am, still in this flesh. So I still struggle, even now with that battle against sin. In helping others in that battle I have noticed that we struggle with either the Cross or with the Resurrection. We either struggle with our Faith, with our trust in God in the eventual complete sanctification when we are judged or we struggle, as I did, with putting our trust in God for our current salvation, in the sanctification we go through in this life. I say theses struggles, these doubts come from pride because they come from the misconception that either is in our hands.

People who doubt the Resurrection, are unsure of that proof for our Life has a tendency to continually ask what they must do to get into heaven which can lead to legalism. They stress in their teachings living as a Christian should so we do not lose this Life. They teach obedience not flowing from a heart of Faith, Hope and Love, but so that you do not lose your salvation. And those who doubt the Cross, unsure that that His work sanctify us, have a tendency to continually ask what do I need to do to put an end to sin in my life which can also lead to legalism. They stress in their teaching living as a Christian should so that we do not again become slaves to sin. They teach obedience not flowing from a heart of Faith, Hope and Love, but so that you do not lose your freedom.

The problem with unbalancing the paradox to one side or the other is, even if we claim otherwise, it makes our salvation, our sanctification either the incomplete now or the final completion, reliant on the work of our hands or minds. From the beginning it is important that we hold on to our Faith, our trust and knowledge of God as the one who saves us. He is the one who freed us from sin so we may be a slave of righteousness. He is the one which continues to sanctify us. And it is God who will raise us in our glorified bodies. (1 Thessalonians 5, 2 Thessalonians 2)

However, that should not be taken as to mean that there is nothing that we should do. Obviously those who say that having a saving experience is enough, do not understand the nature of salvation, if they themselves have Faith. To be born-again, regenerated, saved and then to walk away from it is near impossible. To be saved is to catch a glimpse of the next age, a imperfect sight of what it will be like to be truly without sin, of love perfected. It is in that hope we have in our Faith. That is the promise which the Cross purchased and the Resurrection proved. That alone is enough to sing praises to God all day long regardless of what may be going on in our lives. (1 Corinthians 13)

As you progress though this work and in your Life I want you to keep in mind that our struggle, our real work is not so much about putting an end to sin, changing our character or going and doing things but is to hold onto the Faith in which these things flow. That at the end of the day, regardless of what path God has you on, sanctification is ultimately about increasing our trust in and reliance on Christ. (James 1)

More words than Sense

I have been spending time being silent, unproductive from the outside. Which means that I have been thinking those deep thoughts that only the insane or the desperate can think. I am both of course. Insane enough to think that my insanity is pure genius. As for desperation, well we will call it a quite type. I am desperate to be sure, just not worried. Then again that just may be my insanity that allows me not to worry. So, if you would be so kind as to pay attention, I will share some of those deep thoughts of the insanely desperate, or is the desperately insane. I do not know which, if you want to know go ask someone who thinks of themselves sane...

Blame. There are those who, when confronted with problems, will look around for someone to blame. At least that is what I do, except I do not look around. My Pride is such that I turn on myself, assuming I must be at fault. Superior ability bread superior arrogance, to go along with that superior ambition, if you are a Star Trek purest. Though this can get out of hand, severally out of hand, starting with myself is usually the best place to start, for I cannot control the behavior and attitudes of others. And when it is not taken too far it goes hand in hand with that whole self-awareness thing.

The problem with self-awareness though is that it can also be taken too far. I can easily say that I am very self-aware, trained since my childhood to be such. While this may create a self-consciousness, that feeling that one must always be paying attention to themselves and their behavior, that is not so much of an issue, in so much is that when it becomes a self-awareness which excludes the awareness of others. For a lack of a better way of putting it, when it interferes with empathy.

Lacking the emotional base that others rely on for empathy, I have relied on the intellect and creativity in my understanding of other people. In essence to understand others I use my imagination to create a 'character' of them in my head. Though not germane, that is why I do greatly enjoy people behaving as individuals. Most people follow such expected behavior, act so much like the character in my head that when people behave outside of their programming it is pleasing. That I find it most interesting when people act contrary to my logical imagination.

Is it not all that interesting those who would call the Cross only a story, simply stolen from earlier days, are also the same ones which will refuse to learn the lesson of the story. Not interesting, not surprising. After all, most of those who know the Cross as true will spend little time with the Truth. I do find it a bit interesting, but not surprising that many of those who spend their life in studying what lesson to human existence which the stories of the past speak of, are unable to apply those lessons to their own lives. Again, many times when we know the truth, when we have knowledge, we do not seek the Truth. Life is an art and art always tells a story.

Yes, life is a story like one which you have never seen before. Sometimes predictable, sometimes with those twists that take you by surprise. Or if you would, a story like ad lib, or table top role-playing, where the theme is set, but the lines and actions of the players are determined on the spot. We each have our parts, our roles to play. But the real question, the one which I am asking at any rate, is who is writing your story. Who is it that is determining what your role is, your part in the Story of Life?

Obviously, some, many, most, let society determine the lines, their part. Products of their environment, making no more decision in determining their actions then whatever their group endorses. To the unenlightened masses, the mob, the herd, that follows the leader up the side of the mountain, or over the cliff, enlightenment is doing and believing whatever the group says is enlightened. And while it is popular to warn masses to be careful of the leader they follow, I find it interesting that no one ever warns the leader. Just because you have found a mob to follow you does not mean you know where you are going.

But maybe though, you have waged that war against the forces that shaped you. Have rebelled against your Warrior-Queen, to take charge of your own life. Determined to be the master of your own fate, to be the authority in which takes responsibility for your actions and beliefs. Oh, I know many believe this about themselves already, and I am not one to point out illusions. Well, at least I am not overly concerned about it anymore, as it is a new act after all. Another chapter has come to a close in my life, and the shift into a new one. Act twelve, scene one. Or is it act fifteen? I have never given it much thought, but there are times in which I feel very much as if living in a movie. Maybe sometimes you feel like that, maybe you do not. But as someone once said, life is but a stage, so you are either a player, or in the audience. Well, that is a Lumpy version of what they said anyway.

That is a feeling though is it not, that life is passing you by. That you are missing out, not only a spectator of your own life, but that you are asleep in the seats. That may be true, maybe you are just being lazy. I am like that sometimes, go through my bouts of being unproductive, getting nothing accomplished. More often though, such times, such feelings produce a frenzy of activity with me. Working, pushing myself day and night, and still accomplishing nothing. Being lazy, being unproductive is fine, it is called relaxing, but that feeling, that guilt preventing us from enjoying not only being unproductive, but our productivity as well.

But where does this idea that we must be productive come from? What is this feeling that the measure of our worth, measure of our Life is based on how much we produce, how much we have acquired? And why cannot I escape it? Is it ambition, Lumpy style? Hundreds of pages of wisdom written and some of them actually have some wisdom on them. Three novels, and two score poems, and maybe even some of it is worth reading. Have done more, seen more, helped more, been more than most will in their lifetime. Yet it is all in the past, it is all nothing to me. Still driven into the future as if my life is still not valid, as if I have accomplished nothing. But it is a new act now, which opens with me picking my nose. But don't ask me what that means, I am not the Director of this movie.

Maybe you are such as me, and live with that as a constant feeling, maybe you avoid that feeling, feeling it only sometimes, or maybe not at all. But it is a feeling which is as important as it is discomforting. It is important to face, to understand and except that regardless of how important we think we are, or even how important society may label us, we are cast in a supportive role. We are extras on the Story of Life, or at least that is the way it should be.

Oh, but we like to take it a step further, do we not? Not only do we want the starring role in our lives, for it is our lives after all, but we also want to write the script as well. How frustrated we get when things do not go according to the way we write the future? How shocked we become when things which we do not foresee happen? We figure if we only work hard enough, produce enough, store enough that our futures will be as we planned them. But then the Storm hits, the market crashes, our credit dries up…our hair starts falling out. And we have to face that undeniable, but forgettable fact that we are not the author of our lives.

This is not the first time I have spoken of such. Neither am I the first, nor the only, nor the last who will speak such. In the Inner-Life one must not only give up trying to write the script of their own lives, but they must give up the lead role as well. Faith, Charity and Hope. Faith requires of us that Christ is the author of the Story of our Life. I mean if your life is doing well in your own hands, I can only shrug and ask how is that working out for you? Can you look to the future with a smile, not matter where the economy goes? Whatever happens to our society in the coming decade or so? Do you know that Hope in which not matter whatever happens, it is good to be alive?

Repentance

Being a Christian Philosopher, an apologist in terms before that became to mean evangelist, I rely heavily on experimental knowledge. We can talk for hours, even for years about theology and morality, what we must believe and what we must do, but when it comes right down to it our Faith, our salvation and Life in Christ is an experience. It is good, very good to turn to Scripture to give direction to our Life, for what we should believe and what we should do, and that being the case should we not be what Scripture tells us we are, the children of God? Should we not be experiencing what Scripture tells us we should be experiencing, that which 'all have become partakers'…conviction.

In Christian philosophy we do rely heavily on what we experience to explain. That is, normal communication is not theological but rather experimental, as with the apple, apologetics required shared experiences in order to communicate. And as our society's shifts into a post-literate culture, experimental theology has gained importance. That is not troublesome in and of itself, for if we are Born of the Spirit, if our experiences are truly produced by God then they will align to Scripture. It is that process which in technical language is called illumination. It is by our experiences, if we are truly in God, by which we understand Scripture, its meaning and truth. It has become, however, a travesty that experimental theology is today more of a theology based on the experiences we have, instead of theology about the experiences we have. In so much that it is generally held by those who have never experienced that conviction, who have never been on the wrong track and had God gently or not so gently bring them back, to form their theology that says such things are not necessary, are not real. A travesty for sure, as many of them are pastors, and many more have been sitting in church for decades and yet are not saved.

I know, I know…how those words burn for those of you who do not know God but are yet convinced that you are saved. I know all the excuses, and I know all the lies, and I know firsthand how your inclination is to attack or ignore those of us who say such things. Indeed, I know how for you 'being led by the Spirit' or the chastening of the Lord 'which all have become partakers' is just 'mystic talk' or some sort of social or cultural metaphor and is not meant to be taken literally, at least not to mean for all Christian. The backlash was enough in the youth of my Faith that I backed down from that position, after all I was preaching it based on my experience. I was told time and time again, by ministers and laypeople alike, that I was just special, I was a mystic and cannot expect other Christians to have such a 'great' union with God as I do. And being young in my Faith, and with just enough humility to accept that maybe I was wrong in this, for a time. After all, I was new to the Faith and there may have been things which I did not understand.

To be sure, over the years, as I matured, I learned that it was pride to expect for everyone saved to experience our Life in the same manner, or I should say perceive it in the same manner as me. Each of us is different, so there is a cornucopia of ways in which our Faith is expressed and so a multitude of ways that we perceive the experiences that are common to all who are born of the Spirit. We all experience the chastening of the Lord, though we do not always perceive it as such. My conversion was by vision, I saw the presence and purpose of Christ in the conviction and forgiveness of sins. Most did not perceive it in the same manner, but all who are saved have the same experience. It may not be as intense or vivid as us born-again types of adult converts. But nonetheless, they came aware of their sins and their need to turn to Christ for forgiveness. That is, we do not all perceive Christ's presence in salvation in the same way, but we still all perceive Him in it. In that same way, we do not all perceive the chastening of the Lord in the same manner but we all perceive the need to repent, to turn from our sins and towards Him.

I started this by refocusing the question of whether you are saved to; Are you placing your trust for your salvation in Jesus Christ? For that is the nature of the repentance when we are born of the Spirit, is it not? The turning away from seeking our salvation, our pleasures, our life in the practices and principles of this world and instead placing that trust in Christ. As St. Augustine would point out that there are those who are part of the visible Church who are not of the mystical Church, who are active and even fervent in practice but who are not saved. It is a great tragedy and sorrow because they want to be saved, they want God but they want Him on their terms. They want and so therefore will not see that placing their trust in practices and methods, no matter how good, is a misplaced trust. That placing their trust in the actions they take, no matter how good is the sin of pride, of playing their trust in themselves. That placing their trust in the rules, in the Law, either that which is discerned from Scripture or those which our local or sect fellowship creates are placing their trust in human endeavors, in themselves, instead of the Cross.

We know that no matter what our Will wills, we cannot save ourselves. Or as we were born into this world we were condemned because it was our will to judge ourselves according to our own Self instead of submitting to the judgment of God. Was that not the chastening of the Lord as we were born of the Spirit? That our sins, our desires, our own view of righteousness and path that we willed for ourselves are utter and complete darkness compered to Christ, the Light and Righteousness of God? Do not the antichrists, many who call themselves Christian, declare that salvation is found in the goodness of their person and not in the Cross? But is not the sin that condemns, our love of the darkness that the pride which places our will, over the Will of God? For it is the will of God that salvation will come only to those who stop placing their trust in themselves, but instead places their trust in Christ for their salvation. The Gospel is the will of God, and Faith is not simply believing it but submitting to that knowledge.

The act of accepting Christ as our savior, is the act of accepting Him as Lord. It is repenting from trying to save ourselves instead placing our trust in Him for our salvation. It is repenting from the fact that we have lived our lives according to our own Will instead of the Will of God. And while it is a great tragedy that there are those who think themselves who are not, because they continue to place their trust in themselves, it is a greater tragedy that we who know that salvation is found through Faith in Christ alone, practices a faith in ourselves instead. Which is another reason in which I say while we may not need to be orthodox in order to be saved but being unorthodox hinders our growth in the Faith. That many of the heresies which have hindered the Church both currently and historically comes from the mistaken belief that repentance is our will choosing God, instead of us surrendering our will to His. The mistaken belief we are saved because we have repented, instead of our repentance being a response to the conviction of the chastening of the Lord when we are born of the Spirit. That a wrong view of repentance, will cause us much grief later on.

This is seen most clearly in those have slipped into some sin will struggle and strive to cleanse themselves of that sin before 'returning' to God. Or those who through avoidance, neglect, or down right stubbornness has learned to ignore that fire of conviction. Those who would rather do it their way, rather learn the hard way that God's way is the best way for our new nature. If it was not possible, if it was not common for us to try to work our sanctification, or maturing in Faith in our own way, according to our flesh, to lose our way by ignoring the Spirit, most of the New Testament would not have been written. Indeed, if the chastening of the Lord was pleasing to our flesh, if we never forget the repentance which Grace brought, there would be no need for terms like 'by the Spirit' in Scripture for there would be no question what choice we would make. To be sure, we have all been like the Galatians at one time another. We begun in the Spirit, we then fall into that trap of trying to be made perfect by the flesh. It might be the tradition of our church, or one we make our own, but we rely on some set of rules to perfect our Faith. It might be one found in the latest popular book, or one as old as time, but we practice some method other than one which is clearly prescribed by Scripture, relying the on the Spirit. But whether we run from it or embrace it, we are still convicted, all who are born of the Spirit have become partakers of the chastening of the Lord.

Love and the Cross

Romans 9: 'I have a great sorrow, and continual grief in my heart. For I could wish that I myself were accursed from Christ for my brethren, my countrymen…'

From time to time, I am reminded why I write Beyond Salvation, and why I am a mystic of the Cross. This time it came in a form of a question basically, asking if you would give up your salvation for another. One hand it did not surprise me that there was no one who said yes, but on the other hand it saddened me a little as it was them basically saying that there was no one in their life they loved enough to make such a sacrifice. There was, of course, a whole lot of that 'me and my salvation' focus that so irritated me about church culture in the youth of my Faith. And it convicted me a bit, as it too of late have been focused on myself, distracted by the dramas and turmoil of the world around me. Working five hours from home, Money issues, an upcoming move, too many people needing ministering to, a suicide in the family…and a nephew who has just hit that nasty time of teenage years. That is, there is plenty of excuses in my life, enough turmoil to want to escape the struggle, to look to the rest that resurrection represents, so it was a good time to be reminded of the Cross. To be reminded that it is not, that nothing is about me.

This is hardly a new topic for me, but this had brought home how bad off the Church is today. For that sorrow in which one 'could wish that I myself were accursed from Christ' for the sake of others is not great love, is not mature love but the beginning and start of Love. It is a feeling we have when we gain our first glimpse of the Cross, when we gain that first understanding of Love, God's Love. And how awesome is His Grace! For we are His, preordained to be transformed into His image. In the image of Christ, whose love was great enough to sacrifice Himself for the sins of the world. God did not do such for the love of self, but from a love for us. And so, in that transformation which the Spirit brings, we grow in Charity, we start to love with His Love. A Love great enough which if we could, if it was possible, we would sacrifice ourselves completely to free others from their sin. It is impossible, of course, but if it was possible, you would make that sacrifice.

For those who are outside of Christ, or immature in the Faith see this as a great love, but as I noted this is just the beginning of Charity. For Faith without works is dead because Love demands action, passion must be expressed for them to be true. As I have oft said, it is easy to be enlightened while living in a cave. But the warm and fuzzy feelings of love are not true unless it motivates us to act. To be a better spouse, to be a better parent or mentor, to preach, to teach, to write. To share the Gospel, to share a cup of water. To be a witness of the Salvation found in Him by both words and deeds. To carry our cross and follow Christ. That in doing so we must die to our pride, for our sacrifices no matter how great cannot take away the sins of another, only God can do that. That no matter how skilled in words we may be, we cannot transform the hearts of others, only God can do that.

That pride is an interesting one. I was so focused on trying to show, trying to explain, trying to get people to understand the wonder of being in Christ, that I got frustrated, lost the wonder. That happens a lot, I think. Teachers getting so focused on theology that turn the bible into a god instead of what God would have us know of Him and His will. Preachers get so focused on reaching the numbers that they forget it is about pointing them to Christ. I get so wrapped up in reasoning out my point that I forget about the edification, going about the comfort and conviction…that we get so focused on the sacrifice that we forget that it is about mercy and not sacrifice. It is not about how great our struggle, or how intense our turmoil but about the needs of the ones we Love. At the end of the road, or I should say as far as I have gotten down the road the sacrifices and struggles are nothings, as Love is a pleasurable feeling , is it not? That when we are motivated by Charity it drowns out and overwhelms the struggles and hardship.

Oh…how wonderful, what bliss it will be to be perfect in Love as we will in the next age. If only…and once I thought the Perfect could be had in this age, but as I noted, Love demands that we leave our caves. And in leaving our cave we learn that we are not perfect in Love, that from time to time to time we are all children that cannot sacrifice ourselves totally, that we need others to sacrifice to us as well. That we are not strong enough, not righteousness enough, not wise enough or loving enough, and need the Cross, need Christ every day.

I once wrote that our cross is not heavy or burdensome, it is all the things we try to carry along with it. Seeking righteousness, you know, putting to death the deeds of the flesh. People His yoke is light indeed, if we but let go of our carnal desires. Pride, of course being my principle vice. In that pride I thought that I could say that my sacrifices taught me, disciplined my will so I could more perfectly show Charity...but I now know that that too is a pride that had to go, has to go. Indeed, it is one of those 'what a fool I have been' kind of things. For a thousand times I have pointed out our righteousness is nothing compared to the Righteousness of God, compared to Christ. For a thousand times I have pointed out our sacrifices are but shadows and dust compared to the Cross. And so, how can we take pride in the love we have if we know God's Love? That to say that we are better than another is to use human standards and not the standards of God.

That was a bit off topic, but still relevant, but let me conclude this. We use a lot of excuse not to Love. As if there is a limit to how much Charity we could have. And there is a lot of pride in judging our Love as better than that of them over there. Which is, as pride often is, simply another way to excuse not Loving more. His Love, as His Righteousness is perfect. Ours never is. That Charity, in a way, is the recognition that our love is not enough. That if we are to love perfectly, it must be God's love according to His Will. That is, we can love to the point which we would gladly give up our salvation for another as surely as this is the Love that God has for us. And this Love, if it be true, motivates us to do what God would have us do to express that Love. Motivates us to do His Will for us, to do our part for the purpose He saved us. That is to say, we were not given the Grace of being in Christ simply to be saved, but so that we may be transformed into His Image in order to show the world His Love.

Hypocrisy, Partiality and Self-Seeking

James 3: who is wise and understanding among you? Let him show by good conduct that his works are done in the meekness of wisdom. But if you have bitter envy and self-seeking in your hearts, do not boast and lie against the truth. This wisdom does not descend from above but is earthly, sensual, demonic. For where envy and self-seeking exist, confusion and every evil thing are there. But the wisdom that is from above is first pure, then peaceable, gentle, willing to yield, full of mercy and good fruits, without partiality and without hypocrisy.

Retuning to my endless road of words, I find myself in the Epistle of James. I always seem to lose a group of readers when I come back around to the book. Not that it matters much anymore, because I have more or less given up hope of being read in my lifetime. But this time around I have been thinking of that relationship between 'bitter envy' and 'self-seeking.' I used to know that envy. You know that question about 'what about me?' I did not really know it before my conversion, as I almost always got what I wanted. But after my conversion my life feel apart, I went from an 'up and coming' to an 'outcast' overnight. Much of it was because God had stripped me of my duplicity, my ability to put on any face I wanted in order to get what I want. And as my Faith matured, as I have become more transformed into His image, He stripped that whole self-seeking thing from me. That is, as I wrote at the conclusion of the Insane Voyages, I am no longer the star of my own life, there is simply no room in the upward call for seeking our own benefit, our own desires, or own welfare. You have your own reason for being among the Outcasts, for me it was in order to be heard today your wisdom has to be earthly, sensual, demonic

Hypocrisy, partiality, self-seeking.... Church culture, for the most part, is built upon them instead of upon Christ. Teachers, of course, focus on the corruption of theology. On how it has become humanistic, about us instead of about Christ. I have a great sympathy for them, as their calling is dependent on church culture. That is, as Teachers of the Word, which is unchanging and absolute, they teach to the Church as a group. When a church culture is self-seeking, they will stand only teaching that will get what they want. A compromised church will not stand for the whole of Scripture, but only those that make them feel good about themselves. But, while I have dealt with groups, my focus is always on the Church as individuals. That is, I have the luxury of not having to 'engage the culture' but simply ask you if you what are your hypocrisy, partiality, self-seeking.

I know, I know, you are all humble and holy….and a liar to think that you are without these sins. See, I have it easy because I can pull a vice out of a hat and, as we are not face to Face there is some way in which we are doing this. I am not self-seeking in the general sense, but in the details of my life there are always those moments in which I will look to my own advantage instead of looking to serve others. But that is why the Prophets, and just not the Teachers are saying that church culture has become corrupt or compromised. Because it promotes vices instead of convicting them, it allows and prefers us conforming to the way of the world rather than to the perfection of the Image of Christ. But for you and me, there is no excuse. For we know Him, and is known by Him. The Spirit of Christ is in us, working in our hearts so that we may know and do His will. We know that we must put to death the deeds of the flesh, to put an end to hypocrisy, partiality, self-seeking, and other vices that no one can see. We know that at the End of the Age, we will be judged not by the cool kids and their tag-alongs but by Christ Himself.

And it is the self-seeking in which we should start, as without it the other two seem to fade. At my conversion God promised me 'a kingdom to rule in His Name.' In less grand language, He promised me wisdom and that He will have me do great things with it. The only stipulation was that I would have to do it His way, that He would be my only Master. That is a post all of its own, but more to the point, I of course envisioned a grand ministry. But suddenly where before my conversion I was a 'golden-child,' afterwards I found that I was now a 'trouble-maker' all for preaching that upward call, for that transformation into His Image, inwardly as well as outwardly. In truth I did not give it much thought until a couple of years ago. Honestly, in spite of the troubles, hardships and struggles, I have always enjoyed living in that insane Faith we have. And I took it all in stride, all in that way we do of using our life to convict us. That is, I had always seen it as simply the way that God broke my pride. After all, during those first ten years I was not all that peaceable, gentle or willing to yield.

But see now, there was that temptation to be self-seeking in those early years. People pressuring me to become a pastor, to 'be heard.' As you know, when I am talking about God I have that passion, that spark that excites people. John knows that temptation more than I do, as he is actually a likable fellow. You may not know it, but for those of us who are 'listened to' knows that subtle pressure to 'advance the Kingdom' by seeking authority or popularity for ourselves. That is, that temptation to be self-seeking. To do those things to be heard, to be read, to market ourselves and our words. And do not mistake me, I am not talking about the actions but the motivations. That it is always a question of whether we are advancing the Kingdom of God, or advancing ourselves in the kingdom of the church popular. Am I seeking wisdom so I can be considered wise, or am I seeking wisdom to help you? Are we striving for that Transformation so that we can be called a Saint, or because we are striving to live the Life of Love He has given us by Grace?

James 2: My Brethren, do not hold the faith of our Lord Jesus Christ, the Lord of Glory, with partiality. For if there should come into your assembly a man with gold rings, in fine apparel, and there should come in a poor man in filthy cloths, and you pay attention to the one wearing the fine cloths and say to him, 'you sit here In a good place.' And say to the poor man, 'you stand there' or sit her at my footstool,' have you not shown partiality among yourself, and become judges with evil thoughts.

If you want an example of partiality simply walk into any ministry or church and watch how they treat their major donors compared to their rank-and-file workers. And again, do not mistake me. Obviously, there are things which need to get done, and we need money to do that. I am pointing the self-serving motivation in partiality. the 'rich man' can do more for us than the 'poor man.' We see that in the World every day. Indeed, I shave and put on one of my suits and I am treated like a demi-god, I go to the same place in my street-cloths and it is business as usual. While such an attitude is acceptable when doing business in the world, is it really Love to judge each other in the Church by what they can do for us, how they can advance our plan, our part? Again, I am speaking of our hearts, of our self-serving motivations. For that is what we should do one for the other, lift each other up, advance each other, but seeking our own advancement hinders us in seeking the advancement of others. Indeed, the Church is in the mess it is in because each are seeking their own gain, seeking to advance their own place in the Kingdom instead of seeking to lift others up….do you see where I am going?

1 Corinthians 4: We are fools for Christ's sake, but you are wise in Christ! We are weak, but you are strong! You are distinguished, but we are dishonored! To the present hour we both hunger and thirst, and we are poorly clothed, and beaten and homeless. And we labor, working with our own hands. Being reviled, we bless; being persecuted, we endure; being defamed, we entreat. We have been made as the filth of the world, the offscouring of all things until now…therefore I urge you to imitate me.

I never had any real temptation to place popularity over God's calling. Besides God stripping my ability, it is my nature to defend the oppressed, the poor, the week. I am that kind of alpha that stands up to the pack leader for the sake of the pack. John calls us sheepdogs, because we sort of sit there until a threat to the group comes along. That is, I fall more into that category of counter-culture elitist, then one of the 'cool kids'. I had no sympathy, no mercy for those who would trade the upward call for the approval of the masses, for a pat on the head of leaders, etc. I had no understanding of their struggle until my mid-life crisis, until the subject of romance came up. I mean, my vows never bothered me all that much, nor that being faithful to God led me to a path in which I became 'the filth of the world', because it is sort of a badge of honor with the Pride of the counter-culture elitism. But I faced that dire struggle in romance, sorely tempted to give up all of this, for after all what kind of life is it to be with me when all I have to offer is wisdom and my heart?

But more to the point, I think that much of our self-seeking, our showing partiality is because we do not want to be trash. It came to light for me with romance because it is the only area in which I have insecurity, the only area in which the judgments of another is important. I am secure in my election and calling because I am secure in Christ, as a person I am one of those 'cool kids' that others want to tag-along with, except of course, tagging along with me means moving in that upward call. In opinion I can argue on almost any subject because I actually do the work to form opinions, but in romance, as 'a man' I friggen don't have a clue. And do not mistake me, there is an obvious partiality needed in romance and marriage, but it should be based on love instead of self-seeking, yes. That is the topic of my next post, but here   I am simply pointing out that partiality comes from the self-seeking of the opinions of others, doing things to elevate the opinion others have of us. In my case it was self-seeking a well opinion of myself, but it is more common the other way.

Mathew 6: Moreover, when you fast, do not be like the hypocrites, with a sad countenance. For they disfigure their faces that they may appear to men to be fasting. Assuredly, I say to you that they have their reward. But you, when you fast, anoint your head and wash your face so that you do not appear to men to be fasting, but to your Father who is in the secret place and your Father who sees in secret will reward you openly.

Obviously, the opinions of others within the Church is important, something we should pay attention to…as long as it is a Godly opinion. But self-seeking slowly and subtly starts to become hypocrisy when our pride has grown so that we start taking the opinions of others as God's approval. I know, much of what I do is conformation, to give opinions on matters of your heart. But while Pupils often rely on the opinions of their Masters, the goal of any Master is to elevate their Pupils to form their own opinions, to form their own views, to seek God's opinion for themselves…to mature in the Faith. And while much of church culture pays lip-service to this, much of it is geared towards keeping people as babes so they do not upset the balance of power. It just will not do if we had a bunch of mature Christians running around thinking that they have a voice in the Church. And it does it by endorsing, and actually encouraging the pride of those whom God has called to preach or teach. By bringing us into that self-serving system, so that we never grow to become fools for Christ, to imitate Paul in becoming trash for the Gospel.

In my opinion they do this to hide their own hypocrisy. For outwardly they talk of humility, of being only a servant but inwardly they think themselves wise, they think their words are important. Should I point to my own hypocrisy, for I am nothing, and my words are nothing, but in my heart I am not perfectly humble. But I want to be…I want to be! Oh, to be perfectly humble like on that glorious day when we will see Him face to Face. That is the point is it not, our longing and arrow? Indeed, our Love for God that is so strong that we desire nothing more, have no greater longing than to know Him, as He knows us. That is what makes us outcasts, for we view virtue as not some law to obey, or some work to do but to know and understand that aspect of God. That narrow path, that upward call, maturing in the Faith, the striving for humility, chastity, generosity, for Faith, Hope and Charity, is not motivated to gain the approval of others, or for our own reward but because they are aspects of God, Whom we greatly desire to know. And it is not just and awesome thing, a most wondrous Gift that we can spend countless hours praising God for, that by Grace we are in Christ and can know Him now, and that each of us will know the virtues of God perfectly on that Day.

Journal of the Poor Knight

I have had to spend some time asking myself a very odd question. Why is it that I am tempted, on the very edge of giving up? You know those thoughts. Have I not done enough, given enough? Let someone else pick up the burden. Not an uncommon question, whether by the will of God or just my own I have lived my life in such a way that I have been pushed to those places where it feels like there is nothing left but to surrender. And in such times, it is not an odd question. Indeed, I think it is odd not to have such thoughts of surrender when the enemy has you down and their boot on your throat. But I think the question does very much reaches to the core of who I am. It is really a question of whether or not to kill the Dreamer. Indeed, as my life is fulfilled, should I exchange the contentment with today, for the turmoil of dreaming of what could be? Should I wake up and reach out my hand to achieve the victory I know I can have? Or hold onto the Dream, knowing full well it is a battle I will lose. My intensity is often a trap, and in the end, what does it really all matter? I will choose what I always choose, the path which I do not know where it leads. To a future which I do not see. To chase the Dream. Alas, the only choice I can really make. As inevitable as it is, it has been difficult to give up the rest of my life for a dream without substance, undefined with unknown purpose and meaning. To jump once more into the fire of obsession, back to living on the razor's edge, back once more to being a Dreamer.

Maybe someday I will grow up, as people put it, and the Dreamer will die. Maybe someday I will fall, tired of struggling with the chaos of my mind for a world who does its best to kill the Dreamer. I cannot help but to think that the world would grow a bit darker on that day. Then again, someday I may slowly slip into a holy insanity, spending my days picking wild flowers with a knowing smile on my face. So much fighting, so much strife, it is often more than my heart can bare. And that is why there is no other choice, why we must fight, why we must Dream. As long as evil exists, a knight must persist…

Great Folly

...Humans are predators, without exception. Without exception! There are movements, as there have always been movements in which to deny this. Those instead who worships the herd instinct. Those who believe by suppressing their predatory instinct they are closer to enlightenment, closer to God. This is only a false enlightenment, as it only the desire not to be prey. It is a false righteousness, as it is an ideal created with no regard for reality...Indeed, true passivism is not a philosophy for the herd. One has a need to embrace the predator instinct as few do. It is to hunt the courage to turn the other cheek, it is to stalk the courage to be able to stand firm while staring death in the eye. To sink our teeth into the Honor that not only refuses to do harm, but stands between the harm and its victim. True passivism is not so passive as to do nothing. It requires one to be aggressive, to stand face to face with the worst the world has to offer and say that before it can harm another, it must first destroy you.... Jesus Christ was a predator, a great a hunter as the world has ever seen. He hunted to heal, to preach, and to die. He stalked the Cross, with a cunning and persistence of a predator...

Humans need to hunt, require the hunt, cannot live without the hunt. There are those who would deny this, and ironically, those who do are often the fiercest hunters...Do not be fooled! The question is not whether or not a human hunts, it is simply a matter of what they hunt. A poet hunts for beauty expressed. A philosopher hunts for an idea understood. A warrior hunts for a peace achieved. A Farmer hunts for the crop stored. A knight hunts Honor, and the tyrant hunts for power...when one stops hunting, when one puts away the predator instinct in favor of that of the herd, when the prey becomes less important than becoming one of the popular mass, they lose their chance for greatness

...Reason is useless without facts. A conclusion is only reliable if the data used to form it is reliable, so for reason, pure logic to work it must examine each fact for its reliability. Testing each piece of data not only for its truthfulness but judge its value in forming the opinion. It is shortcoming of many programs meant to teach critical reasoning to rely too heavily on logic. The ability to examine an idea, proposal or opinion relies as much on creativity as

An Endless Road of Words

it does on reason. Logic, the examination of our reason, has several shortcomings which only creativity can overcome. The chief of these is pride. It is simply illogical to believe that the most logical conclusion could not also be the most correct. Logic simply does not allow for the fact that logic can be wrong. It must be true, of course, when our reasoning is limited to concrete and well-defined values, such as in mathematical formulas. Yet when dealing with the majority of life, with the abstract realities of our world, our reason gets bogged down.

The shortcoming of logic is that reason requires not only data in order to function, but a framework, a world-view in order to give data its meaning. Three plus two is five, is only possible because we already know the value of three, two and five. But what does Kor plus Tym equal? Indeed, what happens when we define Tym in different ways, or that we experience Kor in different way? What value, how important do we consider our internal struggle between good and evil? How much value should be given to Love? to Hope? Faith? The feelings and emotional needs of others? To these and many others, logic can give a value only within the framework, within a world view. Given value only in relation to what it is we desire, by what we already consider to be important, or unimportant…

…It is irrational to think that the great masses will ever be rational. It is even too much to hope that all those who claim to love reason, will be reasonable. The human condition is such that it is a constant battle between the animalistic passions and the higher reasoning of the human, between the barbarian and the poet…It is a common mistake to favor one over the other, to think that reason should prevail over passion, or that our passions should rule. But we need both, we need our Warrior passion to give energy and force to our actions, but we need our poetic reason to give them form and direction.

Reasonable thought? Reason, is as unnatural to humans as it is to any other animal. People have taught apes and other animals some amazing things. Animals have been taught to do math and even to paint, but these are only tricks. That animals to an existent can be taught these tricks a clear indication that what the majority of people call reasoning is simply tricks that they have learned. On this level the only advantage a human has is that we can learn more tricks.

Reason as it is commonly known is nothing more than a bag of tricks. It is obvious because the marks of the training for those tricks can be seen in the words we use, and even on our views on how words must be used. Each system of teaching leaves upon the learner certain conditioning. Patterns which never truly leaves us. I bare the marks of how I was trained, and those who have been trained by me have many of those same marks. Knowing that you will have to defend in depth any opinion you bring to me, you form your opinion on the grounds of the most defendable. You rarely go out to risk yourself by expressing that which you cannot show clearly. I risk even less, rarely forming an opinion and instead simply question and inject other facts within the opinion you have formed. And we both bare that mark that a successful argument requires Understanding of the Enemy.

The person who seeks Understanding, to truly know what others base their views on is always going to have an advantage over those who simply try to prove their point. Strategically, it is as simply the fact that by understanding your enemy, to understand the way that they think you will then understand their weaknesses in order to exploit them. Or to avoid their strengths. But beyond scoring points in a debate, or swaying public opinion, Understanding is also important to apologetics, the explaining of what we want others to understand. While there is honor in the defeat of an enemy in proportion to their strength, it is far nobler to elevate an ally to be your equal.

While this philosophy obviously has advantage and use in war and debate, it is one which is equally important in apologetics, in explaining and in teaching. It is simply often abused, used to exploit rather than edify. Classes in apologetics are typically barbaric in their nature, so see Understanding only as a barbarian does. A way to conquer the other person, if not seeing the other person as the opposition at least their beliefs as something needing to be destroyed. It is only natural, of course, our carnal mind is xenophobic. We simply do not like ideas which differ from our own, those which challenge our own views. But such classes, and those with such views cannot achieve Understanding, only knowledge of processes and procedures. If they say this, you say that, they do this, you do that. Understanding, in order to truly Understand your enemies, and even your friends, must be willing to accept the possibility that their views and opinions maybe more sound then our own…

Freedom

…Children do not understand the world of adults. They do not understand much beyond their small circle. Children rarely understand what it is that adults are talking about…but they do listen, and they do remember. I remember. I remember sitting at the kitchen table listening to mother and grandmother Wasik conversing. It was my thing, the thing I liked to do instead of playing with the other children. I do not remember what was ever said, but I remember the awe I would feel of watching a world that I did not understand. that feeling has never really left me, that awe, that wonder, that panic which comes from the constant awareness that no matter how much I learn, no matter how enlightened I become, I am but stuck in a self-made illusion. That I am still very much a child.

I know, I know. You are an adult and live in reality. I can only shrug my shoulders and repeat children do not always understand the world of adults. And as I have already stated that I am still a child forgive my childish notions. That it is far better to live in the constant doubt, and yes, even that bit of fear and pain of a world which is always just out of reach of our understanding…and control. Far better that, then to live a monotonous and drab life created from the illusions that we know how the world is, or should be. With the knowledge of perpetual childhood, comes the sublime pleasure of understanding that the struggles which tests our strengths so are but a pale-moon shadow compared to all of time, and so are nothings from the view of eternity. That the wars we fight so fiercely today can only be seen in the light the child throwing a tantrum for being refused a piece of candy. Forgive me that my aspirations of tomorrow are only that our world will be bit larger, that there should be some frontier we may explore. That my greatest ambition is to find that struggle I am not prepared for, that battle in which I must give it my all. Where I must fight with the strength beyond that which I am capable, to grow, to mature. Indeed, for the only thing which can destroy the child is a world they understand, a world in which there is no need to keep growing.

...It may happen slowly or in one instant, when one breaks a chain which binds them to the civilization-illusion. Either way, you cannot mistake the moment it happens, that moment which the illusion is shattered forever. Disillusionment, tun wu, an awakening...some believe the worst of these is the time is when you first come to know fear. Maybe you can suppress that fear, maybe you learn to live with it. To find peace with those moments of terror, or constant awareness that evil exists in the world...That under the polish and trim of the civilized is the heart of the barbarian. That behind the person next to you in the elevator, that person behind you in line...is a soul capable of doing anything...which all the laws and customs cannot stop them from doing harm to you, that legislators and courts are meaningless, that the system is only capable of creating an illusion of safety, unable to prevent the harm, unable to do a thing if that person next to you decides to act, useless until after the harm has been done...so you hide in fear or pick up the sword and practice, learn to defend yourself, learn to defend others...but then you learn a harsher truth, one far more terrifying then the first, one much harder to face, to live in peace with...that day you wake up and realize beneath all your honor, that behind all your virtue, underneath the polish and trim of your civilized exterior, also is found the barbarian.

That you too are capable of doing anything, despite all law and custom, despite any will you might have to the contrary, you learn that you too are capable of harming another, destroying another for no better reason than your own benefit....thus is the sword stroke which finally destroys the illusion-innocence, and thus is the pain and struggle which buys your freedom from the society-illusion, or creates a slave of a different kind....

Returning To the Road

We cannot expect that our lives to be like those heroes in the movies. Such heroes are two-dimensional, only heroic within context of the story. While they may face overwhelming odds, even if they fail, we know in the end that they will prevail because it is a movie, or if they fail in the end, the story is best served. Likewise, we cannot expect that our lives will be like those great people who are so praised in popular lore. Such greatness is also two-dimensional, only great within the confines of their specialty, the world in which they are bound. The politician, the person of business, yes, even the philosopher or pastor, once they have achieved their success never again venture away from their castle, never straying into areas in which they are not their own lord. Such people do not live the Life of High Adventure, know not what it means to serve the King of the Golden City. For as you can now see, once we have mastered our skills where there is none who can challenge us, our King will move us into a battle in which we must once again rely on Him, and our fellow knights…

…Everyone has a price, everyone can be bought. A knight is no different. But it is honesty which is our wealth. It is our understanding which binds us. It is fellowship, the revealing of each other's hearts, exposing the weakness as well of the strengths which is the coin that purchases us. Show me what is behind your mask and you will own my heart. Seek to understand me and you will have my loyalty…

…As it is pleasing to me at the moment not to entertain myself with those debates which the rabble find so interesting, I climb up the high hill of paradox, of mystery, of Faith. I climb the Hill of the Golden City to visit my grave. To remember the pains, struggles and tears it took to climb the Hill the first time. To remember the days (and the friends) long dead and long buried. To remember the dead whose graves cannot be found on the Hill. To remember why I fight, and to shed new tears…I climbed to the Golden City to visit the graveyard upon the Hill. I climbed to stand on my grave and read those three lines on my tombstone once again. For when the sting of the collee has worn off and there is the need to refresh our memory of why we took our oath…Everything has its cost, and there can be no Life without death. And in that graveyard Grace, the poem written on the Tomb reminds us that Faith is nihilistic and morbid, meaningful and redemptive. That in our tear-blurred sight, when there is nothing left to see except the blood soaked Cross and that empty grave upon the Hill we understand once again…I climbed the Hill to listen to the song of the Saints of yesteryear to ease my turmoil. To listen to the voices of the past singing a single song, of defeat and victory, of pain and joy. A song which chorus is but a singular idea: We are already dead and buried, and what lives now, lives in Christ....Will you be so kind as to play me a dirge for my sorrow? Or if you lack the talent, dance with me on our graves. Or at least, for your own sake, wait at the gates. We can walk back down the Hill together, and with a wink and a nod chase the devil out of our dreams with some old-fashion Dixieland laughter. Oh, then again, forget all I have said. Humor is only beneficial to those who know how to be serious, and words are just the symbols we use for those things too difficult to put into words....

...For seven years the Poet sat unmoving on the side of the road of endless words. For seven years he had no tears to ink my pen. It has been long enough to give up hope of the dream, to even give up the hope of the dream of hope. When all is said, by and by, it will probably call the time in which the Warrior was tamed, finally willing to settled down. It is strange to think that as the Poet sat pouting on the side of the road and the Warrior had free range in my life, he chooses not to charge forward but instead to have what most would call a normal life.

It is not really strange. Though we may think that the Warrior is the risk taker, it is the Poet that dreams, is idealistic, and have those visions for which risks are worth taking. The Warrior fights when he has to, takes risks when he has to. For him it is a practical matter, and without the Poet's grand visions of beauty, there is no real reason to fight. I have fought enough that the honor of the Warrior is satisfied. With glass of wine, cigar and feet propped up he was content to go peaceful into that dark night.

But suddenly, and without warning, the Poet jumped up, pointed with a shout "Rage. Rage! Here comes the Muse." In which the warrior responded as he always does in such a situation. He punched the Poet in the face, and then stood there, staring stoic and stone-faced, while she walked by. For as you know, there is nothing in the world the Warrior fears, except a woman who inspires the Poet. And as I mentioned the Warrior is not a risk taker. Once she passed, he pulled the Poet to his feet and the two returned to their travel down the road of endless words.

Epilogue

The endless road of words began with *Emails to John*, and continued for a decade more. It represents years of adventures and misadventures of digging through my heart as I sought to understand what it meant to be alive in Christ, to mature in the faith, and to minister.

It come to an abrupt end when the road led me to an unexpected place, the Dream. A new chapter began, a new folder created. But, the words did not come. The pain and struggle was too fierce, too personal, too private. That it was time for me to deal with the Wound That Will Not Heal.

The months went by digging into my heart until I reached the Wound itself. Until that was all that was left, and years went by with that Wound, that pain always just below the surface. It was a wall I could not get through. A chain on my heart I could not break, no matter how hard I tried. Then the Muse walked into, and out of my life, and gave me the what I was lacking. A reminder of the importance of The Dream. Of why I have fought so hard for so many years. And just as importantly she gave me the motivation to face the Wound, to struggle through the pain and fear, to find the words to express my heart. And in doing so, destroying the last and thickest chain preventing me from having the heart of Love that I want. So, once again I am a Dreamer and am looking forward to expressing the hardships and struggles that will come along with the Dream…and, of course to the dreams themselves.

www.ingramcontent.com/pod-product-compliance
Lightning Source LLC
Chambersburg PA
CBHW061818040426

42447CB00012B/2705